COLIN BLYTHE

by the same author

Fisherman's Friend, a life of Stephen Reynolds

(*edited*) A Poor Man's House by Stephen Reynolds

COLIN BLYTHE

lament for a legend

Christopher Scoble

SPORTS
BOOKS

Published in Great Britain by
SportsBooks Limited
PO Box 422
Cheltenham
GL50 2YN

© Christopher Scoble 2005
First Published April 2005

Front cover designed by Kath Northam.

A catalogue record for this book is available from
the British Library.
ISBN 1 899807 31 4

Printed by Compass Press.

Contents

Illustrations

Acknowledgements

Though Colin Blythe left few traces – even his cricket memorabilia were mostly lost in a burglary on the family home in the 1920s – I am greatly indebted to members of the family for rounding up what bits and pieces remain: in particular to Sheila Wadsworth and her brother, Michael Blythe, the grandchildren of Colin's brother, Charles, who have been indefatigable in their help and support; and to Edward Gosnell, the step-grandson of Janet Blythe, who salvaged for me her first passport and a few other papers. Other members of the family to whom I am most grateful are Phyllis Spellar, Jenny Morritt and Mrs C B Smart. I have received help too from Richard Seymour, the grandson of Colin's close colleague, Jim Seymour, and from his wife, Helen; and from Jean Brown and Josephine Barratt, the daughters of Claud Woolley. I am grateful too for their permission to reproduce photographs from their respective family collections.

So far as institutional help is concerned, my greatest debt inevitably is to David Robertson, honorary curator at the Kent County Cricket Club. He has been tireless in gathering together books and documents for my use, in fielding my (at times hopeless) questions, in suggesting useful paths to follow. It has been a great pleasure to work at Canterbury under his guiding hand. My thanks also to Jean Owens of the club for help with photographs. I am, of course, grateful to the club itself for permission to quote from its management papers and to reproduce the Chevallier Tayler picture of 1906 and many items from its photographic collection.

I am indebted to Derek Carlaw who has most generously made available to me the fruits of his own researches; and also to Frank Stevens, the leading authority on the Kent Fortress Engineers. I have also received considerable help from Shaw McCloghry of Bloxham School; British Library; British Newspaper Library, Colindale; Jackie Withers of the Commonwealth War

Graves Commission; Defence Storage and Distribution Agency, Llanelli; Eton College Library; Greenwich Heritage Centre; Sarah Paterson and staff of the Imperial War Museum; Dick Whittington and staff of the Centre for Kentish Studies, Maidstone; John Coulter of the Lewisham Local Studies Centre; Light Infantry Office (Yorkshire); London Metropolitan Archives; Glenys Williams and Ken Daldry of the MCC Library, Lord's; National Archives, Kew; National Army Museum; Northampton library; Craig Bowen of the Royal Engineers Museum, Gillingham; John Miller of the Stephens Museum, Tenterden; Sturminster Newton library; Tunbridge Wells library; and West Yorkshire Archive Service.

My thanks go also to all the others who have helped along the way: in particular, Alan Ball, Roger Day, David England, John Gilkes, Bill Mitchinson, Colin Spiro and Bernard Thomson. And last, but not least, to Sheelagh Hunter who has borne with great fortitude the gestation of this book though she cannot tell a wicket from an over.

CLS
31 October 2004

to the memory of
my father
1905 – 1993

Death kills time and enthrones, enhances place.
Could death reward by changing time?

John Fowles, *The Journals*

Chapter 1

Monument

I lost her wedding ring in the garden today, just four days since I had taken to wearing it. It's thin and gold and covered in spiky suns like those on the Dauphin's armour at the Battle of Agincourt. Most of those suns, and the tiny stars that circle round them, have been worn smooth now by thirty years of the friction that is married life. She had bought it herself in that snobby little Sussex town a few days before the wedding while I was away working in London. We couldn't afford much in those days, so I knew it was cheap. A few weeks ago, when I had already begun to covet it, I recalled it had cost only twenty four pounds. "No, sixteen" she said, sitting bolt upright in bed like a white angel, and smiled – smiled with surprise that the memory was still so clear.

It's not cheap to me now. Lord, no. I would give up all my possessions, like in the Bible, to be certain of just this one.

I had been out there mowing the lawn for the first time this spring, with my ancient handmower, not one of those stinking, noisy modern contraptions. The gentle exertion and the pattern of green corridors as I pushed along them under the apple trees was strangely calming – a calmness that has eluded me these past agonising weeks. More than once I had to stoop to clear the damp grass from the cutters and tighten the slippery nuts. It must have happened then.

Back indoors in the gathering dusk, stretched out by the flickering log fire as the television news washed over me, I felt a subtle lightness in my left hand and, looking down, saw the little finger was naked. Naked finger, naked panic. In seconds my hands were scouring the fireside rug, the carpet, the chair, the sofa. I rushed upstairs to comb the bathroom floor. Then up the final flight of dusty wooden steps to my study in the attic where I had been trying, hopelessly and helplessly, to work that afternoon. I pulled madly at books and papers on the shelves until the floor was knee-deep in the wild confetti. But as I knelt there looking out over the freshly cropped front lawn, the penny dropped. Now in a more controlled panic, I rushed out to the garage in the misty twilight to rummage around in mowing machine and grassbox, certain in the knowledge that this had been a gardening disaster.

And then, as the Romans say, wonderful to relate, as I bent over the machine with thumping heart and encircling despair, that strange calmness suddenly took hold once more. I straightened up and, slowly but deliberately, walked round to the front lawn to a spot that was not of my choosing. I thrust my hand deep into the new-mown grass and lifted it out in one smooth movement. I had touched the ring some seconds before I saw it.

She had led me to the spot – there was no doubting it; the first of many little miracles that I now see clearly the future will bring. She promised with a laugh just a week ago that she would sit on my shoulder to keep me in check; but now I see she was promising something quite different – her protection, the same she had always given me in life… .

Ascending the attic stairs this evening to make good the whirlwind havoc of the afternoon, I still felt the power of this fragile new assurance. And as I knelt once more among the cyclone of dusty papers, my mind began to drift on a sea of nostalgic distraction as each new item held up to the light shook out its own stardust of ancient significances waiting for recapture.

It was then that I pulled out the picture, or rather the flaking yellow leaf that had once been the picture. A cricket ground on a sunny summer's afternoon, the boundary lined with trees and tents, beside an all too familiarly statuesque pavilion. Something false about the fielders crouching expectantly round the bat, as though each had been parachuted in from above in his own ready-made configuration. An unsettling intertwining of sleepy somnolence with an almost menacing tension. The slightly feminine figure of the bowler frozen in his delivery stride, leaning gently backwards before the deadly left arm comes over.

Monument

Something in that once familiar landscape, the shape of the arch perhaps above the pavilion gate, seemed to draw me back through fifty years of time to the smell of damp grass newly mown, of battered wholemeal sandwiches held fast with salad cream, to the dull thud of studded boots pounding round the boundary to cut off a four. For a moment I seemed to see clearly how the drama of death can refresh our perspective on life, reaching back to memories of the past as if to defend us from the sorrows of the present. Had the hand that turned up this picture also turned up the ring?

There were words pencilled in the margin which I strove to decipher – my own words of thirty or more years ago but in a seemingly unfamiliar hand. What was it? *Cricket and Death*. And underneath *CB bowls out the last of the golden overs as the Somme and Passchendaele hover overhead*. Well, there's nothing like a false antithesis to spark a youthful imagination, and this perhaps seemed rather sharp at the time, though painfully hackneyed now. And cricket was an overwhelming passion then about which I knew a lot … though little enough of death. Today the roles are reversed. I know less about cricket now despite the untiring efforts of Channel 4 to strangulate the game rather than let it breathe. And yes, over the past few months I have learned for the first time of death – a perverse pupil strapped unwillingly to his desk, I have learned nonetheless.

And on the back of the sheet, some further jottings. *CB elusive character, more myth than man. Intriguing hints of cultivation and neurotic illness. Seemingly left little behind but love. Apart from shrapnel riddled wallet in pavilion. Probably no letters but perhaps the beginnings of a…* . Even more elusive, I guess, thirty years on, as those who knew him have slowly died out. But perhaps we don't need many traces to go on nowadays. History, we are told by the so-called postmodernists, is no longer an objective past, the *before now* of children's stories, but merely the feeble subjective scribblings of the historians. So we can all be our own historian now, attacking the past in our own way, drawing on the traces in our minds.

And there may be something in that antithesis, after all. Cricket, like most games but even more assuredly, takes us out of the world we live in and averts our eyes from the minor miseries of the day to day. More assuredly perhaps, because the special world it fabricates, with its own esoteric rules of deportment, is somehow more self-sufficient than the others and eats up more time – three, four or five days at a stretch. And for the real *aficionados*, in their *Wisden*-lined studies, Life becomes a sort of timeless Test. We are cushioned safely enough from Death even in the brisk non-cricketing world out there, how much more so in the womb of the Long Room at Lord's.

Perhaps, then, we do have here the beginnings of (dare we whisper it?) a book. A strategy for coping with the emptiness and further self-inflicted panics of the months to come. A way through. For she was part of both worlds. She loved Life, but she also loved cricket – especially when Graham Thorpe was at the crease; or Jeff Crowe leading his troops back to the pavilion at Christchurch. And this second love she had wrested from me, so gently and so sweetly.

And what do I have to guide me through? Well, little really – just the handful of her paintings that remain, the wound on my shoulder where she perches … and a wedding ring studded with spiky suns.

The cracked brown leaves swirl in whirlpools round my feet and splinter under every step into a thousand shelly fragments. Their younger sisters see-saw down in lazy pendulum swings from the perches they have held all summer, gazing out across the shimmering roofs to the might of Bell Harry. The avenue of horse chestnuts up to the pavilion seems miserably curtailed compared with those expansive days of fifty years ago, when a small boy wondered how such a grand entrance could lead only to the *back* of such a grand building.

I climb the creaky modern stairs to the committee room where scorebooks and sepia prints await me, set out in tidy welcoming rows. I walk to the front window, looking out over the nets and the windswept square, to get my bearings. It's an unaccustomed back-to-front view, staring the Nackington Road in the face – a view, in those old days, for the privileged few. The ground looks empty and dejected, a colosseum that has lost its purpose; no ball has been bowled here in anger for five weeks at least.

The sacred square, like the high altar during Lent, commands a special genuflection despite the fragility of its protectors – a few rickety iron posts holding hands with the slenderest of ropes. Within the boundary at third man stands the historic lime tree, guardian of a hundred anecdotes, mostly apocryphal; I never once saw a four scored off it. At fine leg, staring back across the void, the thin white boards of the ladies' enclosure, built in 1897 for grass-trailed skirts and parasols and a philosophy of sexual segregation that was to outlive the oldest suffragette. But waiting for tea on a sizzling summer afternoon, what would I not have given for just ten minutes of its apple-tree shade.

Behind the midwicket boundary the west bank rises gently like an iron age earthwork, the one-time vantage point for cars of yesteryear, from which massed ranks of squared up Fords and Austins peer mole-like out through rectangular windscreens on another marathon partnership from Todd and Fagg. And on that boundary, the archetypal square leg fielder scudding forward, arms together and outstretched, to swallow the ballooning loop of some mistimed hook as it curvets through the cool evening air. Jack Cheetham took one there in 1951 which travelled so fast it seemed to disappear right up the sleeves of his sweater.

But where, at the far end, the gently rising tiers of narrow plank benches inhabited by those alternative club members, the fresh air ones, who, like their wealthier brothers in the pavilion, know you can only truly watch a match from behind the bowler's arm? All cleared away, *hélas*, to make room for a modern drive-in experience of sun-flashing windscreens to turn a new generation of batsmen to despair. Yet what of that small boy there in the front row, chewing guiltily on congealed cheese sandwiches ten minutes before the luncheon interval would allow, and pulling on his bottle of Bing?

But there we get ahead of ourselves… .

30 August 1950. A bicycle not made for two freewheels down

Colin Blythe

St Stephen's Hill long before universities have been thought of or medieval tile kilns Time Teamed back into existence. The square wicker basket, filled with my father's black oilskins, crackles and shudders on the back as the wind rushes up through my face and I pray he will apply the brakes in time. We pass the Olde Beverlie where bat and trap still plays. A policeman stops us in Palace Street – a mundane occurrence – and my father lifts me wearily up off the crossbar to disclose a neat leather saddle with tiny iron stirrups suspended. It's OK. We are legal.

We navigate successfully the shuffling crowds along the Old Dover Road and the distant buzz of many thousand voices grabs at my throat. He pushes me on the bicycle through the gate into the field to the right of the main entrance and we park against the brick wall just inside. Everything else is swimming before me in its novelty, but this field suggests a fixity, a sense of place.

It was used at the turn of the 19th century too to store bicycles during Cricket Week, but was rented then from Walter Hearne, landlord of the Bat and Ball across the road, who followed the tradition of indigent Kent professionals by keeping the licensed trade up his sleeve as a sideline. In 1902 the Kent Committee called a special meeting to agree its purchase for £1,000, hoping the rent for bicycles, tennis courts and stabling during matches would pay the interest on the purchase money. The plans fell through then and bore no fruit till 1922, but for the next few years Hearne continued to badger for a sale. Meadow land they called it then, and sweet meadow land it seemed when first I walked upon it.

Our entrance to the ground proper is barred by a bank of hungry-looking turnstiles under a flat-roofed porch, fearsome iron beasts who gnash their ratcheted teeth on each customer as they suck him through into the dark maw. I am small enough to creep through beneath them, but fear evaporates before the bantering chat of the gentle operators under their flat brown cloth-caps, that familiar uniform of all the Kentish labourers I have ever seen walking to work through the autumn fields. They turn the deadly ratchet noise into a child's game of laughter.

Released from this traumatic constriction, as from the

confessional box on a Saturday evening, we burst with relief
into the free expanse of air and climb the grassy bank towards
the multitude of grey heads and backs that groan or roar with
every sound of bat on ball. We circle behind them straining
our necks for a furtive glimpse of white flannel while our fellow travellers strive to find their bearings in the match with
whispered interrogatives – "Who's in?", "What's the score?",
"Who's that facing now?". We find an alleyway between the
rows of ghostly bodies and press boldly into the forest to claim
a slice of grey plank for ourselves.

The West Indies are in and galloping towards a first innings
total of 265. To signal the extraordinary status of a contest that
pits a county against a country the up-to-date scorecard, hur-
riedly purchased for three pence, proclaims in banner head-
lines GRAND CRICKET MATCH. Towards the end of the tea
interval, we take our expectant places beside the roped-off
lane leading from the pavilion to watch the teams come out.
We wait in particular for a close-up of one of the batsmen –
L R Pierre – jet black in a team of disappointingly white or
coffee-coloured faces. The first black face, or so it seems, ever
to be seen in darkest East Kent – a distant world of polite curiosity where latent racism is friendly and unthreatening. And
then the nervous race to the boundary line before the first ball
can be bowled.

It is the first game that the 17-year-old Colin Cowdrey, fresh
from Tonbridge School, has played at Canterbury. He is about
to make his mark with a cool 25 in the Kent first innings, but
is quite unknown to most of the devotees of the Nackington
Road end. He stands a tall, svelte figure ruminating, left hand
under right elbow, on the boundary line at long on, no hint of
the waistline to come that will root him forever to first slip.
A voice on the back row of plank benches is proudly in the
know: "Good man, that Cow-dee. Good man!"

Close of play we pack up cushions and plastic macs and
make for the gates, the long journey ahead made bearable by
the excitations of the afternoon. As I close my tired eyes, sitting on the cross-bar, all I can see is blinding white figures
dancing on a backcloth of emerald green. And as we push
wearily back up St Stephen's we both can smell that plate of

runner beans fresh from the garden, dripping with butter and grilled cheese, which will greet our safe arrival home.

But that first match marks the beginning of something else – an awakening of voices from the past that reach forward through the subconscious to embrace these new found faces in the present. As we leave the ground, I spot out of the corner of my eye a white stone object ringed with chain rails, and with people. It has all the outward appearance of a war memorial, like the familiar one beside the Whitstable library, the dusty old house where we change our books every Tuesday and Friday. But what can one of those strange objects be doing here, tucked away in the corner of a cricket ground?

Full of curiosity, I grab my father's hand and tug towards it. Inside the low chain rail are two steps up to an octagonal base about four feet high on which stands a square plinth supporting a small pointed obelisk. It is all in white stone, neatly proportioned, with much of the feeling of the Dane John monument back down the road where the Baedeker bomb sites lie waiting for redevelopment.

But this records an altogether earlier engagement. I strain myopically to decipher the faded block letters on the west face of the plinth.

TO THE MEMORY OF
COLIN BLYTHE
OF THE KENT ELEVEN WHO VOLUNTEERED FOR ACTIVE
SERVICE UPON THE OUTBREAK OF HOSTILITIES IN THE
GREAT WAR OF 1914-18 AND WAS KILLED AT YPRES ON
THE 18TH NOV. 1917.
AGED 38
HE WAS UNSURPASSED AMONG THE FAMOUS BOWLERS OF
THE PERIOD AND BELOVED BY HIS FELLOW CRICKETERS

The small boy who read the words on the plinth that day was puzzled by this odd conjunction of cricket and war ... and, yes, of death. And those two words, unsurpassed and beloved. It was at once both frightening and beautiful, like death itself. The monument recorded an event of only thirty years before but to the small boy it might have been three thousand.

Monument

23 August 1919 – the christening of the monument to the fallen. How important are dates – 23 August is the birthday too of my fallen angel. A small, rather sombre, group of people gather this Saturday afternoon round the shining white obelisk, pristine in its newness. The bigwigs from the present and the past are all there – Lord George Hamilton, the current President of the club, the ageing Lord Harris who ran it for so long, Lionel Troughton, the wartime captain, and most of the second team mingling with members of the Band of Brothers.

And in the centre, the still figure of a tall young woman with misty grey eyes, just 30 years old, who has come alone to mourn one man while all the rest are mourning a generation. The current of her life is shattered and she is floundering still in the restless waters, searching for the new perspective. She is approaching the end of her second year – the year of healing, some say – but she knows that this is one wound that will never really heal. She hears with half an ear the President mouth his dutiful text – England the home of sport to which no locality has contributed more than Kent; the qualities engendered by sport the national bulwark in the darkest days of war. And then the recital of names, her lover's first – the best slow bowler the county ever produced.

But her mind is elsewhere. As she stares at this expensive white memorial, shimmering in the luminous light, she sees only a simple wooden cross in a makeshift cemetery of countless wooden crosses where she stood, alone there too, just a week ago. She has seen the country of his fall, even now, two years on, barely recovering from the mire of mud and stench of death. So different from this neat and tidy cricket ground with its green and manicured square.

And how did he die? She knows only what she has been told. Not for her the questionable comfort of the watch at the bedside, the sound of movement in the throat, the tortured wait for that frightening last breath. Frightening yet beautiful. But there is no beauty in this death or the thousands of others all around him. Was it truly the hot steel shell bursting nearby, blasting everyone to fragments, as the story went, and as the two punctured wallets rescued from the body seem to bear awful witness? Or was it all a dire dream?

Like most of her fellow widows, she cannot be certain of what they have told her, of information pieced together not in a climate of deceit but one of hopeless, well-meaning ignorance. Not for her then the simple, certain closure of the witness at the bedside. But at least he was not among those countless others whose end could never be tidily explained, even in the formal War Office letter – poor bastards sucked into cruel black whirl-pools of mud, spiralling down to oblivion, lost without trace. At least for her there is a body and a resting-place.

And a date – dates are important. He was killed on 8 November, two days before the final push on the Passchendaele Ridge, while the generals back in the safety of GHQ – those generals who ten years before had gloried in the subtleties of his length and flight from the window of the Long Room at Lord's – were quietly choreographing his slaughter. But wait a minute! The date it says here was the *eighteenth* of November. As she reads the gentle words on the plinth, her mind is too fragile to take it all in, certainly too *distrait* to spot the deliber-ate mistake. Irony of ironies, with all these dignitaries stand-ing round in mournful tribute, they had got the date wrong! Someone had blundered.

In other times and other climes, it might have mattered more – a careless insult to a memory, some might have said. But after all, as if we did not know it already, even the high authorities are fallible. In times of such uncertainty, perhaps even dates themselves become a little less certain. So no-one read it mindfully or questioned it. There is something quaint and very English about it all, a curiosity inscribed in stone that has gone unremarked for more than eighty years.

And now, fifty years on from my own first sighting of this stone, with time put squarely in her place, I read those words again on an autumn afternoon, the brown leaves scudding round my feet and a chill in the wind. And just behind me, a tall, young woman with misty grey eyes, looking over my shoulder to read them too once more. I cannot detach from her and she cannot detach from me.

Monument

Who is to comfort and console her? How will she reconstruct *her* life out of the remains? And indeed what does still remain of him who has gone? Well, little really – just a couple of violins, a set of scorebooks, the photo of herself he kept in the wallet over his heart, with the face symbolically shot clean away. And now, this monument. But out of all this must she reconstruct.

For he now is dead. Unsurpassed and beloved. *And when he died his spirit reached out to me and has been with me ever since.*

Chapter 2

Nursery

Colin Blythe was born on 30 May 1879 at No. 78, Evelyn Street, the main arterial road that runs parallel with the Thames through the ancient district of Deptford. On the same day in 1593, Christopher Marlowe was murdered in the tavern of Eleanor Bull just a stone's throw away. Marlowe was born in Canterbury but his spirit set free in Deptford. Blythe was born in Deptford but his spirit lingers on in Canterbury.

In Marlowe's day Evelyn Street was still the Old Deptford Road, a dark and dangerous place, notorious for highway robberies. The name was changed in the mid 19th century to commemorate John Evelyn, the diarist, who lived at Sayers Court in Deptford for forty years in the late 17th century. When the Blythe family came to live there, it was a buzzing community of old houses, shops and small businesses. For centuries workers had been drawn to Deptford by the heavy industry there. The Royal Dockyard founded by Henry VIII and the Woolwich Arsenal established in John Evelyn's time both provided thousands of jobs, and gave birth to many small ancillary businesses and related Government organisations, like Her Majesty's Victualling Yard close to Blythe's birthplace.

Blythe's paternal grandfather, another Colin, was born in Rochester in 1808 and, like so many in the 1840s, was sucked in to the metropolis by the lure of employment. He settled in Deptford where he flourished as a shirt maker and dealer in silk goods, and then later ran a warehousing business in

Gresham Street in the City of London. He had a typically large Victorian family of three sons and six daughters. The third son, Walter, the cricketer's father, was born in Deptford in 1854 and on leaving school became an engineer fitter. In 1878 he married Elizabeth Dready, a year younger than himself, who was the daughter of a cooper and came from a family that had lived in Deptford for generations – her grandfather enjoyed the dashing title of "leading man of stores" in the Victualling Yard.

It was a shotgun wedding. They escaped to the privacy of Kensington where they were married at St Clement's Church on Christmas Day 1878. By that time Elizabeth was already four months pregnant with Colin, but peace was no doubt soon made with the families as they settled back into Deptford in the new year. While it is perhaps too colourful to say, as Neville Cardus has done, that Colin Blythe was born "in a slum", there is no doubt that Deptford, then as now, was an area of some deprivation. The closing down of the Dockyard in 1867, because it was unsuitable for building the new iron ships, was a severe blow to the local economy. In 1887, when Colin was eight, the unemployment rate in North Deptford where he lived was more than 32 per cent, according to a parliamentary enquiry into the conditions of the working class in London which had deliberately targeted the area as one of the most deprived.

Although Walter Blythe was fortunate to be a skilled artisan in an area where industry needed engineers, the growth of his family over the next twenty years must have put severe pressure on the domestic purse. From the arrival of Colin until 1902, Elizabeth Blythe gave birth to six more sons and six daughters. He had already been playing three seasons for Kent when his last sister, Nellie, was born. The fact that only one of these thirteen children died in infancy is sufficient indication they were much better fed and housed than the average working class family in East London, where infant mortality hit phenomenal rates at the end of the century.

As the family expanded, larger accommodation was required. In the year after Colin's birth they moved west up Evelyn Street to No. 206 and were to stay in that close vicinity for the next ten years. In the mid 1880s, they moved off the main road to 63 Rolt Street where they stayed for a couple of years, and then round the corner to 39 Gosterwood Street, which was clean and eminently respectable; then finally to 36 Wotton Road where Colin was to live out the 1890s.

In such a large family it was fortunate for him to be followed by three sisters, Jessie, Florrie and May, a triumvirate who as time went on would be qualified by their sex to look after the other children. Colin was seven before his privileged position as sole male heir was challenged by the appearance of another brother, Walter. But his position as eldest child of a rapidly expanding family would put pressure on him later to leave school and start earning money at the earliest possible juncture.

His education began at Duke Street Infants School in the early 1880s where he was subject to the firm discipline and learning by rote that was standard at the time. Six weeks before his eighth birthday he moved on to Alverton Street School at the bottom of Gosterwood Street, where he was to remain for the next five years. In April 1892, just a few weeks before his 13th birthday, the statutory minimum age, he finally left school, no doubt because the family, with seven children then to feed, sorely needed a new breadwinner.

He was then apprenticed as a trainee engineer fitter and turner at the Woolwich Arsenal, following in his father's footsteps. He loved his work and, as later with his cricket, threw himself into it body and soul, determined to learn and to improve. He set himself to study for a Whitworth scholarship but, as a result of the pressures of working and studying at the same time, his health broke down. It seems likely, in view of the later history, that this was the first major onset of the epilepsy that was to dog him in his Test career, for he gave up the studying and his doctor advised him strongly to get out into the open air as much as he could.

In the Blythe mythology it was this advice that made him a cricketer. According to this account, he never played cricket at school, and the day he was "discovered" by Captain McCanlis at 18 was almost the first time he had turned his arm over. This seems, however, to be the kind of distortion that naturally occurs when someone's life takes off as miraculously as his, and the world looks round for material to embellish the story further. In another, perhaps more reliable, version, he used to play cricket and football in the boys clubs around Blackheath, but was 11 before he started to bowl and find the natural rhythms essential to that art.

Later, his obituary in the *Kentish Mercury* hinted that he had played as a schoolboy for the local team of St Luke's, though this has never been corroborated. Given his occupation, it is possible also that he played at some time for one of the two Ordnance Department teams on their Royal Arsenal ground, but if he did, there is no record of a regular appearance in the side. Perhaps the general lack of hard evidence of his cricket before joining Kent supports the broad assertion that he did not play competitively very much.

Certainly, his surroundings were perfect for semi-organised matches. The vast stretches of Blackheath, which had been synonymous with cricket since the early 18th century, lay on his doorstep, and scratch games there were a common part of life for the boys of Deptford. So popular was the sport in Blythe's day that up to thirty games could be playing on the heath at the same time. The impossible pitches were no good to train a batsman on, but tailor-made for a spin bowler with a natural flair for exploiting bad wickets.

Although there were two county grounds within walking distance of his home, at Catford and the Rectory Field, Blackheath, Blythe, with his eyes fixed firmly on his engineering studies, seems never to have seen Kent play in the 1890s until, that is, the day that changed his life. On 15 July 1897 Kent opened a match against Somerset at the Rectory Field. It was beautiful weather but the attendance very small because of a more compelling attraction down the road – Surrey were playing Middlesex at Lord's. Kent quickly knocked up 282 and by close of play had Somerset 73 for 4. The following day the visitors crawled to within 29 of the Kent score thanks to a brilliant 92 by S M J Woods. Jack Mason followed suit with an equally brilliant century for Kent, who ended the second day on 217 for 7, 246 runs ahead. Mason was then 105 not out, with the ageing Kent all-rounder, Walter Wright, due in next.

Colin Blythe

Saturday 17 July was a holiday for Blythe from the sweated labour of the Arsenal and, with the final day of the game promising an interesting finish, he made his way to the Rectory Field to join the tiny crowd already there. The usual morning nets were in train when Walter Wright, nervously awaiting his call to the wicket, stepped out of the pavilion looking for someone to bowl at him. Blythe tells the story in his own words: "I don't think there were many more spectators than players. Walter Wright came out to practise and asked me to 'bowl him a few'." The young man responded as best he could; he had no idea of anything so sophisticated as length, but merely tried to hit the wicket.

Standing by was the veteran Captain William McCanlis, one of the last of the underhand lob bowlers, who had served the Kent club since the 1860s as cricketer, adviser and later coach, and now took on the chance role of talent spotter: "I noticed a lad, one of the crowd, bowl a few balls to Walter Wright, and was impressed with his delivery. I spoke to him and arranged for him to come and bowl to me one evening".

It was a chance find out of a clear blue sky. Without that surprise request to "bowl a few", it is possible that the 18-year-old engineer would have gone back to his engineering and stayed there for the rest of his life. He must have watched the cricket that day with only half a mind to the scoreboard. There was excitement on the field, but it was nothing to the churning excitement within himself. His few practice balls to Walter Wright seem to have paid off – the No. 9 scored an unaccustomed 18 and the last three Kent wickets put on 118 in all. Mason, shortly to become Blythe's first captain, hit cleanly all round the wicket and made his highest score of 183, till he was bowled by a deceptive lob from Palairet.

Somerset were set 365 to win and by four o'clock had reached a careful 94 for 3, seeming certain to save the match. But Jack Mason, not content with his heroics with the bat, then came on to bowl and took five of the last seven wickets for 20 runs. He finished with 5 for 23 and Somerset were beaten by 213 runs. It was a thrilling display for the 18-year-old as he packed up his things and made his way home to Deptford, burning to tell the unbelievable news of his chance to join these heroes.

Nursery

Events now proceeded fast. He kept the appointment at Charlton Park, where McCanlis skippered his local team, to bowl at the bearded veteran, who the more he tested him, the more convinced he became that this boy's natural ability needed only proper development for him to do great things. He recommended him for a trial at the Tonbridge "nursery", which he passed with flying colours and was signed up at once to train that autumn in preparation for the season of 1898. The laconic remarks in the trials book pointed to the possibility of future success: "Bowls slow left. Very useful bowler".

The Tonbridge nursery was not a purely Kent invention (Surrey had just started a similar operation for training young professionals) but it was the best publicised, and generally credited with creating the backbone of the team that was to take Kent to such unexpected success in the Edwardian period. It had been born out of necessity. Kent had, in the past, been largely dependent on amateurs for the limited success it had achieved. In general, it was the swashbuckling batsmen, mostly amateur, who gave the media sparkle to cricket and created the public following. Bowlers, usually professional, were the industrial workhorses of the game, lobbing up the balls for the spectacular, and amateur, hitters.

The problem in each cricket season was one of timing. It was not until July and August, when the universities came down and businessmen were free to take their long summer holidays, that the market was suddenly flooded with a surfeit of talented amateurs. This had two unwelcome effects for a county side of any ambition. First, many of the professionals, who had toiled through the heats of May and June, were forced to stand aside and make way for these seasonal birds of passage; this was no way to convince the young among them that county cricket could offer a stable career. Second, the great victories that were thus constructed in August were never sufficient to balance out the more mundane draws and losses of the first three-quarters of the season. This was a serious matter as the fight for the county championship took on a more competitive edge, and success in that competition became the talisman for success at the turnstile and in enrolling club members. In short, the traditional easygoing

17

management of the cricketing labour force was now threatening the economic survival of the clubs.

By the mid-1890s, it soon became apparent to the Kent Committee that the county's poor showing in the championship might well have to do with the balance of a team that as often as not put out two or three professionals to eight or nine amateurs. And, surprise surprise, whereas it was easy to recruit more amateurs, it was much more difficult to find young professionals who wished to join such a lop-sided enterprise. If championship success were the goal, a special initiative was needed.

On 4 August 1896 the Committee met in the tent of its chairman, Lord Harris, at the St Lawrence Ground during a break in the Canterbury Cricket Week. The captain, Frank Marchant, a swashbuckler himself *par excellence*, put forward a formal proposal that the County should enter negotiations with the Tonbridge Cricket Club for placing some young players on its Angel Ground the following season, leaving the details to be worked out by a newly established Young Players Committee. By November, the club was able to announce that the arrangements would be in place early the following season and to call for recommendations of promising players.

Thus the Tonbridge nursery was born. Tonbridge seems a strange choice since the Canterbury ground had only recently been purchased and had long been the *de facto* headquarters of Kent cricket. But the guiding force behind the new initiative was the Kent general manager, Tom Pawley, who as a Tonbridge man himself knew the local club well and was keen to build up his home town as a centre of cricketing excellence. That winter George Webb, the coach at Tonbridge School, was put in charge of coaching at the new nursery at a salary of 30 shillings a week. When in 1900 it became apparent that Webb's full time duties at the school were hampering his nursery role, Captain McCanlis took over from him in a stint that was to last until 1912.

In the course of 1897, six young players, including Blythe, had been engaged on the Tonbridge ground, of whom the fast bowler Arthur Fielder was the only other to make it permanently into the Kent team. A hundred pounds had been put into the enterprise that year, and to tide over the winter months Lord Harris wrote to local employers, seeking work for the young players and offering the bait of an attractive contribution from the club towards their wages. It seems that Blythe continued with his engineering job that winter, living as usual at home, but took lodgings in Tonbridge the following year. While maintaining his base in Deptford for some years still, Tonbridge was to become his spiritual, and later his real, home for the whole of his cricketing life.

1898 was Blythe's first year in Kent cricket and the routine at Tonbridge was relentless. Practice would start at 10.30 in the morning, in one or two nets according to the numbers available, with each trainee taking turns at batting and bowling for about a quarter of an hour at a time. Those neither batting nor bowling would have to field until lunch was taken at one. In the early part of the season, a further net would be held in the afternoon. Later on in the year, the young players would bowl through the afternoon, two at a time, to members looking for practice, but care was taken not to overbowl them for too long spells.

The grind of daily nets was alleviated by opportunities to play full games for the Tonbridge club, and for clubs in the locality who were invited to apply for players. In this second year, such was the success of the scheme that it was found impossible to send a man to meet every application. And the demand for nursery places soon became highly competitive; in 1898 forty-four aspiring young players were given trials for the very few places available.

This was the insistent background against which Colin Blythe learned his cricketing skills – the impeccable length born of perpetual practice, the fast turn and bounce developed through concentration on technique, and the final flourishes of pace, flight and swing. What stood out about this unassuming young man was his total dedication to the task, his quiet ambition and resolve to become a professional cricketer of quality. He showed a great anxiety to learn from his coaches and a determination to unlearn everything which might stand in the way of his future success.

Colin Blythe

A reporter on the *Kentish Express* recalled how he looked in these first days of his apprenticeship before the eyes of the world had fallen upon him.

> Well can I remember seeing him bowling away in the nets early that summer – a loosely-built, lean youngster, with always a happy look about his face, but a difficult bowler for any batsman to play. Obviously, he only wanted experience.

By 1899, his second season at Tonbridge, he was already gaining that experience and was much in demand for local matches. In these he bowled more than 600 overs, and took 105 wickets at an average of just over 13. Only his new friend, the fast bowler Arthur Fielder, with 91 wickets at 18 apiece, came anywhere near him. And even his batting this year seemed to bear out Captain McCanlis' assertion that "Blythe is not half a bad batsman when he goes in with the intention of staying; and yet, when he came to Tonbridge he had no idea whatever of batting". Those hours in the nets were paying off. In 22 local innings this year he made 230 runs, with a top score of 44 not out, and a respectable average of 16.42. It was another five seasons before he would come close to matching that average in first class cricket.

1899 was the most successful year of the nursery to date. Of the six young professionals on the books, four were given the opportunity to play for the county, and for Colin Blythe the call-up came on Monday 21 August, against Yorkshire at his now "home" ground of Tonbridge. At just 20, he was to join a team of his boyhood heroes, soon to become his regular colleagues – the captain, Jack Mason, the dashing bat and fast bowler whose impact on the side was dramatic even when later on his appearances became irregular; Alec Hearne, the principal professional, doughty opening bat and off-break bowler who would often open the bowling with Blythe; Cuthbert Burnup, the recently arrived top order batsman who on his day was unbeatable; Bill Bradley, the fast bowling complement to Mason; and Fred Huish behind the stumps, the first in a long line of Kent wicketkeepers that were best in the land. To add to this intimidating list, he was to face the one player with whom his name would always be linked in competition, the legendary slow left-armer, Wilfred Rhodes.

Kent came into the match with a fairly mediocre season behind them as the performance of their professional bowlers Fred Martin, Walter Wright and even Alec Hearne fell away. Yorkshire by contrast, with 14 victories already under their belt, were the hottest favourites to take the championship. The Yorkshire innings made a disastrous start. On a good hard batting pitch, they lost Jackson, Tunnicliffe and Denton to the pace of Jack Mason for just one run. But Frank Mitchell came in and was soon hitting Mason, Bradley and Alec Hearne all round the ground. With support from both Wainwright and later Hirst, he had steadied the Yorkshire ship and put it on course for a decent score.

With Yorkshire on 86 for 4 and Mitchell 55 not out, the point had now been reached when Mason could call only upon Blythe. It was to be the first sight in county cricket of that gentle run-up, easy turn of the arm and devastating spin. And, as the local reporter witnessed, the miraculous happened.

> Then the young colt was given the ball. I can see the suppressed excitement now – all the Tonbridgians anxious as to the result of the Kent skipper's experiment. Towards the bowling crease trotted Blythe, as innocent-looking as a babe. The ball pitched just off the wicket, the burly Yorkshireman played forward, but the leg bail fell, and Blythe had phenomenally taken a wicket – and a good wicket too – from the first ball he ever bowled for his county. He has done many brave things since then, he has been cheered to the echo in field and in pavilion, but never, I feel sure, has he experienced such a proud moment of his life, nor heard such joyous music as the shouts that greeted him on the old Angel ground that sunny afternoon in August 1899.

Strangely, the only bowler before him to take a wicket with his first ball for Kent was George McCanlis, the younger brother of his discoverer, back in 1873 at the Oval. For the young man, it was a remarkable opening, and something more – a declaration of intent.

He was to perform no further miracles that match. The Yorkshire batsmen then began to get after him and he was taken off after four overs had conceded 25 runs. In the second innings, however, in which he took the last wicket to fall, he managed to hold a Yorkshire batting attack on the rampage to just three runs an over. Thanks to Bradley and Mason, the visitors were dismissed in the first innings for 164 on a good wicket and Kent replied with 369, by dint of a magnificent 171 by Burnup. Yorkshire's 325 in the second innings left Kent with just 120 to win, which they managed with the loss of only two wickets. It was Kent's greatest triumph of the season and marked the end of Yorkshire's title hopes. For the young aspirant, playing the first match for his county, it was a remarkably exciting launch pad.

He played in the three remaining matches of the season and added a further 12 wickets to his tally. In the drawn match against Surrey at his other "home" ground of Blackheath, there was a hint of things to come. In the first innings he took 3 for 15 off 5 overs, and in the second 3 for 24 off 24 overs – wicket taking and economy, his hallmarks for the next fifteen years. In *Wisden* that year the Kent entry drew attention to the discovery of this "new and promising" bowler, but stopped short on so little evidence of predicting a great future. It took only one more season to throw such caution to the winds.

Chapter 3

The Week

The Nackington Road end. That small society of hunched expectant figures, seated on folded grey raincoats to save their bottoms from the numbing properties of those narrow plank benches. Silent and concentrated, but for the odd caustic quip from a Kentish cloth cap in the back row. Silent, that is, until a wicket fell, when the roar would be followed by a chatter of excitement as the very English ice was broken, neighbour enquiring of neighbour was it caught or lbw? who caught it? what did he make? And the small boys among us rushed to complete the careful entry in the scorecard before the next ball could be bowled.

The images have stuck in our brains like those white figures glued to our retina after close of play. Fred Ridgway, red in the face and dripping with sweat on a sultry summer afternoon, glaring straight at us as he made the great wheeling turn at the end of his long walk back. It was a look of some subtlety, a combination of contempt for soft livers who sat and watched while he worked his guts out, and a plea to be released from the agonising prospect of another six overs. Then, just before he turned, the human look suddenly shut off and the automaton took over, concentrating on delivery of the next ball. Occasionally, someone would cry out from the crowd a few words of encouragement, or some joking reference to his toil, and for one split second it seemed the façade would crack open and he would give full vent to all those suppressed feelings, or leap into the crowd and murder someone.

Then Fred would be replaced by Ray Dovey, tall, bespectacled, stiff and balding, who took just a few mechanical steps before the arm came lazily over. Slow bowlers were always a let-down for us kids, fast bowling the only true currency. Perhaps it was the macho nature of that art, the promise of spectacular wicket-taking that it held out; perhaps we had not the patience nor eyesight to be moved by the subtleties of turn and length. To us, Ray Dovey's incipient baldness and the few crumbling steps to the wicket made him seem unconscionably old and ineffectual. We therefore dozed, or reached for our sweaty sandwiches or the bottle of fizzy orange Bing, with the china stopper on its wire frame that fitted back over the top like the seal of a champagne cork.

What went on at the pavilion end was a distant mystery, except when Doug Wright came on to bowl, with his extraordinary run, all looping leaps and flailing arms like a bouncing windmill. We all tried to imitate it in the lunch hour at school and found to our astonishment that, if you really bounced into it with a will (not Colin Cowdrey's flat imitation to lighten the close of a boring draw), it invariably delivered a good length and a sharpish leg-break.

No matter that we could not, from our end, see the ball pitch, turn and leap; we heard the sudden flurry of boot on earth, saw the blind swing of bat and the Godfrey Evans dive. The occasional ball did so much that, particularly in the early overs before Godfrey had got his eye in, it would beat the lot – bat, stumps and blushes of England wicketkeeper. As the ball suddenly appeared over Godfrey's left shoulder, everyone on the pitch and in the crowd was transfixed with shocked laughter – no matter for the byes, here were wickets in prospect!

In all of this, the opposition might not have existed; it was only our heroes we noticed. When they were performing, their past great feats, personal records that schoolboys took glory from knowing, came flooding back to the forefront of our minds. If Doug Wright were on, we remembered the world record of seven hat-tricks and wondered would he add to it today. When Arthur Fagg was approaching his century, we thought of that game at Colchester in 1938 when he had made a double century in each innings, a record whose special thrill lay in the fact it could never be broken.

For most of the 1950s, or so it seemed, our two opponents in Cricket Week were always the same, a circumstance which, win or lose, made them both in our eyes inexorably slow, boring and mediocre. From Saturday to Tuesday it would be Hampshire; from Wednesday to Friday Middlesex. Neither seemed to us to have class players. The highpoint of the Hampshire innings was always when Desmond Eager marched jauntily to the wicket to a chorus of jeers, flaunting his multi-coloured quartered Harlequin cap, and returned just as jauntily, having been out first ball. In my memory at least, he was *always* out first ball.

Our image of both teams was formed by just two players who seemed irremovably determined to ruin any game of cricket. When Hampshire were on the run with five wickets down cheaply, who would arrive at the wicket but Peter Sainsbury. For Middlesex, it would be Fred Titmus. Both would bring the game to an instant grinding halt, with dead bat performances that made Trevor Bailey look like Victor Trumper. On and on they would grind for what seemed eternity, driving crowd and Kent players to distraction. And when Kent were running away with the bat some twenty overs into an innings, they would both go on at the pavilion end to audible groans, close the game down and empty the terraces.

It was at such moments that one's eye moved away from the action, or reverse of it, out on the square to take in the ground, its buildings and the timeless atmosphere they so powerfully exuded. To the right stood the Annexe, built in 1909, originally intended as an extension of the pavilion, but finally erected as a stand alone to save the lime trees between it and the older building. For the Kent Committee trees always came first. Its two storeys were beautifully proportioned, the slender white pillars leading up to a roof of delicate pink tiles which contrasted perfectly in the sun with its white boarding. It was always in the eye because the main scoreboard sprouted like an overgrown ear from its left hand side. Behind it stood the white printing shed of Messrs. J A Jennings, where we queued patiently at the end of a match while they printed the vital bowling analyses for our close of play scorecards.

To the left stood the Concrete Stand, built in 1927, one of the largest cantilever structures of its day, and acknowledged as an eyesore by everyone but myself. It was long and thin and badly proportioned with its top storey jutting out threateningly over the lower. Close up, the rough grey concrete filled with tiny pebbles seemed from an age of aboriginal building before the science of materials had been properly learned. Its internal spaces were vast and chill, like a barren desert; on a still day the applause of the spectators within it echoed round the bare walls like a death knell. And that was its attraction – a sense of mystery and foreboding, a bomb shelter above ground, rushed up in a blind panic of national emergency.

And then in the middle, the pavilion. What can one say of a building that gave the whole ground and the game played upon it its character and its beauty? Built in the winter of 1899-1900, its style and pink-white colouring is similar to the Annexe of nine years later. But where the latter takes its beauty from straight up and down simplicity, the pavilion takes its from the odd rococo touches, the slight curve of the arches on the lower storey, the Doric arch over the entrance, the famous clock on its white baroque pediment, that several batsmen had cleared with the ball but only Les Ames had managed to hit.

The spate of building at the turn of the century had been conditioned by one act. In 1895 the owner of the ground, Lord Sondes, offered it for sale to the Kent Club and after some haggling a deal was struck the following February on a sum of £4,500 for the 13 acres. Now the ground was its own property, the club looked to make its own permanent improvements. In September 1896 it was agreed to add 630 free seats to the facilities. The major enterprise of a pavilion was discussed, but shelved in favour of a cheaper option until the ground had been fully paid for – the building of a stand of brick and iron on the former members enclosure, to provide a maximum of 315 seats. Thus was born the Iron Stand, or ladies enclosure, at the Nackington Road end.

Two years later the Committee was able to make its move. In November 1899 estimates were approved for a pavilion to be built on the site of the old thatched shed that had served the purpose up till then, and the building went up that winter – a committee room, dressing rooms for the players, and most important of all a luncheon room, players having previously had to cadge their lunchtime refreshment from friends in private or club tents, or pay for it themselves at the Bat and Ball over the road. For the members, there was seating for an additional 500 in the upper storey and under the verandah in front of the building. The whole project cost a little over £2,600, more than half the cost of the ground itself. Minor touches came later. It was not until November 1900 that a member of the committee suggested a clock on the pediment of the building and the Vice-Presidents agreed to pay the £80 required as a gift to the club.

Thus when Blythe played his first county match at Canterbury in August 1900, the pavilion was playing its first match too; though from the Nackington Road perspective of the 1950s that seemed to be truly impossible. For us, the unapproachable building, with its curving white arches leading into dusty, darkened recesses that echoed with boots on boards, was an enchanted palace constructed way before time began. And in the haze of a summer's afternoon, as the slowness of the game brought time to a halt, the pavilion stood there across the green outfield like the core of some great illusion, firm yet fragile, solid yet susceptible. It approached, it receded, in the heatstrokes of the mind. It shimmered in the dazzling white of the sun; it faded, ghost-like, in the folds of evening shadows. It held one's eye in its hypnotic gaze and took possession of one's soul.

For me, that distant building across the turf had another quite separate and secret existence which gave further force to this mystical, dream-like illusion. I had discovered it in a picture in a book at home, *my* picture, a snapshot apparently of a moment in time, but which, as I found out much later with some disenchantment, had been deceitfully contrived a year afterwards to give the appearance of that moment in time. An impressionist work which fed me the right impression, and confirmed what I always knew – that what lay before my eyes on those summer afternoons was no more than an image, an everlasting image with no conceivable roots in time or reality. The fielders crouch round the bat, the high left arm is about to come over, framed in the darkness of the pavilion entrance. And the perspective is ours of the Nackington Road.

That timeless feeling of cricket at Canterbury was, from a more mundane perspective, also an illusion. In Blythe's day the cricket there was a comparatively recent growth, or rather should one say, transplant. For the traditional centre of Kent cricket had always been the geographic centre of the county, Maidstone and the Wealden villages like Penshurst and Benenden. Just before the middle of the 19th century, when Kent cricket began to take on its modern shape, it might well have claimed to be Town Malling, to which the redoubtable batsman and cricket impresario, Fuller Pilch, had been induced by money to come and reside, away from his native Norfolk. In 1839 and 1840, Kent played at Town Malling their grand matches against England.

But where money had spoken once, it could speak again. In 1841, a Canterbury clergyman, the Rev. John Baker, who had founded the local Beverley Club back in 1835, together with some cricketing and acting friends from Cambridge invited Pilch for a salary to come and live in Canterbury and support the cricket there. As a consequence, the first match at Canterbury between Kent and England, a return for the match at Lord's earlier in the year, was played in 1841 on a ground near the cavalry barracks newly leased by Baker's club. The local Beverley Club at St Stephen's, where bat and trap had played since ancient times, thus became, to all intents and purposes, the county club.

Baker and his distinguished Cambridge friends decided that the best way to promote the cricket at Canterbury and to pay its way was to invite, with suitable social inducements, the local county families and members of the MCC to take part in a regular gala week of first rate cricket between Kent and England, and the Gentlemen of Kent and Gentlemen of England. Canterbury Cricket Week was born.

The Week

The first took place in 1842 and was immediately a huge success. The matches continued to be played on the ground by the military barracks and, because of the interest of the Baker circle in private theatricals, were backed up in the evenings by plays, with professional actresses brought down from London, and by two balls. Once started, the proceedings seemed to run of themselves. The hotels were overflowing, and soon the local townspeople got in on the act with special decorations and illuminations along the main streets, processions and military bands, and picnics at the ground. In 1847 the cricket moved to the newly opened St Lawrence Ground, leased from the tenant of Winter's Farm, Nackington and named after the site of the medieval St Lawrence Priory which it adjoined. This was the start of my own personal dream.

As the 19th century progressed, so the Week flourished. Accommodation expanded to house the visitors and, with the onset of the railway age, crowds flooded in on cheap excursions from London, and holiday-makers from Margate and Ramsgate. The amateur actors soon formed themselves into the Old Stagers troupe and the evening performances at the New Theatre in Orange Street grew in accomplishment and prestige. The cricket teams themselves would take the stage for a bow at the end of the performance. By 1900 Canterbury Week was an event to rival Ascot and Goodwood in the summer calendar, and the show of fashion on Ladies' Day, always the Thursday, was a sight to compete with the ladies' promenade at Lord's during the Eton and Harrow or Varsity matches.

Like them, it was widely reported in the national press. As the Kent team of the Blythe era proceeded from triumph to triumph, so did their success become even more closely associated with Canterbury. By 1910 the *Times* correspondent had begun to see The Week as the archetypal tourist attraction and the quintessence of Englishness.

It has been said with some measure of truth that Kent cricket is different from other cricket, and Canterbury is different from other Kent cricket. Certainly there is nothing more delightful. If one wished to show an intelligent (*sic*) foreigner something essentially

Colin Blythe

English and quite unlike anything he could see in his own country, one could not do better than take him to the St. Lawrence Ground.

It was a lot to live up to. For any new player to the county side, the matches of Canterbury Week were the real test of both ability and acceptance.

Since his promising start in the final matches of 1899, the summer of 1900 was to mark Colin Blythe's first full season of county cricket. By the end of that summer, the few dancing steps to the wicket, the little chassée before the long last stride brought the windmill left arm over, had become imprinted on the collective mind of every ground in the country. It was to remain a symbolic spectacle of English cricket for another fourteen seasons to come.

His impact that wet summer was immediate. In Kent's second match against Gloucestershire at Catford, though ruined by rain, he took 5-71 in the first innings, his first five wicket haul, and three of the four wickets that fell in the second for just 13 runs. It was a warning signal of what was in store. Against Middlesex at Tonbridge in June he took 5-46 in the first innings and against Yorkshire at Headingley in July 5-41, his best analysis to date. By the second week of August, as he faced with nervous expectation his first match at Canterbury, he had already taken 56 wickets in 14 matches at a cost of 22.5. Canterbury was the turning point. In the last 8 matches of the season, he was to take a further 58 wickets for 14.5 runs apiece.

Canterbury Week was due to open that year on Monday 6 August with the match against Lancashire, the symbolic opponents of the Edwardian "Week". The Boer War had cast an inevitable shadow over proceedings, with so many members of Kent families away at the front, that the usual dances were cancelled. There was general anxiety in the city over the fate of Colonel Frith, the popular commandant of the Canterbury depot, who had narrowly survived a serious carriage accident, and as a result the military withdrew their attendance from the matches. To compound matters, on the

The Week

Tuesday afternoon came news of the death of Quintin Twiss who for 25 years had been the mainstay of the Old Stagers company, and that night's theatrical performance was also cancelled.

The weather seemed determined to match these peripheral disasters. On the Friday evening before the Week, just after the tents had been put up, a violent storm arose and blew them all down again. Monday started fine with sunshine but by breakfast time black clouds loomed ominously across the sky. Despite the poor prospects for play, crowds flocked in from all over the county, some in brakes, smart traps, farm carts, bicycles, tricycles, and some by rail.

By 11am there were more than 4,000 in the ground, all staring in wonder at the new pavilion, standing in the place where the I Zingari tent used to be. The general reaction to this beautiful new building was conservative in the extreme. *The Times* called it rather defensively "an extremely useful pavilion, which has in no sense destroyed the picturesqueness of the famous old scene". The *Kent Messenger* thought otherwise. It was "a solid looking building and although it supplies a long felt want cannot be looked upon as adding artistic beauty to the ground".

Play started on time with Kent winning the toss and electing to bat. When the first rain came down fifty minutes later they had made 23 for the loss of Cuthbert Burnup. After lunch the rain set in, and the crowds had already begun gradually to drift away, when play was abandoned at a quarter past three. The traditional illuminations on the Dane John and the rest of the city were likewise abandoned that evening because of the incessant rain.

Tuesday dawned bright, but with a violent wind still blowing. All but two or three of the tents had blown down again in the storm of the previous day, but when the wind finally subsided at lunch time the majority had been put up again and the ground resumed its usual appearance of pastoral elegance. The drying wicket was playing devilishly when Kent resumed. Alec Hearne hung on grimly and was at the crease for almost three hours for his 29. This contrasted so strongly with the captain, Jack Mason, in brilliant form that summer, whose faultless 73 out of 97 was made with singular ease in just an hour and a quarter. Kent were 138 for 4 and going well, when disaster struck. Suddenly they too were all blown away in a fine spell of bowling by Webb, the last six wickets falling just before lunch for the addition of a single run. That single was made by Colin Blythe, who was not out at the close.

Seeing the problem of the wicket, the Lancashire batsmen determined to make a game of it and hit their way out of any trouble. But the new slow left-arm bowler, whom none had seen on the ground before, took the new ball from the pavilion end and started in deadly form. He deceived Hallows with a straight ball and bowled him when the score was six. At 11 he had Ward out to a tame stroke, caught by Mason at slip. He had Eccles at 39 and Hearne bowled MacLaren at the same score for a duck. When he finally bowled Tyldesley for 26, Lancashire were 59 for 5 and Blythe had taken 4 wickets for 5 runs in 4 overs.

Hartley, who had been dropped by Perkins at cover point when 11, now proceeded to set about Blythe and ruin his analysis. He hit three fours off his next over and another three off the next over from Hearne. The following Blythe over was even more remarkable. Hartley hit him again for three fours, two of which landed on the roof of the new pavilion – these were the days, of course, when a six had to be hit right out of the ground. Thus was inaugurated the perennial challenge for Kent batsmen and their opponents of hitting right over the pavilion, which was to produce that celebrated occasion when Les Ames smashed the clock.

Throughout his career Blythe could never be hit off his line and length. He responded to big hitting, not by low defensive trajectories, but by more teasing, attacking high lobs. But he was a young bowler finding his feet and Mason, fearing the damage that might be done to him psychologically, took him off. Nonetheless, the lower order batsmen continued the attack. The seventh wicket put on 46 and when a seemingly unbreakable eighth wicket partnership had already put on 32, Blythe was called back again. With his first ball he had Sharp stumped by Fred Huish and with his fourth bowled

Pennington for a duck. Bradley took the final wicket the following over. Lancashire in two hours had scored 158 and Blythe, despite being hit by Hartley for six fours in two overs, finished with figures of 6 for 40, his best to date.

In the seventy minutes of the day remaining, the Kent opening pair put on 61 and by close of play the side had made 81 for 1, a lead of 62. It was the first fine evening of the week and, as the crowds made their way to the organ recital in the cathedral, the lights shone out at last from the Dane John, the gas jets hissed from the Westgate Towers and coloured lamps bounced and flickered all along the front of the Weavers. Kent and its new bowler had done well, but no-one dared hope for victory the following day.

On the Wednesday morning, Kent hit out and by lunch had made 218 for 7. Though the match seemed safe, Mason, with the Lancashire first innings in mind, was nervous of leaving his opponents a score of less than 80 or 90 an hour. So he batted on after lunch and the last wicket pair of Blythe and Bradley consumed a further ten overs. When the innings closed at 279, Blythe was 13 not out, two short of his highest score. With less than two and a quarter hours to play, Lancashire could not possibly make the 261 runs needed for victory, but thought they were safe at least.

Blythe opened the bowling again from the pavilion end and Hearne from the Nackington Road. Lancashire were determined to defend and only four runs came off the first seven overs. Blythe was bowling superbly to a perfect length and turning the ball consistently in both directions. MacLaren, who had gone in up the order with Ward, found himself in all kinds of trouble and, when the score was 10, received a devastating curler from Blythe that pitched on the leg stump and came back to take the off. At 39 Blythe had Tyldesley caught by Mason at slip, and at 51 Eccles caught by Huish behind. He bowled Hallows second ball for a duck. Then at last came revenge on Hartley for the first innings treatment; when Blythe clean bowled him for a duck, the crowd went mad. Lancashire were 59 for 5 again and there were still 50 minutes left to play. It was Blythe's arm ball that had done most of the damage; he had taken 5 for 16.

But the victory so clearly in sight was not to be. Ward and Cuttell were even more determined to retrench, and managed to bat out the next 25 minutes without further loss. Blythe's luck evaded him, as a number of times he beat the bat and the wicket as well. When the score reached 71, Mason replaced him but without any immediate success. Lancashire were saved above all by a plucky innings from Albert Ward, who batted for over two hours and was only defeated ten minutes from the close. They escaped by the skin of their teeth on 82 for 8.

It was, as *The Times* remarked, a personal triumph for Blythe, who had completed his first ever match in Canterbury Week with an analysis of 11 wickets for 72 runs. The Kent crowd too knew that something special had occurred. Though victory had been missed by just two wickets, the emotional scenes when Blythe arrived back in the pavilion could not have been greater had Kent won. In a spontaneous upsurge of feeling from the members, the hat was passed round and the shy 21-year-old presented with a handsome collection of £7 1s 6d. It was an unparalleled act to mark an unparalleled performance.

The *Kentish Express* saw what all this meant for the Kent cricket of the future.

> Blythe was the hero of the match. He has proved himself the best colt of the year and certainly Kent has seen no one to equal him for many years. Throughout the Lancashire match he kept a perfect length and it was only the want of a little experience that let him be hit about so unmercifully by Hartley. The latter had got the exact pitch of the ball, and an experienced bowler would have at once used discretion and varied his pace. But diplomacy will come in time and then Blythe will be the deadliest bowler in England.

The second match of the Canterbury Week, against Surrey, was even more of a washout. Little more than an hour's play was possible on the first two days in which Kent made 37 for 1. Ironically, the final Saturday was dry and sunny and Kent declared before lunch at 169 for 8, with Blythe 11 not out.

Towards the end of the Surrey innings of 171, Blythe once again could not be mastered, taking 6 for 73. The three innings in which he had bowled that week had produced a bag of 17 wickets. Even his batting at No. 9 had shown some surprising sparkle: in the three innings he had scored 25 runs and remained undefeated in all of them.

The remaining matches of the season brought a further five 5-wicket hauls. As an experiment, perhaps to make full use of the new facilities at the ground, the Kent Committee had arranged for the first time a further county match at Canterbury after the Week, this time against Worcestershire. It was an unqualified success, and despite rain on the first morning there was time to complete an easy Kent victory by 231 runs. Blythe scored 20 runs with the bat, but his bowling was again the decisive factor in the Kent win, taking 6 for 63 in the first innings and 6 for 60 in the second.

The summer of 1900 thus marked the uncompromising arrival of Blythe upon the English cricket scene. Kent finished third in the county championship, a position they had not achieved since 1890. And the reason for this sudden improvement? When the Kent bowling averages came to be computed, at the head of the table stood Colin Blythe with 114 wickets at a cost of 18.47. The Kent Committee pointed to his success as an encouraging indication of what the Tonbridge nursery had achieved, and might continue to achieve in future. And he had saved his best for Canterbury, the Lord's of Kent cricket. It was the beginning of an emotional relationship with the cricket ground at the heart of his career, a relationship that would survive him well beyond the grave.

Chapter 4

Celebrity

September arrived and the drama of his first season's successes began to fade into unreal memory. While the well-heeled amateur players went back to school or university teaching, or the professions that had been held open for them through the summer, Blythe for the first time faced winter obscurity with the perennial worries of the hard-pressed professional – how to survive economically the dead months of the year while still maintaining fitness and the mental strength to bounce back in the spring.

Fortunately for him, the market value of the promising young professional was high at that period, especially in Kent. The Kent Committee had not invested heavily in the Tonbridge nursery only to allow that investment to wither away in winter; it would continue the nursing long after its babies had been weaned. Thus grew up that system of paternalistic rule, like the one Fabian socialists had in mind for the working classes in general, which was to dog the lives of professional cricketers for many years to come. It was on the surface a liberal development, well-intentioned and designed to provide a smidgeon of economic security in an uncertain world, but it treated its subjects at best like schoolchildren and at worst like chattels. Blythe was one of the few to stand up to the system and maintain his self-respect.

It was as late as September 1897, when the Kent Committee was beginning to recognise the need for a permanent professional core, that it had decided to introduce winter payments for its professionals, in line with the initiative started recently by Lord Hawke in Yorkshire. But while concurring in the decision, Lord Harris was evidently concerned that such an innovation might encourage a life of subsidised idleness. He proposed as a condition that all recipients of winter payments should guarantee to be available the following season and be willing to work at their own trade during the winter months, propositions wisely sidestepped by the other members of the Committee.

Thus it was that, from mid September 1900 to mid April the following year, Blythe was the proud recipient of 20 shillings a week, half the winter payment handed out in Yorkshire. It was the barest survival wage for the poorest manual labourer of the period, and a decent addition to it had to be sought elsewhere. But the 21-year-old Blythe was still living that winter at his parents' home in Wotton Road, along with his ten brothers and sisters, and he carried on with his engineering work at Woolwich Arsenal to help keep the family afloat. For a professional cricketer, even with a dazzling first season behind him, life was far from certain. When Walter, his father, came to fill in his census form the following spring, he had not yet the faith to assign his eldest son the occupation "professional cricketer" but subscribed him "engineer fitter" like himself.

He could not, however, have worked the whole of that winter for he seems to have been quite badly ill for some part of it. It may just have been the usual winter ailment to which a fairly susceptible constitution was prone; or it may have been the onset of the epilepsy of which we have no firm record until later in his life. Most likely, perhaps, the first full year of county cricket had put a special strain on his nerves, as the intense concentration demanded of the spin bowler came for the first time under the unrelenting microscope of public attention. It was this particular form of nervous disability which was later to become the bane of his Test career.

Whatever the cause, it was a serious enough illness for the Kent authorities to sit up and take notice. In March 1901 the Committee decided to repeat its pre-season arrangements of the previous year and send Blythe to Canterbury, along with Huish and Humphreys, for four weeks coaching by Fred Martin and Walter Hearne. But there was a further formal proposition on the table that "as Blythe has wintered badly he should be sent to the seaside for a fortnight". It was agreed that he should first be examined by a doctor and that the arrangements for his trip should be made by the general manager, Tom Pawley. It was a unique piece of cossetting which paid tribute not only to Blythe's importance to the side but also to the special appeal of his personality, even in these early days. If anyone deserved it, it was him.

This illness may have played some part in the relative falling off of his performance in 1901; he took 93 wickets against the 114 of his first season. But probably the most influential factor was the fine summer which that year produced hard wickets, tailor-made for hard hitting Edwardian batsmen. On the occasional wicket that gave him assistance that year he proved as deadly as ever; witness the match against Surrey at the Oval where he took 7 for 64 in the first innings and would have had more if the Kent fielders had held on to their catches. In the same match he suffered the indignity of being hit by the powerful Frank Crawford for five fours and a single in one over, another lesson for the future. In Kent's massacre of the touring South Africans at Beckenham, he took nine wickets overall, eight of them clean bowled, and three in four balls. Against Somerset at Taunton he bowled unchanged throughout the match, the first of five occasions in his career on which he was to perform this feat. And even when on hard wickets he finished with a poor analysis, his economy was often remarkable. Against Essex at Leyton in May, his match analysis was 3 for 97, but those runs came off 62 overs, an economy rate of just 26 runs per hundred balls.

Despite his growing maturity as a first class professional, he was still, notionally at least, a member of the Tonbridge nursery and played a few local matches there in 1901, taking 29 wickets at an average of 12.06. It was on the strength of his achievement in these first two seasons that he was picked for the 1901-2 MacLaren tour of Australia. The natural choice of left-arm spinner would, of course, have been Wilfred Rhodes, but when Lord Hawke refused to release Hirst and Rhodes

for what was a *private* tour, it spoke a lot for Blythe's achievement and promise that he, at the age of 22, should be regarded
as the natural replacement. Kent were pleased to grant permission for him to go but, true to form, withheld his winter
money while he was out of the country, a policy he was to
challenge as an older player on later tours.

This overseas tour, the first of four he was to make with
the national team, was an opening of new horizons to a
young man whose mental life was still the narrow confines
of Deptford; he took part fully in the social aspects of the
tour, even finishing up at half-back in a soccer match between
England and Fremantle, for which he received a gold medal.
But the cricket was for the most part dismal. In the first match
against South Australia he took 5 for 45 in the second innings,
but the tourists still lost. His first Test at Sydney in December
was a brilliant victory. England won the toss and MacLaren
and Hayward put on 154 for the first wicket. There followed
a mini-collapse and at close of play the tourists were 272 for
six. On the second day, however, the last four wickets were to
add a further 192, with Blythe as last man in making a remarkable Test batting debut by equalling his then highest first class
score of 20. In reply to England's 464, Australia had made
103 for 3.

In a remarkable collapse on the third day, four more
Australian wickets fell at 112, with Blythe and Barnes taking
two apiece. Seventeen Australian wickets were to fall that day
and England won by an innings and 124 runs. Blythe bowled
beautifully throughout, taking 7 for 56 in the match off 29
overs, and was afterwards presented with a gold pocket watch
in which was engraved those magic words, seven wickets and
fifty six runs. No-one could have wished for a more promising
Test debut.

But from then on it was downhill all the way, on wickets
that never really suited him. England lost the last four Tests
and, although he was never really mastered by the Australian
batsmen, Blythe's wicket-taking fell away – a disappointing
haul of just six in the last three Tests for an average of 44. In
the third Test at Adelaide, he split a finger of his bowling hand,
which prevented him putting any spin on the ball, delivering

all of his overs from the palm of his hand. This more than anything else seems to have been the turning point of his decline, for even in the next Test he had to bowl with two fingers of his bowling hand strapped together. Whether or not this tour was also the beginning of that strain that Test cricket was later to impose upon his nerves, it certainly marked the start of a history of apparent under-achievement at the highest levels of the game, particularly on tours abroad.

What was incontrovertible, however, was that the antipodean climate and extra summer had done wonders for his fragile health. The new environment had braced him up and he came back filled out bodily, and physically stronger than he had ever been before. Certainly, in the photographs of this period he is fatter in the face than in later years. It was in some ways a strange face, rather cranial in form, with slightly pinched features grouped closely together between a broad rounded forehead and firm determined chin. His thin lips when sloping downward gave his face a truculent air, and sometimes his raw, uneven mouth, when straining open on the delivery stride, seemed to be emitting a skeletal shriek. But at other times, the hint of a smile in that slightly lopsided mouth, allied to the twinkle in the half-shuttered eyes, made a face of elfin humour, the outward sign of the cheeky cockney personality within.

His hair was thin and receding at an early age, which is why perhaps we rarely catch him bare-headed, always bowling with the tiny cap of the period that fitted so tightly over the skull. A working man's face, then, but with bags of personality, humour and determination, and a rather detached, faraway look in the eyes. Someone keen, too, to make the best of his appearance; in the few pictures we have of him in civilian clothes, there is always the touch of the dandy – the high collar, the flourish of the cravat, the flamboyance of the hat – all out to make the same statement, the shy man's way of letting his presence, and *real* personality, be known.

In the warm-up to the 1902 season, he was no longer required to go down to Canterbury for coaching with Martin and Hearne; as an England Test player, he was now finally out of the nursery and determined to show it. 1902 was a summer of almost constant wet weather and difficult pitches, and thus helped Blythe return to the successes of 1900, with 127 wickets overall at an average of 15.47. The two defeats of Worcestershire were typical of his performance this season. At Worcester in June he took 10 wickets in the match, but fared even better in the return fixture at Tonbridge in August. In the first innings, the visitors were so powerless against him that they lost their first nine wickets for 65, Blythe eventually posting an analysis of 5 for 60. In the second, he even improved it with 6 for 61, an instrumental contribution to victory in a match that Worcester seemed always likely to save.

His best performance of the year was saved for Somerset at Maidstone at the end of July. As a result of the all too predictable rain, only three hours play was possible on the first day. Kent batted first and lost Dillon when the score was only 1. Burnup and Marsham, however, put on 121 for the second wicket and, with their traditional fast scoring, Kent had by close of play made 209 for 7. The hard hitting continued the next morning when Kent were all out for 299. On the same wicket, Somerset were completely outclassed. Their first innings was a triumph for Alec Hearne who took 7 for 34, and Blythe 3 for 42, in a rout that had the visitors dismissed for 100 in 30 overs.

Following on, Somerset were bowled out in an hour and a quarter for 97, the match finishing at half past four on the second day. Hearne and Blythe bowled unchanged throughout the innings, but this time roles were reversed. Hearne took 2 for 55 while Blythe at the other end was on top form. He took a wicket with the third ball of his first over and the first ball of his second; in his last seven overs he took 6 for 29, finishing with 8 for 42 overall off 12.4 overs. The collapse of both Somerset innings in a matter of hours was a foretaste of similar events to come, culminating in the sensation at Northampton in 1907. But for now, 8 for 42 were his best bowling figures to date, a record destined to last no more than a further year.

His surprise batting performance in the first Test down under seems to have given more confidence to the No. 10 right-handed batsman. Despite the bad wickets, this year he made a total of 249 runs, far better than his previous seasons.

Colin Blythe

At Tonbridge in June against Gloucestershire he made 23 out of a small Kent total of 207, putting on 50 with Fred Huish for the ninth wicket; and he made the same score against the same team at Bristol a week later. Batting against Hampshire at Tunbridge Wells in July he made another stand of 54 with Huish, hitting no less than six fours in his top score to date of 31. It was a sign that he was maturing and giving himself the mental space to concentrate on his batting and enjoy it.

At the end of the season the Kent Committee patted itself on the back for its bold decision in allowing such a young man, with a history of illness, to tour Australia the previous winter and still perform better this season than in 1901. "While bearing in mind the fact that the general condition of the grounds during the past season was more favourable than that of 1901 for his style of bowling, the Committee are gratified to find that no deteriorating effect has resulted from the permission given for his inclusion in the team that visited Australia in 1901-2".

By now the cricket grounds of England were becoming accustomed to this young willowy figure who opened the bowling for Kent with, following the tradition of the day, a fast bowler at the other end – whether Bradley, Mason or Fielder. What was it like that familiar run-up, and what was the recipe for his constant success?

The few steps he took to the wicket were marked by a gentle rhythm and grace, an almost feminine sensibility. They were dancing steps, culminating in a little chassée before the long last stride from toe to toe, more like a ballet dancer than a runner. Such was the interest in his run up that one magazine even published a footprint map of its choreography. Arriving at the wicket he would fling back his left arm till it was bent tight behind his back, almost under his right armpit, and as he began his final stride his back was half turned towards the batsman allowing a glimpse of the tucked up bowling arm. Then he would throw his right arm high and forward to balance his left, swivel his body round as the high left arm came over, with a quick finish to the swing which gave a lively quality even to his slowest ball.

The most lyrical description flows from the pen of G D Martineau.

> As he trod his measure to the wicket, it was as though he stepped to a tune played on his own violin. Then the left arm whipped round behind his back and came up and over in a curve as beautiful as the swoop of a gull. The ball seemed to float for an instant, then struck down and upwards – a thing of beauty.

He was a master of variable flight, often tossing the ball up with a lot of air and disguised pace so batsmen found the movement of the ball impossible to gauge. What appeared to be a half-volley through the air became a good length ball when landing on the pitch. The hard-hitting Essex batsman and later journalist, Edward Sewell was the first to document the importance of this skill to Blythe's success.

> Blythe's bowling had everything a slow left hander's bowling ought to have. But above and before all it had Flight – that precious gift only imitations of which can be acquired.

Sewell remembered one morning at the Oval when Blythe served up half a dozen deliberate full tosses in the first twenty minutes to Tom Hayward, and the batsman failed to score a run off any of them. It was this mastery of flight, his key asset as a bowler, that kept him on the attack on plumb wickets while other bowlers were resorting to defence, and which above all entrenched his reputation as probably the greatest left-arm spinner on good wickets that the game has ever seen.

His accuracy too was phenomenal. Bill Fairservice remembered him pitching five balls out of six on a football, which gives credence to the story that once bowling a full toss in Canterbury Cricket Week in early August, he remarked "I think that's the first bad ball I've bowled this year!".

Colin Blythe

Bowling normally to a full length, his deliveries on landing were marked by a very sharp and sudden spin from leg to off and a high bounce which produced catches behind the wicket at waist height or higher. On sticky wickets there was often a pronounced kick as the ball hit the ground, which made the spin even more difficult to play. With the new ball he bowled very distinct swingers which, because the swing did not start until the ball had very nearly pitched, were extremely difficult to follow.

This combination of variable flight, good length, late swing, very fast spin and high bounce, delivered in a deceptively easy and graceful manner, made him virtually unplayable on a drying or crumbling pitch. And his accuracy was such, he did not need much of the pitch to work on.

> Blythe does not require the whole wicket to be bad before he becomes almost irresistible; it is enough for him if a very little piece of it wears badly. In this he is like the famous bowlers of former days – Alfred Shaw, Attewell, Morley, Spofforth, Jim Lillywhite, and Turner – who were so accurate that they could make use of even the smallest flaw in a wicket.

The ball which left the right-handed bat was something of a rarity in Edwardian cricket, when most bowling consisted of breakbacks, inswingers, off-breaks and googlies. Blythe and his fellow slow left-armers seemed to have the monopoly of the ball that moved away outside the off-stump to be gobbled up in the slips. But as well as the standard delivery, he had a deadly arm ball which approached a fast bowler's pace without any discernible change of action. In some of his most spectacular performances, it was the unexpected arm ball that did all the damage.

It is Edward Sewell who sums up the authentic batsman's view from the popping crease of this blistering array of weaponry.

> Blythe used to sort of step-dance up to the bowling crease, starting from behind the umpire and delivering off the seventh step or thereabouts. He made good

use of the length of the crease and, at a guess, I should say that he, like Rhodes, never bowled a no-ball.

Then, his left hand went right back beyond his buttocks and up towards his right arm-pit. The swing back for the final swing forward was so fast as to induce a feeling in Mr Striker that the ball would be faster than it really was in most cases. But when Blythe wanted to bowl what we must call his fast one, he could do so at his chosen moment without giving the show away by noticeable change of action, thanks to his long final swing. There followed in the case of his ordinary ball a kind of curved flight, which called for all the gauging the batsman could give it if he wanted to stay in for long, before the ball – which was finger-spun and turning like a propeller – dropped a very good length when not a perfect one.

Of course Blythe here and there bowled a plain straight one which, to use the old, and correct, verbiage "went with his arm", and which pitching on the off stump would, if unimpeded, hit the leg stump. In addition to which he could, and did, bowl true in-swerve now and then. To top up with, he could bowl the yorker. In sum, a Parfait Bowler.

In addition to this remarkable armoury, he had an almost intuitive skill in attuning each delivery to the individual batsman and the state of the pitch. On a good hard wicket, he showed the same brilliant skills, bowling a little short and on a slightly lower trajectory which made it hard to advance out to him and prevented the drive.

Slow bowling is even more of a psychological battle than fast, both with the opposing batsman and with oneself, and Colin Blythe was personally very well equipped to take batsmen on when he came under challenge. In the first place, he was remarkably brave. When being hit off his line and length all around the ground, he did not run for cover like most bowlers, sheltering behind short, fast low-trajectory deliveries. Quite the reverse. He would continue to toss up high tempting lobs, putting on extra spin, on the philosophy that a batsman was at

Colin Blythe

his most vulnerable when the adrenalin was flowing. And eventually this bold perseverance would succeed with a wicket.

Such careless bravery was all of a part with his apparently gentle, relaxed personality. Though his bowling was menacing in the extreme, he himself was the least menacing of men. It was the cheerful cockney demeanour and accent, as much a part of his cricket as his life, that earned him his nickname of Charlie, the name by which he was known to all players up and down the country, both friend and foe alike. He was always Colin at home, where he lived with his own brother Charles, a cricketer also, ten years his junior. In Deptford it was Charles Blythe who was always called by his diminutive; within the bowels of the Blythe family he was, to coin a phrase, the proper Charlie. But out on the cricket fields of Kent it was the name that seemed best to suit the personality of the elder brother.

Colin Blythe (as we must call him) enjoyed the game so much that he seemed genuinely to treat it for what it was – a game. The psychological pressure he put on batsmen sprang purely from his skills as a bowler, not from his behaviour as a man. There are countless anecdotes about his gentle, guileless approach to opponents. Neville Cardus recalled that once when he bowled Archie MacLaren Blythe walked down the wicket to him as if to apologise. And there is the famous story of how the dashing Lancashire batsman, Reggie Spooner, at Canterbury hit him out of the ground for six, and Blythe applauded him saying "Oh, Mr Spooner, I'd give all my bowling to bat like that". This was honest and genuinely meant, but for a batsman used to a vicious competitive edge from bowlers may have been as effective a destabilisation ploy as the heaviest sledging from the Australian slips.

And he treated his Kent colleagues in the same way, never losing his temper with their failures. One remembered a particular instance.

> He was ever generous to an opponent, and I have heard him say to a comrade who apologised for missing a catch, "Never mind. How about that 'scorcher' you held

at the Oval which gave me a wicket". There in a nutshell you have Blythe's temperament.

It was because of this naturally laid-back approach to the game at a personal level that Blythe never seemed to get wound up by opponents, and could approach the delivery of the next ball with as much calmness and boldness when he had just been hit for three sixes as when he had just taken three wickets. But he was far from laid back in his approach to the technical skills of bowling, on which he practised incessantly, and was constantly plotting and planning each variation of delivery while a game was in progress. He gave the impression of never being lost for resources. In the few records that we have of his technical approach, he always comes over as highly thoughtful and keen to embrace the unorthodox. This on variation of length and pace:

> Bowling an occasional ball from a yard or two behind the crease is a very good plan to adopt, and by bowling to a quick-footed batsman a slow left-hander will learn that he will have to bowl slightly faster to some batsmen than to others.

It was the concentration required in this continual search for the right variation, ball by ball, while maintaining perfect line and length, that was his undoing in the more competitive world of Test cricket. Such an intense approach to perfecting technique, combined with his natural sensitivity, was to lead to nervous exhaustion. But in county cricket, these skills continued to be deployed to supreme effect over many years, and 1903 was the year in which his name was finally made.

Where were the golden summers of Edwardian legend? Certainly not around at the beginning of the decade. 1903 was another appallingly wet summer, with June providing three times the average rainfall, and July twice. Kent rather lost their way in the county championship when Jack Mason, who had captained the side since Blythe joined the team, had to relinquish the captaincy to devote more time to his business following a collapse in his father's financial fortunes. With Cuthbert Burnup leading the team, the Kent batsmen struggled to find their form in the earlier part of the season, and it was only a resurgence in August, in which Blythe played the leading role, that enabled them to clock up seven wins and joint eighth place in the championship.

This was the first season in which Blythe took a wicket in every match he played, a feat he was to repeat for the next seven summers. Seven times he took ten wickets or more in a match, and his tally for the season as a whole was 142 wickets at an average of 13.75, a step up from his previous best. Most impressively, half those wickets were taken in the month of August.

Inevitably, it was at Canterbury Cricket Week at the beginning of the month that he set his best analysis to date. Keeping a perfect length and making liberal use of his deadly arm ball, he took 9 for 67 as Kent dismissed Essex for 121 in their first innings. Edward Sewell has left us with a graphic account of how it felt to be on the receiving end of such a performance, trying to spot the arm ball against the murky gloom of the pavilion at Canterbury. He noticed how Blythe, "one of the cutest bowling brains the game ever knew", used the full width of the recently extended bowling crease to make the most of the poor background.

> He was wont to hide behind the umpire and then, as though part of some pastoral ballet, would perform a *pas seul* to the bowling crease, and after in some quite unbelievable manner tucking his left arm under his right armpit, would proceed to deal out destruction in what, innocent looks and *pas seul* duly considered, seemed a most unfair manner. Perhaps he was the cause of the introduction of a band of musicians at Canterbury's festival – and how he made batsmen dance.
>
> At least I remember thinking so on one occasion when, having tried to sock him into the Dane John, I hit noth-

ing at all, and was duly adjudged lbw. As in that innings his hand came plumb out of a black window which was yards clear of the end of a quite useless screen, and as he took nine wickets in the innings for 67 runs, I struck the air in a pretty goodly company. His bag included Fane, Perrin, McGahey, Lucas, Douglas, Reeves, Young and Mead, in the course of 28 overs.

It was the first of six nine-wicket hauls in his career and was to be bettered the following season. When the by now standard collection went round for Alec Hearne and the other professionals at the ground, Blythe netted a useful seven pounds.

His two most spectacular successes of the season took place in back to back matches in the third week of August. On 17 August Kent opened the batting against Surrey at the Oval at half past twelve because heavy overnight rain had prevented a normal start. Burnup was out in the first over, Seymour was caught at mid-off at 7, and soon after Hearne and Dillon were out to good catches at slip. In less than an hour, Kent found themselves 20 for 4. Then, as the wicket improved, the Surrey bowlers lost their length and the fielders began to drop their catches. Day, who had been dropped at 1, 11 and 16, put on 69 for the fifth wicket with Mason, and in the fast scoring tradition of contemporary Kent batsmen, 87 with Blaker for the seventh wicket in just over three quarters of an hour. After such a poor start, Kent had managed a total of 222. Surrey went in a few minutes before five, and when bad light stopped play a little after six had made 62 for 4, with Blythe taking 2 for 28.

Tuesday 18 August was one of those phenomenal days in the Blythe calendar which were to occur more frequently as his career progressed. Heavy rain had fallen again overnight and the pitch was soft and tailor-made for him. Surrey collapsed from 64 for 4 to 75 for 9 and by ten past twelve had lost their last six wickets for 27 runs. In a fast morning's work, Blythe had taken 5 for 13 off 4.3 overs.

In their second innings, Kent batted steadily at first, but when Dillon joined Burnup, the third wicket pair, oblivious of the tricky pitch, proceeded to put on 99 in about an hour.

Colin Blythe

At four o'clock with Kent 211 for 8, Burnup declared to minimise the risk that bad weather might rob them of victory. Chasing 345 to win, Surrey went in to bat without opener Tom Hayward who had just had an abscess removed from his eye. Once again Blythe and Hearne bowled unchanged through the innings and in the space of just 23 overs put Surrey out for 52, giving Kent victory by 292 runs. It was a superlative performance from Blythe, who took 5 for 26 in the second innings and whose figures for the day made up a remarkable 16.3 overs, 4 maidens, 10 for 39.

Burnup's declaration proved well-judged, for it rained solidly throughout the Wednesday, the day off Kent had earned to travel down to Canterbury for their home fixture against Yorkshire. Rain prevented play for two thirds of this match, but once again contrived a thrilling finish. On Thursday 20 August heavy early morning rain made the wicket unusable until after lunch and also interrupted the afternoon play. In the less than two hours that was possible, Blythe continued where he had left off at the Oval on Tuesday, putting a prodigious turn on his standard break to the off which completely defeated the opposition. Yorkshire lost their first three wickets for 21 and, despite a stand by Smith and Hirst for the fourth wicket, by close of play were 73 for 9. Blythe bowled unchanged from the pavilion end and had taken 6 for 31.

Rain fell again overnight, but despite several hours strong sun the pitch was so wet that not a ball could be bowled on the Friday. Anticipating a likely draw, the captains agreed to start at 10.45am on the Saturday and complete by 5.15pm. Burnup's consent to this early finish in the event cost Kent the match. The new start time was, in fact, delayed by more rain on Saturday morning when Yorkshire added a further six runs before Lord Hawke ran himself out. They had made just 79 runs, the first time the team had been dismissed for under a hundred all season. Hearne and Burnup hit 95 before lunch, and afterwards, in an attempt to force the pace, Kent lost seven wickets in an hour. They declared at 181, leaving Yorkshire 102 runs to avoid an innings defeat.

With only an hour and three-quarters to go, it seemed certain that Yorkshire would save the match, but Blythe thought otherwise. He took a wicket with his first ball and one in each of his next two overs. In less than 30 minutes half the side were out for 16, and in his seven overs Blythe had taken 4 for 10. But then Wilkinson and Rhodes spent an hour apiece at the wicket, for just 24 runs, which was enough to save the match. When stumps were drawn early under the special arrangement, Yorkshire were 51 for 8 and staring certain defeat in the face. Though disappointing for Kent, it was a thrilling finish and yet another superb effort from Blythe, who in the second innings took 7 for 26. In less than three-and-a-half days of cricket that rain-sodden week, he had taken 25 wickets at a cost of just 5 runs apiece.

It was sumptuous performances such as this that August that led *Wisden* to choose Blythe as one of their five players of the year, and finally underwrite his growing celebrity. Though mistakenly naming him Charles (a product of the nickname of Charlie) they noted the elevated place he had now earned for himself among English bowlers and pointed to a highly successful career in prospect. The 24-year-old bowler, so well known and regarded in Kent for the past four seasons, had in the eyes of the cricketing establishment finally arrived.

Chapter 5

Champion

I stand under the awning of a shop in St John's Wood High Street, sheltering from the rain, as I wait to join a party for the customary tour of Lord's. The incessant raindrops plashing in the puddles at my feet and dripping from the iron joists are surrogates now for the tears I can no longer make. They send a shiver down my spine to meet the sinking feeling in my stomach.

Through this depressive mist of cold and wet, I look across the road and see a small girl in a white dress, of a style that resonates the First World War, come skipping out of a shop into the summer sun, a bag of Saturday morning sweets clutched tightly in her hand. She stops at the kerb and looks across at me, and I sense a moment of recognition. She smiles directly at me, hovers for a second more, and then dances off round the corner into Barrow Hill Road, and is gone.

Despite the rain I have used my waiting time responsibly to fulfil a mission of love for that little girl, who is also now dead. She died exactly a week before the one whose ring I lost and found. A death long awaited, much like a birth, creates an excitement that has to be communicated. When news came through that my mother had died, I rushed upstairs to tell her as she lay there looking up to the ceiling, as though essential she should know before too late. She heard me in silence, then simply turned her head away, as if to say "Why do you tell me this? Too much. Too much".

Champion

Too much for me too; in all the trauma of recent months, I have yet to catch up with my mother. But perhaps today I have made a start. For some years I had intended to visit the house in Culworth Street where she was born and lived till her early twenties. Just a stone's throw from the zoo and the lions that roared when the Zeppelin bombs fell, and more significant for me, a stone's throw from Lord's. She had begun to talk about it a lot in late years, how she as a young child, rejected by her father as a "mistake", had found a new protector in her crippled grandfather, imprisoned in the attic at the top of the house, to whom she carried up the daily meals, and remained there spellbound by tales of his youth in Cornwall in the 1840s and the guns his firm supplied to the Russians in the Crimean War.

I fully intended to take a photo of the four storey Georgian house, wrapped in its cloak of Virginia creeper, to reassure her that nothing had changed since the First World War – but other people's nostalgia is never so compelling as one's own, so this was one intention that had fallen by the way. Just as well, as it has turned out. As I came upon the little street this morning, I found to my horror that all the homely domestic dwellings of the old sepia photographs had translated into high rise office blocks and flats, of the anonymous soulless kind that could have been fixed to any date between 1940 and 1980. An attempt to photograph that scene would have smashed my camera. Thank God she had gone with her image of it still intact.

But the grandfather stories came from her old age when people turn to their own grandparents for identity and solace. The big cricketing story of her life in that street was told when I was young. It was, I think, in the early summer of 1928 that, returning home with her close girlfriend from a play or a concert, they came upon two young men chatting together on the corner of the street. They somehow got into conversation, from which it soon emerged that the men were cricketers currently working on the Lord's ground staff. The very tall, well-built one with the strong, rather equine face already played cricket for Gloucestershire, and was on a kind of year's sabbatical to recharge his batteries, improve his bowling and help

Colin Blythe

others in the nets. It was Tom Goddard, the trundling right-arm fast county bowler in the year of his metamorphosis into Tom Goddard, the deadly slow off-spin Test bowler.

He was in digs across the road in Newcourt Street, and from that evening encounter they began to go out together. Summer romances were, then as now, difficult for professional cricketers with their habitual no fixed abode, but this summer Tom Goddard was well grounded on his St John's Wood base. Though with no prior knowledge or interest in cricket, she was soon sucked into this strange exclusive world, knitting her way through Middlesex home matches, travelling at weekends with the ground staff team to play local clubs, averting her eyes from the backbiting and jealousies of the pavilion. At 18 it was her first relationship, and that summer cricket was not the main thing on her mind.

Ten years older, he was deeply interested in her; and she in him, perhaps more than she was later to let on. But the season came to an end, he returned to Gloucester and the romance became more distant, dictated by the postman and the occasional cricketing visit to London. They were still in touch a year later when he sent her from South Africa the team photograph of the England touring side of 1930/31 of which he was now a shining star. That photograph became my own proud possession at the age of eight. Then she met my father and her life took a different road, though one that, as a cricket-mad child, I found difficult to comprehend. It took a lot to persuade me that, had she done the obvious thing and married the England Test cricketer, the product would not have been me!

Which is why, standing in St John's Wood High Street for the first time, the damp air is full of her young life, on which I shall never be able to question her more.

It must have been about that time when she first told me of Tom Goddard that I was given for a birthday the 1947 edition of Neville Cardus' *English Cricket*. It was a puzzling book that I found difficult to read, so much emphasis on the distant origins of the game as against the current realities. Who could enthuse over the Kent v Sussex match of 1773 when Walcott and Weekes were batting at Canterbury? And yet, turning to

1 *The young bowler in his Australian tour blazer, about 1902.*

2 *Two views of Evelyn Street in Deptford. (above) a few doors up from Blythe's birthplace, long since demolished. (below) the other side of the street.*

3 *Blythe's Deptford. 1. His birthplace. 2. Alverton Street School. 3. St Luke's Church. 4. H M Victualling Yard.*

4 The celebrated painting by Chevallier Tayler, Canterbury, 10 August 1906. Ted Humphreys (mid-on), Ted Dillon (long-on), William Findlay (non-striker and absentee on the day), A J Affield (umpire), CB, Johnny Tyldesley (batting), Dick Blaker (mid-off), Fred Huish (wicket-keeper), Ken Hutchings (on boundary), Slug Marsham (extra-cover), Arthur Fielder (point), Jack Mason (slip), Pinkie Burnup (cover), Jim Seymour (third man).

5 *The St Lawrence Ground with the Blythe memorial in the top right hand corner.*

(left) **6** *31 August 1950, Kent v West Indies. Colin Cowdrey makes his Canterbury debut.*
(right) **7** *Captain McCanlis, the discoverer of Blythe.*

8 *MacLaren's XI in Australia 1901-02. (standing) John Gunn, CB, Sydney Barnes, Dick Lilley, Tom Hayward, Len Braund (seated) Harold Garnett, Charlie McGahey, Archie MacLaren, Charles Robson, Arthur Jones (on ground) Willie Quaife, Johnny Tyldesley.*

9 *England in Australia 1907-08 (standing) Dick Young, Ernie Hayes, Arthur Fielder, CB, Joe Humphries, Jack Hobbs (seated) Jack Crawford, Len Braund, Arthur Jones, Frederick Fane, Kenneth Hutchings, Wilfred Rhodes (on ground) Sydney Barnes, Joe Hardstaff, Col. Philip Trevor (manager), George Gunn.*

10 *Four studies of the bowler at work.*

11 *Canterbury Cricket Week 1905.*

F.H.HUISH
E.HUMPHREYS
C.BLYTHE
A.FIELDER

LORD HARRIS DISTRIBUTES THE MONEY COLLECTED ON
TUESDAY AND THURSDAY FOR THE KENTISH PROFESSIONALS

12 *Canterbury Cricket Week 1906. Lord Harris shares out the spoils (see page 71).*

*(left) **13** The promising young batsman at Tonbridge. (right) **14** The dandy in his Australian tour hat, 1901-02.*

15 *The Kent team that played Sussex at Canterbury, August 1908. (standing) Frank Woolley, Jim Seymour, CB, Wally Hardinge (seated) Ken Hutchings, Jack Mason, Slug Marsham, Sammy Day, Fred Huish (on ground) Bill Fairservice, Ted Humphreys.*
Hutchings dislocated a finger fielding and could not bat.

16 *Janet Blythe in the summer of 1919, before her pilgrimage to Flanders.*

(left) **17** *Charlie Blythe, the younger brother and failed cricketer. (right)* **18** *40 St Mary's Road, Tonbridge where the Blythes lived from 1907 to 1911.*

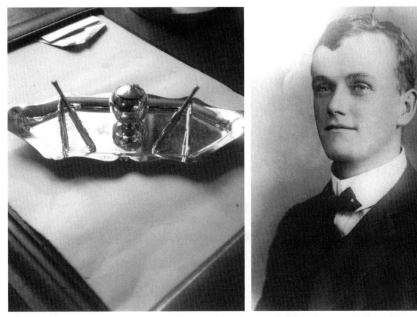

(left) **19** *The silver inkstand presented to Blythe for winning the championship in 1909. (right)* **20** *The famous cricketer off duty.*

21 *Colin Blythe about 1906, proudly sporting his MCC blazer from the South African tour.*

page 35, there it was – that picture that immediately struck a chord in me and has struck similar chords in cricketing generations still to come. It stood above the gnomic title "Cricket Match at Canterbury, 1906. J.T.Tyldesley batting" .

No mention of the teams that were at play; more important, no mention of the bowler. Nor anything in the text to explain its significance, why it was there. What hit the eye was not the eager expectation of the fielders crouching round the bat, nor the menacing shadows of the trees and foreground, but the sight of that strangely elegant pavilion, shimmering in the sun, giving the comfort of familiarity to the fearful undertones of a past now long dead, most of the players long dead too. The thrill lay in this bridge to the past, the novel recognition that something apparently modern and familiar could still have existed, modern and familiar then too, so many aeons ago. And there peeping through the trees, the cathedral tower of Bell Harry – the two most precious buildings of my childhood enthroned in a single work of art.

At last the rain seems about to stop, and I move out from my sentry post to cover the few hundred yards to the Grace gates. I have latched on to this official tour party so I can remain anonymous, scud round the margins of the group and look at what *I* want to see. I shall have the chance to sus out the library without betraying my purpose. We are shown proudly the new extension to the pavilion and then enter the Long Room, which instantly reminds me of a previous long-forgotten visit back in the '60s, having dinner with the Hampshire team straight from a hard day in the field against Middlesex.

Finally we make the Museum and are shown the traditional artefacts, the sparrow killed by the ball in 1936, the tiny urn of the Ashes. I see in snatched glimpses, hovering above me on the first floor landing, that picture, which I have half forgotten is here, but which is actually the main unconscious reason for my visit. I cannot wait to climb the stairs to study it more closely.

And here it is, a sudden burst of primary colour before my eyes, the original of an image that has been with me for more than fifty years. There is something unfamiliar here and

Colin Blythe

I am slow to puzzle it out. Of course, the image I have grown up with is the black and white engraving, and this the original oil painting, losing in subtlety what it gains in strength. Nonetheless, the size and the colour is overwhelming, as is the fact of its originality – like meeting a film star one has worshipped from afar.

We come to it late in our tour of the Museum and I wait expectantly for our guide's introduction. It is perfunctory and disappointing; clearly this picture means more to me than anyone else round here. His words are also predictable: "A Kent match at Canterbury with Charlie Blythe bowling, soon to head off for the First World War and meet his death". A distorted, concertina view of history in which we anticipate death by a decade, while all the time engrossed in a quiet game of cricket. Yet he has hit the popular stance correctly; posthumously the death takes precedence in the mind over the bowling average. And he has at least chosen the bowler, not the batsman, as the guiding force behind this work of art.

———————————

By contrast with the previous two seasons, 1904 was a dry summer of good, firm wickets, kind to batsmen and spectators, but tough on spin bowlers. The 138 wickets Blythe took this year was confirmation, if any were needed, that he was not just a fair weather success. When wickets were difficult to come by, he could keep the runs down far better than most. In the drawn match against Sussex at Tunbridge Wells in July, when more than a thousand runs were scored, of the 29 overs he bowled in the first innings, 18 were maidens. He bowled for an hour without conceding a run, and for 12 overs conceding only one.

As in 1900, Kent came third again in the county championship, the best position achieved since the advent of Blythe, and much of it was due to sterling performances by Ted Humphreys and Jim Seymour, the two young professional batsmen who had grown up with him at the Tonbridge nursery and were now coming into their own. Whether it was the firm wickets, or merely a maturing confidence, Blythe's own batting went through a minor revolution this summer, enough to justify that McCanlis view that he was "not half a bad batsman when he goes in with the intention of staying". In the Kent victory over Hampshire in early June he bowled unchanged through both innings and took 13 wickets for 91 runs, but he also made his highest first class score of 34.

It was a record destined to survive only two more matches. When Kent played at Nottingham in mid June, the home side batting first made 602 in a day-and-a-half. When Blythe came in, Kent were eight wickets down for 206 and seemed likely to lose the match; but he and Fairservice set about the Nottinghamshire bowling, and by close of play they had reached 240 for 8 with Fairservice promisingly poised on 17 and Blythe 15. They continued to hit out the following morning, and in a remarkable ninth wicket stand put on a mighty 106. Then Blythe and Fielder made a further 44 for the tenth wicket. Blythe's innings was the surprise of the match, and of the season. Though making a few false strokes, he managed to notch up 82 not out, and was set fair for a hundred had he not run out of partners. It was the highest first class score of his career.

A spectator from Nottingham wrote to the *Tuesday Express* full of admiration: "In your Kent eleven you have the smartest young crew in England. Blythe batted in absolutely first-class style, but they tell me he never takes batting seriously. All I can say is that he ought to. His strokes were excellent, and he hardly let off a loose ball".

But it was no flash in the pan, and the Kent captain that season had now to take some account of the capability of this new young batsman. In the second innings against Yorkshire in July, he was promoted to number four in the order and made 42 not out; and he now became the first contender for night-watchman when one was needed. He had a second brilliant success in the victory over Somerset at Taunton in August. Kent were put in to bat and were 80 for 9 when Blythe joined Fairservice at the crease. The pair proceeded to put on 98 for the last wicket, of which Blythe made 70 in an hour, and with scarcely a mistake until he was bowled. The partnership crucially changed the balance of the match. He scored nearly 400 runs in the county championship this summer, and his average leapt from 12 to 18 – not bad for a number 10 or 11.

Just as he had been nominated one of the players of the year by *Wisden* in 1903, he received a similar honour at the end of this season as subject of one of the prestigious profile articles in *Cricket* magazine, where his batting achievements did not go unremarked.

> This season Blythe has again been in the very front rank of bowlers, and some of his performances have been astonishingly good. He has, moreover, shone as a batsman on two or three occasions when runs were very badly wanted indeed, and in the course of these hard-hitting displays of his he has shown clearly enough that he would probably be a great batsman if he were not a great bowler.

Hyperbole perhaps, for he was never to achieve such batting heights again. As a batsman he hit the ball hard and seemed to revel in the hit or miss ethos of the tail-ender. Batting for him was an opportunity to relax from the intense concentration of his bowling. He enjoyed cricket *as a game* and knew where his priorities lay. Had he spent many hours in the nets, as tail-enders do today, honing his batting technique, it could well have impacted on his bowling.

He took his 121 championship wickets this summer by dint of consistent accumulation rather than the great flashes of brilliance of recent wet seasons. Yet there *were* a few spectacular performances. By strange coincidence, as in the previous year, his most remarkable feat came on 18 August. It was the last home match of the championship season and Kent were playing Hampshire at Tonbridge. So difficult was the wicket that three innings were completed in the single day, and Kent needed only 45 minutes the following morning to knock off the runs for victory.

When Hampshire batted first, they found Blythe in devastating form on a wet pitch made treacherous by the sun. His length and turn were wonderful to behold. Fielder took the first wicket, bowling Bowell for 2, and then all the rest went to Blythe, five bowled, three caught and one lbw. Hampshire were all out for 91, giving Blythe a new personal best of 9 for 30, which he was only to better once more in his career. Kent fared almost as badly and were swiftly dismissed for 114, though the lead of 23 seemed likely to prove vital.

The Hampshire second innings started even more disastrously than the first. In less than half an hour they lost half their side for 14, four of them to Blythe who had a new record well within his sights. Thanks, however, to a gutsy performance by Bowell, who made 42 runs out of the next 46 in half an hour, once hitting Blythe for six right out of the ground, the visiting team were able to limp by close of play to 85 all out. Blythe bowled unchanged again and took 6 for 46. In an altogether sensational day, he had bowled 38 overs and taken 15 wickets for 76.

1905 was another fine season for Blythe, who took 149 wickets in all, his largest tally yet. His good form won him a home Test place for the first time, against the Australians at Leeds, where he took three quick wickets in the second innings and caused a momentary panic in the Australian ranks. Kent fell to sixth place in the county table, mainly by losing more matches than the previous season. By common consent they were one of the most attractive sides to watch, but the batting dropped off a little and Blythe received less quality support than usual from the other bowlers.

Canterbury Cricket Week that year proved more of a showcase for Blythe, the right-handed batsman than Blythe, the left-arm bowler. In the first match against Essex he did manage to take 10 wickets, but for a total of 150 runs. More memorable was his cavalier knock of 17 not out in the first innings when he put on 48 for the last wicket with Blaker. In his accustomed style, he had a real flail at the bowling, which produced a surfeit of amusement all round the ground: "Blythe smiled when he hit the ball, and enjoyed the joke when he didn't".

Lancashire were the visitors in the second match of the week, the first of a trio of such encounters at Canterbury in consecutive years. It turned out an unmitigated disaster for the home team. Kent won the toss and put Lancashire in to bat, hoping that the rain of the previous day would make the pitch unplayable. But the pitch never became difficult, Blythe bowled badly for him, taking 2 for 104, and by close on the first day the visitors had made 467 for 7. Kent were bowled out for 162 in their first innings and left 317 to avoid an innings defeat.

When Blythe joined Fairservice on 221 for 8, that defeat seemed certain, but he opted to play his normal game and hit his way out of trouble. As a result, the two put on an astonishing 120 in 75 minutes for the ninth wicket, and complete humiliation was avoided. Blythe himself hit 13 fours in his 75, before he was bowled by Walter Brearley. It seemed for a moment like a throwback to the batting successes of 1904, and the beginning of a more consistent batting career, but as it turned out this was the swansong of his really big scores. The defeat by eight wickets was a shameful display by Kent, who had to wait for the following season to take their revenge.

At the end of August there occurred another strange landmark in his career – the only tied match he ever played in, and it was his bowling that was instrumental in bringing it about. Kent were put in by Surrey at the Oval and dismissed for 202; Blythe bowled superbly in the Surrey innings, taking 5 for 45 and limiting their total to 125. That lead of 77 in a low-scoring match looked a winning advantage, but was put firmly into perspective by a dismal performance from Kent in the second innings, as they collapsed from 52 for 2 to 84 all out. The 162 that Surrey needed for victory seemed well within their grasp when they ended the second day on 116 for 4.

But they had calculated without Blythe. In the space of six overs on the final morning he took four quick wickets for 12 runs, and with Surrey needing 18 to get with two wickets left, the game hung finely in the balance. At this point Humphreys made a bad mistake, dropping "Razor" Smith at long-off off Blythe's bowling. It was an error that cost Kent the match. When Knox, the last Surrey batsman, joined Smith, eight runs were still needed for victory and the match was poised like a modern one day game.

In one over from Alec Hearne, Smith took a four, a two and then a single. Only one was now needed as Blythe took the ball, but he kept his head and saw his opportunity. Knowing the tension the batsman was under with only one run for victory, for the second ball of the over he tossed up a tempting delivery just wide of off stump. Smith hit out and the ball spiralled high into the air to Murrell at third man. The numerous anecdotes to which this exciting finish gave rise all spoke to Kent's coolness under fire. While the ball was in the air, Murrell is said to have calmly rubbed his hands on his trousers to ensure they were dry, and Blythe, who was known for his quiet ways and close observation, remarked to a colleague, as the ball was coming down : "I've never played in a tie match before today!".

On the strength of his performances in the previous few seasons, Blythe was selected once again to go on winter tour, this time with the official MCC party to South Africa. He attempted a spot of unofficial Kent business as well, inviting the young South African fast bowler, C J Nicholls, to join the county, but without success. It was in general a satisfactory tour that added to his international reputation, though the English side were heavily defeated by four Tests to one. Blythe seemed to take to the matting pitches, securing a total of 113 wickets in all matches played and 57 in the first class ones. In the only Test that England won, he took 6 for 68 in the first innings and 5 for 50 in the second. Perhaps he sent home to a girlfriend waiting back in England a proud official photo of the MCC team, like the one my mother was to receive in 1930.

Before the tour, there occurred a small incident which showed both that Blythe was one professional prepared to stand up to the traditional paternalism of the county committees, and also how the balance of power had shifted towards him in the past four years as a result of his successes on the field. In 1901, when he had toured Australia with MacLaren's XI, his winter payments of 20 shillings a week were suspended for the period he was out of the country. At face value this might have seemed fair enough, since he was paid quite generously by the tour organisers. But in reality, the winter money was intended only as a small-scale retainer which he continued to receive alongside his full-time winter wage, working at the Woolwich Arsenal. It seemed harsh that the Kent Committee should stop these payments just when his winter work, and all the experience it would bring, was set to benefit the Kent side.

When the Kent managing committee met under Lord Harris on 6 November 1905 it heard that Blythe was about to be invited to tour South Africa and that he was keen to go, provided his winter money could continue to be paid. When professionals at this period held out their bowls and asked for more, they generally got short shrift. But this time Blythe's boldness paid off.

There was clearly some argument about acceding to the request, for it was agreed only on a majority vote. And Lord Harris's opinion, that seems to have swung the committee in Blythe's favour, left no doubt as to who was in charge, and the proper place of professionals, even talented ones, in the order of things. He told the committee "it would be a good thing to let Blythe go, and that what he does with his winter money is no concern of the Committee so long as he behaves himself, and that if he chose to winter abroad no one could object, and no one could object if he was earning money for himself in addition to what he receives by way of winter money". When liberality was dispensed in such a grudging fashion, it could not help but leave a slightly sour taste.

The pointed caveat "so long as he behaves himself" may have had a very current significance. At the same meeting there was another small agenda item headed "Behaviour of the Professionals". The somewhat gnomic minute read:

> Complaints were made respecting the behaviour of three of the professionals, and it was decided that they should be brought before the Committee and spoken to by the Chairman before the beginning of the next Season.

The committee had rather high standards and strong views with regard to behaviour. These even reached out to embrace the general public. In 1912, for example, the committee held a discussion of barracking on Kent grounds, concluding the occurrence of "this objectionable behaviour" had not been so serious as to warrant drastic action. The behaviour of the professionals on this particular occasion may not have been so very bad by modern standards, but since there was only a handful of young professionals on the county books and Blythe was noted for his cheeky personality, it is not beyond the bounds of possibility that one of the three malfeasants was Blythe himself.

1906 was the *annus mirabilis* of Kent county cricket. For the previous two decades the county championship had been monopolised by Surrey, with nine championships, and Yorkshire with seven. Kent became champions this year for the first time in their history, just beating Yorkshire by the skin of their teeth. In the early matches the season held out little promise of the great things that were to come, but gradually the wealth of batting and bowling talent in the side began to make itself felt. The mainstays of a thrilling batting side were Kenneth Hutchings and Cuthbert Burnup who at the end of the season posted averages of 69 and 64 respectively. And the bowling support for Blythe was strengthened by a marked improvement all round, especially on the part of the fast bowler Arthur Fielder. What may have tipped the balance in both bowling and batting, however, was the first appearance of a 19-year-old professional, fresh from the Tonbridge nursery, by the name of Frank Woolley.

Ironically, this year of such brilliant achievement for Kent was one of mixed fortunes for Colin Blythe – the only season from 1902 to 1914 in which he failed to take a hundred championship wickets. It started well enough when in the home match against Yorkshire in May he took ten wickets, though Kent were soundly beaten. But on 5 June, in the match against Sussex at Hove, he suffered a devastating blow. He took 6 for 37 in the first innings, helping Kent towards an innings victory, at the close of which the correspondent of *The Times* pontificated: "Kent have often caused the leading side of the year trouble, but the inability of the best amateurs to play regularly will always prevent them from winning the championship". He had saved his prediction for the right year.

Colin Blythe

It was the final day and Kent were well on their way to the win when disaster struck. At the start of the Sussex second innings, Blythe took a blinding catch at point to dismiss Robert Relf with the score on 7. When the fifth wicket had fallen for 53, he tried to perform a similar feat in response to a fearsomely hot return from Albert Relf, Robert's elder brother. Blythe seemed to lose the ball in the dark background of the stand and, as a result, split the second finger of his bowling hand very badly. He sat out the next three matches, but his return in the Hampshire match on 18 June, which Kent again won by an innings, was clearly premature. At first the injury seemed to be holding up well: he bowled 17 overs in the first innings without taking a wicket and on the second morning knocked up 24 runs in double quick time. But the injury had evidently not healed sufficiently, for that afternoon, in fielding a ball at mid-off, he split his hand open again at the very same spot and had to retire from the field. It was clear he might be out for some time.

Playing him so soon was a gamble that had not paid off and safety first was called for now. At a meeting of the Kent Committee three days later it was decided that he should not be allowed to play again until a written certificate had been received from his doctor. This was not just a psychological blow, but one to the pocket as well; under the existing Kent rules injured players received only half their ground pay and half match pay for the period of their injury.

He remained on half pay for a further three-and-a-half weeks, missing four more matches. But his return on 12 July to play the West Indies at Catford was finally proof that he was back to total fitness; he bowled 60 overs and took 10 wickets. The one redeeming feature of this injury was that it gave a chance in the first team to Frank Woolley, initially as slow left-arm replacement but soon as dominant all-rounder. Woolley, a Tonbridge man born and bred, had been hanging around the Angel Ground there for most of his boyhood. In 1903 he was finally invited to help out at the morning practice sessions, and by 1904 had become a fully paid-up member of the nursery. He had watched Blythe with admiration for many seasons and modelled his bowling on him. In the early days the two went around a lot together; Blythe coached him and became his general mentor.

The 19-year-old proved a more than adequate substitute for his boyhood hero. In the seven matches Blythe missed, Woolley made 287 runs and took 28 wickets, a foretaste of the brilliant career ahead. But the absence of Blythe was still keenly felt by the Kent side who won only three of those matches, lost one and drew three. From his return in mid July to the end of the season, they played 12 further matches, Blythe took 82 wickets, and they won the lot.

Surrey came to Blackheath on 30 July fresh from a brilliant victory over their nearest rivals, Yorkshire. The fate of the championship was now seen by many to hang on this match with Kent. The home side went to lunch on the first day on a workmanlike 103 for 4, but collapsed after the break to 136 all out. In fits and starts, Surrey managed a first innings lead of 83 and seemed on their way to victory as Kent lost half their second innings wickets while still only 57 runs ahead. But fine late order innings by Woolley, Humphreys and Blaker saw Kent move on to 327. Surrey were set 245 to win and although they lost Hobbs cheaply in the twelve minutes batting that second evening, they seemed certain to knock off the 234 needed on the final day.

There was no problem with the wicket. Goatly and Strudwick batted for the first three quarters of an hour without fuss and put on a further 17 runs. Then Fielder struck, bowling Goatly neck and crop, and the floodgates opened. In the next hour, Surrey lost their remaining eight wickets for 52 runs, Blythe bowling unchanged throughout the innings and taking 5 for 25 off 20 overs. While not the most spectacular set of figures, it was a superb performance on a perfectly good wicket, and the decisive factor in the Kent victory. Whether receiving from him or not, the Surrey batsmen had crumbled mentally in the face of his deceptive flight and occasional use of the fast arm ball.

Kent played consistently well through August, but so did Yorkshire and Surrey, and the championship was a nailbiter right up to the finish. The turning point came on 25 August when Kent beat Worcestershire at Canterbury and Yorkshire lost surprisingly to Gloucestershire at Bristol by the margin of a single run. It proved the most important run in Kent history. Going into the final week of the season, they found themselves at last at the head of the table, with only Middlesex and Hampshire to play. Before a packed house at Lord's, Kent's batting was mediocre but established a useful first innings lead; but another devastating display by Blythe in the second innings ripped the Middlesex order apart. He took 7 for 66 and left Kent with a simple 59 to win.

All eyes were now on the final match at Bournemouth, with Kent needing only a draw to secure the championship. On an excellent batting wicket, the result was set up in the first two hours by Kent's two best bowlers of the season, Blythe and Fielder, reducing Hampshire to 75 for 8. In the final total of 163, Blythe took 6 for 67. It was fitting too that in the 610 runs that Kent knocked up in the next six hours their two best batsmen of the season, Burnup and Hutchings, made 179 and 124 respectively. Having been shown how good the wicket was, the Hampshire batsman now collared the Kent bowling, but their four hundred runs was never going to be enough to save the innings defeat. Amidst all the euphoria of the Kent achievement, one fact stood out – Blythe had taken yet another twelve wicket haul for the match.

In September the congratulatory telegrams came pouring in from cricket enthusiasts worldwide. Kent had been seen for some years as a marvellously entertaining side, but one that did not quite have the staying power to see off Yorkshire and Surrey. Now they had done it for the first time, everyone put aside their traditional allegiances to share in the excitement of this much under-rated team.

It was decided to make a bonus payment of £10 to each of the professionals in recognition of their championship. It was not much even in Edwardian currency. In 1906 a Kent player received in what was called "ground pay" a basic 10 shillings per match day, up to a maximum of 50 shillings a week. Those playing in first eleven matches were paid an extra five pounds per match, with an additional one pound for a win. These payments were supplemented by personal talent money of seven shillings and sixpence for 50 runs and the same for 5 wickets, though this was never settled up until the end of the season. So the bonus Blythe received was rather less than a single week's normal wage, not the most magnanimous of gifts, and not even enough to cover the money he had lost through injury.

The Kent players ate their way through the autumn of that year as local municipalities and groups of members vied with one another to put on the best celebratory dinner. On 10 October the mayor of Maidstone presided over an immense banquet at the Corn Exchange there at which the traditional souvenirs were handed out. On 1 November there was a dinner given by the six Christopherson brothers, that incomparable Kent cricketing brotherhood, in Blythe's backyard of Blackheath. On 6 November the champions were invited as guests of honour, along with C B Fry, Plum Warner and Gilbert Jessop, to the ninth annual dinner of the Association of Men of Kent and Kentish Men at the Holborn Restaurant in London where every course was packed with Kentish delights from Whitstable oysters to Orpington chicken, from Ramsgate scallops to Dover sole.

The centrepiece of these celebrations came on 11 October when the members gave a dinner at the Hotel Cecil in London in honour of the players. It was a brilliant gathering of 550 souls, presided over by the chairman of the club, Lord Harris, and, with many old players of past years present, a fitting way to end a remarkable season. There must have been some uneasy stomachs among the players coming straight from the Maidstone banquet of the previous day, but they managed to munch their way in good Edwardian style through dishes of consommé and turbot, chicken and lamb, roast pheasant and York ham, while the Band of the Royal East Kent Imperial Yeomanry played the overture from *Tancredi* and the intermezzo from *Cavalleria Rusticana*.

In a break between the fourteen speeches, Lady Harris presented each player with a set of gold cufflinks; emblazoned on the oval heads of one set were the words *Champions 1906 C Blythe*. They were passed down to Colin's brother, Charles, and are still in use by his grandson today.

———————

Colin Blythe

The dinner was to give rise to something more substantial than a set of cufflinks and more lasting than fine speeches of celebration. Since the last match at Bournemouth, Lord Harris had been casting round for ideas for a memento that would set this historic achievement in concrete for all time. The usual team photograph, taken every year irrespective of success or failure, was not enough. Towards the end of his speech he made the suggestion that the members might commission a picture of the eleven from the well-known cricket painter, Chevallier Tayler. It would not be a portrait of a mere team line-up, but an action painting of the side in the field. He made only two stipulations: the ground should be Canterbury and the bowler should be Blythe.

Thus came to pass the commissioning of one of the most famous cricket pictures ever painted, capturing all the atmosphere of the St Lawrence Ground in Edwardian dress, and the tense expectation of a team straining every nerve to win the supreme cricket prize. The selection of Blythe as the key figure was no mere chance. Harris saw clearly that the young, gifted and popular bowler was already a poignant symbol of the Kent cricket of that day, just as his early death and the nostalgia of later generations were to turn him into the even more poignant symbol of the whole "Golden Age".

At a meeting of the Managing Committee on 5 November it was agreed to pursue the Chairman's proposal further, and on 10 December the General Committee decided formally to commission the artist for 200 guineas, and grant him a share of the proceeds from the subsequent photogravure of the painting, up to a further 150 guineas.

The recipient of this commission, Albert Chevallier Tayler, was an artist with a colourful bohemian background, who in his youth had held out much promise as a groundbreaker. Now in middle age, he had succumbed to the inevitable acceptance world in which money flowed easiest through religious and fashionable society commissions, and his current little niche of cricketing paintings. He had been born in 1862, the son of a London solicitor, and was a lively pupil at Bloxham School in Oxfordshire where his drawing talent was first recognised. From there he won a scholarship to the Slade

and went on to Paris in the early 1880s to work in the studios
of Jean Paul Laurens and later Carlos Duran, where he met
and became close friends with Stanhope Forbes. He joined
Forbes in Cornwall in 1884 where, along with other friends,
he started the Newlyn School which first brought the radi-
cal *plein air* movement to England. His paintings at this time
proved difficult to sell and he tended to keep in touch with
London rather more than the other Newlyn colleagues. In
1895 he returned to the metropolis for good.

The members of the Newlyn school were well known too
for *plein airiste* leisure occupations – swimming, sailing, walking. Cricket was an obsession common to most of them and
they formed together a fairly creditable Newlyn team whose
central focus was the annual games against St Ives, home and
away. Tayler, the batsman, was more keen than most. When
he left Newlyn for a painting commission in Venice in 1887,
Forbes recalled : "He was in high glee for he had played in a
cricket match in the afternoon, and made top score". At the
beginning of the Golden Age, he put his cricketing enthusiasm
to good commercial use. In 1905 he had exhibited no less than
100 original portraits, drawn from life, of famous English and
colonial cricketers under the title "The Empire's Cricketers",
and it was the publicity from this event that had obviously
caught Lord Harris's eye.

If the picture commissioned were to represent action in a
real match, and nothing less would do, Harris and Tayler had
now to decide which that match should be. There had been only
three matches at Canterbury that summer, two in the Week and
one against Worcestershire in late August. The choice was not
easy for it had been a truly vintage Week that year.

In the first match, Sussex had been stuffed by an innings
and 131 runs, and the Kent innings had been little short of sensational. After two and a quarter hours on the first day Kent
were 145 for 5, a snail's pace by their standards; the remainder
of the day added a further 307 runs for the loss of only two
more wickets! Blythe walked out to join Marsham on the second morning on a score of 457 for 8. Fifty runs were hit off the
first five overs that day and the pair added 111 in 35 minutes.
Blythe finished with 53, his highest score of the season, and

Colin Blythe

Kent with 568 all out in five and a half hours. What added to the hilarity and joy of the home spectators was the sight of Sussex in such desperation that they were forced to bowl all of their players, except the wicketkeeper Butt. Ten bowlers in an innings is the stuff of fantasy itself.

Coming down to earth, however, Blythe's batting had been more memorable than his bowling in that match, whereas in the Lancashire game that followed he had at least taken eight wickets. This, therefore, seemed the right one to choose. In February 1907 the Lancashire President, A N Hornby, of poetic legend, gave his consent to a representation of the Lancashire match.

Thursday 9 August 1906 was the traditional Ladies' Day and 13,000 people packed the St Lawrence Ground, a new record. The start was delayed until half past twelve to await the Lancashire team, held up on their long journey down from a defeat in the Roses match at Old Trafford. Burnup, Seymour and Hutchings batted in their usual flamboyant style and the score was 208 for 2 when Burnup was run out, gallantly surrendering his own wicket to Hutchings. In the last hour and three quarters of play, Hutchings and Mason put on 201, and in the shortened day Kent had built a score of 409 for 3.

Kent hit out the next morning and were finally dismissed for 479, Frank Harry of Lancashire taking five wickets in his last three overs. It was a perfect day for cricket, marred only by a late shower that held up play between four and five in the afternoon. Quieter than Ladies' Day, there were seven or eight thousand on the ground. Lancashire began their innings at midday and, though batting courageously, fine bowling by Blythe and Fielder soon destroyed any hopes they had of saving the game. The Kent fielding was brilliant in the extreme, epitomised by Seymour's diving slip catch off a full-blooded cut from Tyldesley in the second innings, which many thought the catch of a lifetime.

The match was decided on this second day. Lancashire were dismissed for 159 by mid afternoon, Blythe taking 5 for 80. A few overs into their second innings they were 20 for 4, and by close of play had crawled to 78 for 4. On the Saturday, Blythe and Fielder bowled as brilliantly as before, and the remaining six wickets fell in half an hour for 37 runs, Kent winning by an innings and 195. A large crowd gathered in front of the pavilion to see the collection of £136 presented by Lord Harris to the county's now growing cohort of ten professionals. Along with Fred Huish and Frank Woolley, Blythe's cut was £15. From the steps of the pavilion, Harris extolled the virtues of the side that year and the fine spirit in which they had played. Whether they won or lost the championship, their great skills would never be forgotten.

Tayler sets his picture on Friday 10 August, the decisive day, some time between midday and the luncheon interval, when Blythe and Fielder were bowling at their best and the Kent fielding was electric. It is not, of course, one of those paintings taken quietly from life sitting at the edge of the boundary, though many viewing it since may well have thought so. It is entirely contrived from an imaginative recollection. The fielding positions of individual players are accurately drawn, but the field overall is compressed to ensure that all eleven Kent players can be seen face on.

Fresh from his portraits of the Empire's cricketers, Tayler was keen to achieve facial accuracy. He arranged individual sittings with most of the Kent team, but in his quest for verisimilitude had more trouble with the Lancashire batsmen. For Johnny Tyldesley, the celebrated Lancashire batsman facing Blythe, only a backview was needed. But the batsman at the bowler's end was Harry Makepeace, the cricketer footballer who had just won the FA Cup with Everton, and with whom, based up north, a personal sitting was more difficult to achieve. So Tayler took a second best course and called in William Findlay, the Lancashire player who had retired at the end of the 1906 season and was now Secretary to Surrey at the Oval, within striking distance of the Tayler studio. The only difficulty was that Findlay, who normally went in No. 8, had not played in the match at all!

The picture was ready by the late summer of 1907 and proved a commercial success. By July 192 engravings of it had been ordered and the receipts of £366 more than paid off the artist. Lancashire were keen to get in on the act, and Johnny Tyldesley himself even offered to sell copies from his shop in Manchester. The picture caused quite a public stir and many wanted to see it in the flesh. So in the spring of 1908 it was loaned to Blackheath, and subsequently to Lord's, where it hung in the pavilion for a few months before finding its natural home back in the pavilion at Canterbury. Still today it retains its iconic status worldwide, and is much in demand as a merchandising aid. The Kent authorities get regular requests for its commercial use, most recently to adorn an Australian biscuit tin and the cover of a French educational book on English *moeurs* entitled *Manuel de civilisation britannique*.

What had been intended merely as a memento of Kent's great achievement that year, a keepsake to mark a very local event, soon became one of the most celebrated of cricket pictures, and the lasting symbol of a cricketing era held later to be without compare. Part of this was due to the atmospheric skill of the painter; but much also to the fact that Colin Blythe was at its heart.

Chapter 6

Northampton

Marriage to a professional cricketer, as my mother may have surmised, was not a step to be taken lightly. In summer they are constantly on the move and home becomes just another cheap hotel. In winter, if any good, they are many thousand miles away, soaking up Australian or South African sun. If only county average, they are at a loose end, bored by a tedious winter job that can only be second best. Most challenging of all is the question of commitment – the woman or the game? To remain top of one's class, whether slow left-arm bowler or leading batsman, the single-minded concentration required leaves little room for a second major obsession.

By the opening of 1907, the leading bowler of the new champion county was 27 years old. He had followed his peripatetic trade for seven full seasons, played in 11 Test matches and been on winter tours to Australia, South Africa and the United States – the short Kent tour to Philadelphia in 1903. Though many players survived longer then than they do today, into their forties and even fifties, it seemed likely that Blythe had now reached the mid-way point in his career. He was living as usual in the winter at his parents' home in New Cross Road and working as an engineer, sometimes back at the Woolwich Arsenal and at others with the Maxim Gun Company.

But this winter was different from the rest. He had met and fallen in love with a woman from his summer hunting ground, Tunbridge Wells, and they were married at Greenwich Registry Office, his home patch, on 11 March 1907. They settled into a little semi-detached house, with traditional Victorian square bay windows, in Tonbridge, the town where he had learnt his cricket. His arrival caused a buzz in the street. Mrs Roe, now still living in the house next door, remembers him as a kindly man who used to give her sweets over the garden fence. They were to remain there at 40, St Mary's Road, half-way down the hill that overlooked the Angel Ground, for the next four years.

His wife, Janet Brown, had been born in Rochdale Road, Tunbridge Wells on 1 February 1889 to Henry Brown, a jour-neyman painter, and Deborah, his wife. She was thus almost ten years younger than her famous husband and, to redress the balance a little, gave her age on marriage as nineteen. By this time her father was already dead, which perhaps explains why the ceremony was held in the groom's home town rather than the bride's.

She was 5 foot 10 inches in height, tall for a woman of the time, and very attractive, with brown hair, big round grey eyes, a strong determined nose and full lips. She had been for-mally christened Janet Gertrude, and was called Janet within her family of birth and then when she married a second time. But for Colin and the rest of the Blythe family she was always Gertrude, and so, like her husband, rejoiced in the luxury of two Christian names.

She is remembered still in the Blythe family today as a kindly, lively woman who loved her husband deeply and cher-ished his memory. She still maintained her links with them long after his death. In the family of her second marriage, she is remembered only as an old woman, and a strong-minded, rather domineering, one at that. She never had children her-self, and did not get on too well with her two stepdaugh-ters, though for any second marriage that is often par for the course.

If even at the tender age of 18 she was the strong-minded woman of later years, that would make sense of marriage to a rather shy, sensitive man ten years her senior. We know she was devoted to him after his death, but nothing more about their marriage to enable us to speculate on the balance within the relationship, except that it lasted till death and produced no offspring.

There are perhaps even fewer grounds on which we can speculate how marriage might have affected Blythe himself, except by deduction from human behaviour in general. Given that the routine stability of a normal marriage is difficult for the travelling professional cricketer, it is possible that the euphoria of the event itself gave way before long to anxiety in face of new domestic pressures, especially if his spouse were a strong personality. What is indubitably true is that the life of complete independence he had enjoyed for some time past was now no longer on offer. And although it may be quite coincidental, it is only from 1907 on that we start to hear the stories of neurotic illness, of his nervous exhaustion after very big matches, of his epilepsy. It is just possible, then, that cricket and the concentration demanded became more of a burden because of the competing responsibilities at home.

But if domestic life had irrevocably changed for better or for worse, his power performance on the field did not waver. 1907 was the year in which Blythe took his one thousandth wicket for Kent, the first bowler ever to do so. Kent entered the season as the brilliant champions of the year before, determined to show that their unexpected success was no chance accident. For the first month they looked certain to prove their case, winning their first three matches by wide margins; but then reality set in. Their two strongest batsmen from 1906 were eclipsed by circumstance. Burnup could spare time to play in only three matches (the curse of the amateur still prevailing) and Hutchings badly injured his hand and was out for a number of games. Jim Seymour was the only one to step in and fill the breach, while the rest of the batsmen, anxious to live up to their reputation for dashing brilliancy, tended to hit out before playing themselves in, with predictable consequences.

Consistently fine bowling performances by Blythe (141 wickets) and Fielder (151) could never be enough to win matches without batsmen, and Kent consequently slumped to eighth place in the championship. But even towards the

end of the season when the team were losing and drawing
a run of matches, the Blythe magic would suddenly super-
vene and Kent would seem like champions again. In back to
back matches against Surrey and Leicestershire in late July, as
a gentle warm-up to his greatest Test performance, he took 23
wickets and scored 37 runs.

The first two days of the Surrey game at Blackheath produced only just over four hours play because of rain. When
Surrey went in to bat at ten to one on the first day, the batsmen
found the timing of Blythe's bowling almost an impossibility. In a
typically devastating performance, he had Jack Hobbs stumped
for 5 in his second over and then took one wicket in each of the
next three. His figures at that stage stood at 5 – 1 – 11 – 4.
In a short space of time Surrey were 32 for 5 and facing their
lowest score of the season.

Desperate measures were called for and when Lord
Dalmeny came in at No. 7 he embarked at once on a sustained
display of powerful and resolute hitting. He took 15 off one
over from Blythe, including a six from a straight drive over
the sight screen and out to the tennis courts beyond. It was
Blythe, however, who got him to miscue the next over and
he was caught by Fred Huish, the wicketkeeper, running
out to short leg. He had made 70 out of 101 in just over an
hour. Surrey were finally bowled out by half past three for
136. Blythe bowled unchanged throughout the innings and,
despite the onslaught from Dalmeny, had taken 7 for 56.

Play was halted for rain on this first day at a quarter past
four with Kent on 28 for 1. The second day was another wash-
out and Dillon and Seymour did not resume their innings
until after four o'clock. By this time the ground was so soft
that the bowlers could scarcely obtain a foothold and the two
batsmen rapidly carried the score to 108, their full partnership adding in typical Kent fashion 102 in 90 minutes. The
pitch proved master in the end, however, and six wickets fell
in the last hour, mostly to Crawford, for the addition of only
30 runs. By close of play Kent were two runs ahead with only
two wickets left and the game, with only one wet day to go,
looked delicately poised for a draw.

But this was to count without the special genius of Blythe.

However unlikely, Kent's natural instinct in these situations was to go all out for a win, and immediately next morning Blythe and Fairservice went on the attack. Blythe was dropped early on – a simple catch to Knox at mid-off – and this error was to have an enormous impact on the game, given the state of the wicket. By dint of fierce hitting he and Fairservice put on 43 runs in 20 minutes for the ninth wicket, giving Kent a first innings lead of 51 with Blythe hitting four fours in his unbeaten 23.

For the Surrey second innings Jack Mason, captaining Kent in the absence of Marsham, immediately put on his two greatest assets, the slow left arms of Blythe and Woolley. Both proved difficult to play, but most especially Blythe with his perfect length and sudden turn and lift. Surrey lost their first four wickets for 15 and after only 75 minutes play were 41 for 8 with an innings defeat staring them in the face. At this point Blythe had taken 5 wickets for 12 runs but, as often happens in such situations, some swift tail-ender hitting brought the analysis back to reality. Smith and Strudwick took 22 off his last two overs and raised the final Surrey total to a more presentable 79, but not enough to save them from defeat by ten wickets. Blythe finished with 5 for 34 and a match analysis of 12 for 90.

He was in red hot form as the team moved on that day to Maidstone to face Leicestershire. The wicket was good and more suitable for fast bowling than for spin, but Blythe in bowling 71 overs in the match showed how quality perseverance could still bring victory in a relatively high-scoring game. In Kent's first innings Seymour, Troughton and Woolley hit out and when Blythe came in at No. 10 Kent had reached 232 for 8. But Blythe and Fairservice were not to be outdone, and put on a vital 52 for the ninth wicket, taking the final Kent total to 285.

Leicestershire, by an odd combination of hard hitting and slow attrition, managed to reach 207 in their first innings, Blythe taking most of the bowling and finishing with 5 for 79. Then Kent collapsed badly in their second innings to 79 for 6, owing to some fine cricket by Jayes who performed the hat-trick in bowling Dillon, Troughton and Woolley. The home side crawled to a total of 130, leaving Leicestershire a comfortably attainable 209 to win. At close on the second day they were 76 for 2 (both wickets to Blythe) with only 133 runs still required.

The final Saturday was a tantalising affair as the initiative swung back and forth, though with Leicestershire in the principal driving seat. With 59 to get they still had five wickets left; with their last three wickets only 29. But Blythe stuck to his last and took the crucial wicket of Coe for 35, the one Leicestershire batsman who seemed determined to win the match. Despite the nervous tension of the finish, Blythe polished off the last two wickets, giving Kent victory by 21 runs. His final analysis of 6 for 96 was not on paper one of his greatest feats, but his eleven wickets in the match, and partnership with Fairservice in the first innings, had made the most substantial contribution to the victory.

With just one day's rest on the Sunday, spent travelling up to Headingley, he then proceeded to lay waste the South African batting in the second Test – which forms a spell-binding story of its own. His tally for these nine consecutive days of cricket was a mere 38 wickets! Yet just two months earlier, in the game with which his memory is irrevocably entwined, he had taken almost half that number in a single day.

Northamptonshire had joined the County Championship from the small fry of the minor counties in 1905. In their first two years they had made a fairly fragile start, losing 8 out of 12 matches in 1905 and 10 out of 16 in 1906. Only one of their batsmen, Charles Pool, seemed capable of standing up to first class bowling, and in their first season they had been bowled out twice by Surrey at the Oval in less than three hours for 55 and 32. Their second season had shown some batting improvement with the team averaging just under 200 for a completed innings, enough to give them the confidence to take on for the first time the big boys of Kent, Lancashire and Gloucestershire. At the beginning of 1907 the cricketing world wondered how they would fare with this new ambitious programme.

Northampton

It did not have long to wait. On 13 May Kent, coming straight from a victory over the MCC at Lord's, played their opening championship fixture at Catford against Northants. They batted first on a difficult wicket that made fast deliveries bounce and kick, but managed to make 259, thanks to a fine attacking innings of 99 by Frank Woolley. Northants were then swept away for a total of 73 in an hour-and-a-half, primarily by the pace of Fielder who took 8 for 42 off 14 overs. At close of play Northants, following on, had made 5 for 1 in their second innings.

Rain prevented play on the second day until ten to four, but it needed only another hour and forty minutes to dismiss the visitors again for 86 and give Kent victory by an innings and 100 runs. Humphreys was the leading wicket-taker in this second innings with 5 for 26, but Blythe, following the normal course, had been deployed to keep up the pressure from the other end. He had bowled unchanged throughout the match, taking 2 for 29 in the first innings and 4 for 37 in the second. But these were paltry figures compared to the next encounter between the two sides.

Ominously for Northants this was set for a fortnight later and happened to be their very next match. So they had to sit out those two weeks, contemplating their likely fate on the next round, while Kent rushed to three brilliant victories and one defeat (against Lancashire) by just six runs. The game was to be played on the County Ground, Northampton which had been the home of Northamptonshire cricket for twenty years, albeit shared with Northampton Town Football Club since 1897.

The omens were not good when Kent arrived at the ground on Thursday 30 May, Blythe's 28th birthday, fresh from a remarkable innings victory over Derbyshire at Chesterfield in less than a full day's play; a game in which the home side had been dismissed for 37 in the second innings, the lowest score of the season so far, and Blythe had returned match figures of 7 for 46. Here at Northampton no play was possible on the first morning, but three hours were squeezed from the afternoon before further rain put paid to play for the day.

Despite the threatening weather, Kent won the toss and made good use of the limited time available. Woolley and Hardinge put on 64 for the first wicket, and then Hardinge and

Colin Blythe

Seymour a further 71 for the second. Despite the good fortune of being dropped at mid-off when 12 and 43, Hardinge made no further errors and had scored 73 when finally dismissed with Kent on 135 for 2. Then came a typical innings full of brilliant driving from Hutchings, who was 49 not out when the rain finally ended the day. In the 180 minutes, Kent had made 212 for 4 and looked well set for the expected victory.

On the second day the weather continued chief player. It rained incessantly from close of play on the first day, throughout the night and right up until two o'clock on the Friday afternoon. The prospects for play then seemed brighter, but a heavy thunderstorm just after three soon put paid to all hope of any cricket. Though for the few miserable spectators who hung on throughout the day (as spectators tend to do) there was apparently no action, this night and day marked the crucial action of the game. The elements were combining to produce the archetypal Blythe wicket.

Saturday 1 June 1907 was too an archetypal Blythe day. When play started on time at 11.35, there was little prospect of bringing the game to a conclusion. With only 212 on the board, Kent could hardly declare, the weather prospects for a full day's play remained uncertain, and the wicket after all that rain was expected to be soft and dead. Nonetheless, these were not (as we have seen already) the circumstances to deter this Kent side with its dashing reputation from going all out for victory. After all, they had started the last day of their previous match against Derbyshire with only two hours play under their belts, and had won it all the same.

The remaining Kent batsmen hit out fearlessly, adding 42 in forty minutes for the last six wickets. On 243 for 8, Blythe came in to join wicketkeeper Fred Huish, who made a sparkling 19 not out. Blythe himself immediately hit out at East with two well-driven twos, and stayed with Huish to make a score of six. He eventually went for a big hit and was caught in the outfield by the Northamptonshire amateur Vials who, for other reasons, was the only person to blight this day of glory for Blythe.

During this Huish-Blythe mini-partnership, there occurred a little cameo incident which shows just how much cricket remains the same from one generation to the next. While Huish was facing, a deceptive ball from East down the leg side put him into two minds, and so unbalanced him that he had to leapfrog the wicket to prevent knocking the stumps down. It caused great hilarity among the crowd, and the report in the *Northampton Chronicle* suddenly rushes us forward more than eighty years to Ian Botham and the Oval of 1991, with Johnston and Agnew in the commentary box erupting like suppressed volcanoes.

> Blythe, the famous slow bowler, off and on drove East for twos, and then Huish caused some amusement by putting his *leg over* the wicket in an attempt to make a leg hit. [*my italics*]

The Northants first innings was an unmitigated disaster for the home side on a wicket that was more slow and puddeny than desperately dangerous. Blythe opened the bowling from the pavilion end and on the fourth ball of his first over had the opening batsman Buswell cleverly stumped by Fred Huish for a duck, deceived by flight and length as he played forward. The next ball caught the shoulder of Pool's bat and reared up to provide a simple catch to Fielder running in from point. Nought for two and the best batsman gone.

Kingston, who now came in, managed to survive the hat-trick, and in Blythe's next over scored the first run of the innings through the slips, to loud ironic cheers from the home spectators. Then in his third over Blythe had Cox, the other opening batsman, stumped in the same manner as Buswell. Kingston and George Thompson ran two leg-byes, and then in his fifth over Blythe bowled Thompson for another duck.

Meanwhile, Fairservice kept up the psychological pressure from the other end, bowling four straight maidens on the trot. This particular spell was broken in his fifth over when Kingston hit him for a single over cover point's head. Blythe's sixth over was a rout. With his first ball, he had Kingston, the only one of the first seven batsmen to score, leg before wicket for 2, and with his third he had Crosse caught by Fairservice at cover point. East hit out at his last ball and skyed it down the leg side where Huish ran out to take a smart catch. He had taken four wickets off his last eight balls, and at this point in the innings Northants were 4 for 7 wickets, and two of those four were extras! Blythe's analysis stood at 6 overs, 5 maidens, 7 wickets for 1 run. All taking part were dumbfounded, as major world records seemed about to topple.

G A T Vials, a very capable batsman, now came in at No. 9, for some reason much lower down the order than usual. He immediately showed his intent by hitting the last ball of the next Fairservice over to the on boundary for four, giving rise to a tremendous round of cheering from the spectators. Thompson drove the first ball of Blythe's next over for a single, and then came the moment that was to turn the Kent bowler's proudest day into a source of future nightmares. Vials was deceived by his first ball from Blythe and sent a high return back down the wicket to the bowler. If not the "sitter" of a catch that Frank Woolley later remembered, it was certainly takeable under normal conditions. He missed it. Whether just a moment of inattention, or the nerves of the situation had got to him, he missed it.

For future generations of cricket statisticians, who love unbeatable records, it was a costly miss. Had he held it the Northants score would have stood at 9 for 8, and Blythe's analysis 8 for 2. A R Thompson at the non-striker's end was 1 not out, Wells the next man in was eventually out to Blythe for a duck (but that was another six overs later) and the last man, Driffield, was no batsman at all. Had the catch been held, there was every probability that Northants would have been bowled out for 9 and Blythe had a return of 10 for 2, or at least something close.

But there is no such thing as probability in cricket, wherein lies the charm. It is not unusual when a side collapses calamitously for tail-enders to make their career best scores. Blythe was intensely keen on cricket records and this important miss, quite understandably, seems to have had an effect on his bowling. Woolley remembered it some thirty years later (though in the wrong context) in affectionate terms: "Poor Charlie! I think that miss so upset him that he could not bowl another ball."

In fact he bowled another nine overs before the last wicket fell, but they might have been from a different game. For if the miss had blighted Blythe, it had given an accretion of confidence to Vials and to Thompson at the other end. Seven runs were now smashed off the remaining three balls of this disastrous seventh over – an incredible strike in the context of the innings so far – and four off his eighth. Great cheers went up as Vials took the score into double figures and Thompson saw them past the Nottinghamshire lowest first class total of 13.

It took a couple of overs, but Blythe eventually regained his confidence. He struck back with two wicket maidens, having Thompson caught by Seymour in the slips for 10 and Wells caught by Humphreys at mid-on for 0. Though the eighth wicket had put on a massive 20 runs, at the end of this over Northants were 26 for 9 and Blythe still had the stupendous analysis of 10 overs, 7 maidens, 9 for 13.

But Vials now turned his attention to Blythe, hitting 12 off his next four overs, as he and the last man Driffield carried the Northants spectators through the next two landmarks, overtaking their previous lowest score of 32 and the lowest score of the season, the 37 by Derbyshire in Kent's previous match. At this point the figure 38 was raised on the scoreboard to deafening cheers.

When the score had reached 41, anxious to take the last wicket before lunch, Ted Dillon, the Kent captain, put on Fielder for Fairservice, but he was hit for nine off his first two overs, while at the other end Vials drove Blythe over cover point's head for four. Northants went to lunch on 54 for 9, and the game had turned on its head. As Vials on 30 and Driffield on 9 walked back to the pavilion they were given a hero's reception by an intensely excited crowd, who had been vigorously cheering every run. It took only three further overs after lunch, however, to bring the innings to a close. At five to three, when the last wicket stand had put on 34 in 12 overs, Blythe finally bowled Driffield for 12. Though the mind-blowing records had evaporated into thin air, he had still taken 10 for 30 off 16 overs.

The taking of all ten wickets in the innings was in itself a remarkable feat, one that Blythe was never to repeat. Journalists rushed to the record books to discover it had been achieved in county cricket by only 11 bowlers in the previous forty years, and also, by coincidence, the previous season by Blythe's professional colleague Arthur Fielder, who had taken 10 for 90 in the Gentlemen and Players match. What always makes the feat remarkable is the question, if the wicket is favourable to bowlers and the batting poor, why no-one else should take a wicket. In this particular case, the only other bowlers tried were the pace of Fairservice and Fielder on a pitch that was not yet all that fast.

This was to change as Northants went in a second time, following on 194 behind. The batsmen had put up a feeble performance in the first innings, but now they could perhaps be forgiven their errors as the wicket had become appreciably faster and the ball came off the ground at great pace. Was it possible that Blythe could take all 20 wickets on such a pitch? As the undefeated champion of the first innings, Vials was promoted to No 1, but in the third over of the innings he mishit a ball from Blythe which went spiralling high into the air on the offside. As Fairservice came running in from mid-off, it looked as though Blythe was on the way again. He got under the ball in time, but then he dropped it.

For a bowler who thrived on records, this was a devastating start to the innings. But worse was to come when on the first ball of the next over Fairservice clean bowled Vials for one. The possibility of a 20 wicket haul had been dashed from him in the most aggravating of circumstances. The batting picked up as Pool on-drove Blythe for 2 in his next over and Cox drove Fairservice twice to the off and once to the on to pick up a further six runs.

But then Blythe got back on message. Off the last two balls of his fourth over he had Pool stumped for 5 (a doubtful decision that caused much surprise) and Kingston lbw for 0. George Thompson survived the hat-trick but three overs later he fell to a fine running catch by Hardinge in the outfield and Cox, who had batted steadily for his 12, was stumped, both off Blythe. The next over Fairservice had East brilliantly caught behind, a decision which the batsman hotly contested. After 16 overs Northants were 21 for 6, and Blythe's personal tally was 4 for 6.

Northampton

The fight was now on once again to save the home side from their own lowest score and the lowest of the season. Buswell and A R Thompson now decided to go on the attack. Buswell hit Blythe to the on-boundary for four and Thompson put him to leg for two, his tenth over conceding seven runs. Then came a run of missed chances. At 29 Humphreys replaced Fairservice, and Buswell was dropped at point off the new bowler. Then on the second ball of the next over Blythe received a gentle return catch from Thompson – and he dropped it. This loss of a simple fifth wicket, coming after Fairservice's miss early on and the seven runs off the last over, was a dreadful reminder of the first innings miss off Vials.

In Humphreys' second over Buswell was dropped once more, this time by Day at long-off, but in Blythe's next over he was finally caught by Woolley at mid-off. When Crosse came in, rain started to fall and it seemed possible that play might have to be halted. He lifted Blythe to the onside for a single but at 35 was well caught by Hardinge on the boundary. Wells played on to Humphreys and, at 35 for 9, Northants were heading for the lowest score of the season after all; but Driffield, with a single to leg off Humphreys, raised the magic figure of 38 once more and the scorers, replete with excitement, did not bother this time to post the numbers up.

Off the first ball of his 16th over, Blythe had Thompson well caught by Humphreys at mid-on and Northants had been routed again in an hour and a quarter for 39. Kent had won by an innings and 155, and afterwards several of their players praised the home side for their sportsmanship in playing on in the drizzle. But the gods were clearly on the Kent side that day. Just after the players left the field at 4.30, the heavens opened and it poured continuously for the next few hours.

Blythe's analysis for the second innings was 15 overs, 7 maidens, 7 for 18; his tally for the match 17 for 48. Again the record-mongers scratched their heads to discover when 17 wickets had last been taken in a county match. By chance, it had happened only two seasons before when the Lancashire bowler Walter Brearley took 17 Somerset wickets at Old Trafford, and before that one had to go back to 1895 when the Essex bowler Walter Mead had performed the feat. But neither bowler's analysis came anything close to Blythe's. Mead got his wickets for 119 runs and Brearley for 137.

Seventeen wickets in a match have been taken since (Tich Freeman did it twice in his career for Kent) but for some time Blythe remained the only person to have performed the feat in the space of one day. This record lasted for 26 years until Hedley Verity, another slow left-armer killed in war, did it against Essex at Leyton in 1933. The only other person to do it was my mother's friend, Tom Goddard, at Bristol in 1939, and the side he decimated on that occasion was ... well yes, Kent.

But today 17 for 48 remains the best ever match analysis in county cricket, and the most wickets for least runs in all first class cricket, apart from Jim Laker's ethereal 19 for 90 against the Australians at Old Trafford in 1956. The two achievements, one in a match against a poor county side and one in a Test match, cannot, of course, be compared. The most remarkable thing about Laker's achievement was that on such a pitch Tony Lock could only rustle up one wicket. Looking at the figures, however, the fact remains that Laker's wickets cost 4.7 apiece, while Blythe's cost 2.8.

The national press was full of luxuriant praise; and even the local press put aside its partisanship. The following week in the *Northampton Independent* there appeared a touching little cartoon of Blythe on a monument, ball in left hand, right hand jauntily on hip, with the whole of the Northants team kneeling in a circle at the foot in submission to the master, some with heads bowed, others looking sheepishly out at the world. It is entitled "Bowing the Knee to Blythe".

As time passed, Blythe's remarkable day at Northampton took on a legendary status that continued to capture the public imagination for many years, in a way that the subsequent performances of 17 in a day have not. This may have to do with the nature of the man, of the specific performance itself, or of the rosy after-glow that has long surrounded Edwardian cricket. That glow was ignited by the horrors of the trenches that so distorted the popular perception of the peacetime world that had gone before. In the same way, Blythe's death amid those trenches has given a special finality to all those cricketing feats in our historical imagination, which in some

BOWING THE KNEE TO BLYTHE

intangible way has made them even more illustrious than they were in actual life.

It is, perhaps, for this reason that all the stories about Northampton have tended to focus on what might have been. Frank Woolley in his reminiscences, pretty consistently unreliable, built up the dropped caught and bowled off Vials as the only thing that had stood in the way of the fabled twenty wicket haul. For this, he transposed the first innings into the second – Blythe had taken ten in the first, and the first seven in the second, and the dropped caught and bowled off Vials would have made the eighteenth! This was not true, but in modern times it has not stopped such luminaries as David Frith from falling for the story. As we have seen, any 20 wicket dream was immediately shattered when Fairservice took the first wicket of the second innings.

This gross distortion of historical fact was not deliberate, nor the product of old-age amnesia – Woolley was then in his middle years. It just goes to show how powerful were the emotions created by that day and how strong the personal image of the man, now dead, no longer in a position to set the record straight. It is also an example of wishful thinking; when someone dies we always want to mould their completed lives after our own image and add that special gloss that they would never recognise themselves. It is perhaps our way of affirming that no-one's life is ever really over.

There was a telling postscript to this day of miracles by the bowler who was now a newly-married man. The Kent team travelled on to Headingley where they were to face their closest championship rivals, Yorkshire, in a game for which the whole country was holding its breath. Blythe arrived at the ground on a dark Monday morning with the rain coming down in buckets, but soon began to feel unwell and was sent to see a doctor. The doctor diagnosed a severe chill and packed him off back to the hotel to bed. He was out for two games.

His absence was heralded as a major blow for the champion county, but in the event the concern proved unwarranted as the Yorkshire match petered out in rain. The Blythe collapse on this occasion may have been no more than the effect of days of exposure in wet outfields and draughty pavilions on a man with a constitution that was none too strong. But it was not just his physical constitution that had its weakness, and it would be no surprise if one contributory factor had been the mental pressures of that Saturday, as cheap wickets piled up behind him and world records beckoned before. His response to the emotional pressures of the game – the pressures of success rather than of failure – now became a significant factor in his career, particularly in cricket at the highest level of all.

Chapter 7

Test

Another Christmas has come and gone, and the anticipated pain of the past at this stocktaking season never quite eventuates. As we stare down the wrong end of the telescope, the black monsters grow smaller and less threatening. The first few days of a new year seem to shed a breath of hope through their apparent vacancy.

The rain has been incessant, like an Edwardian cricket match. Down by the bridge at the bottom of the hill the river has broken its banks, disseminating the tears of yesterday across the countryside of today to feed the pastures of tomorrow. Through the twisted leafless fretwork of the high-banked hedges a cerulean sky pierces the vaporous trails of white cloud.

I follow the mud-strewn wintry lanes on my quotidian path round Banbury hill – not *the* Banbury Hill, of course, just mine. The low white light of the afternoon sun kisses the gentle slopes of green meadow rising up to the small dark clump of trees, huddling inwards, gnarled arms around each other's necks, to protect their great secret – that here two thousand years and more ago lived people, lived and moved, whose individual lives are lost forever, as ours soon shall be too. No secret now to us as we rush past in our self-importance, just another minor Iron Age fort. But still a secret to the trees, a mystery worth preserving.

Home to tea and log fire, I turn the paper and see, in the

obituaries, that Richard Davis has died. Died aged 37 of a brain tumour – a low grade tumour, it says, and operated on, but he died nonetheless. "After having surgery last summer, he went to watch Kent play at the St Lawrence ground, Canterbury." I knew of him vaguely but, just to show how out of touch I am with cricket these days, I may have seen him in the odd one-day match on television, but no more than that. He joined Kent as a slow left-armer in 1986 in the intimidating shadow of Derek Underwood, that brilliant modern pretender to the mantle of Colin Blythe. This seems to have blighted his self-belief and later his career; after Kent released him, he played for four more counties in almost as many years. His best of 7 for 64 against Durham in 1992 is not perhaps so far distant, as a modern equivalent, from a haul of 10 for 30 against Northants on the uncovered wickets of 1907.

But wait a minute! A Kent slow left-armer who dies at 37, it says further on he was unable to drive because of epileptic fits – "seizures" it calls them in the euphemistic way of obituaries. A player whose epilepsy stopped him from driving but not from bowling. No explanation of this as the side-effect of tumours; and equally no discussion here how, even in his last few matches, such a disability might touch his play, his self-confidence, the control of emotion under pressure. And no mention by this obituary writer of the striking resonance with another past – because the past is now a forgotten territory, bounded by dark trees, close and impenetrable.

In Blythe's day epilepsy was less understood than it is today. It was seen as an hereditary disease rather than the paroxysmal disorder that it is, and the causes were put down to quite specific factors, such as chronic alcoholism in the patient's parents, syphilis, alcohol or blows to the head. Lack of self-control was seen as a prominent feature of epileptics and thus for child sufferers strict discipline was regarded as essential from an early age. But, as today, stress or sleeplessness was recognised as a major factor in the onset of attacks, so for those same children competitive examinations were ruled out – hence perhaps Blythe's abandonment of the work for his scholarship. For the adult Blythe, it was eventually Test matches that were seen as the culprit. Patients were treated with bromide, not the successful menu of drugs available today.

There was also, of course, at this period a social stigma attaching to any illness connected with the brain, and an individual's epilepsy would rarely be discussed in public. It is most obviously for this reason that we know so little of the circumstances of Blythe's illness. Given the fact that he was able to play a public sport with confidence, it seems unlikely that he suffered from the most serious form of the disorder with convulsive falling fits. More likely, he was prone to *petit mal*, resulting in minor lapses of consciousness for a matter of minutes.

Blythe was sensitive and highly strung, and it seems to have been generally accepted by commentators, especially after the Edgbaston Test of 1909 when the issue was widely discussed, that the tension and stress of Test cricket in particular was likely to lead in his case to nervous indisposition. But there are scarcely any documented occasions when he is said to have had an epileptic fit in the course of a match. C B Fry, the Sussex batsman, all-round sportsman and journalist, once mentioned Blythe as having had such a fit at Headingley, which can only refer to the 1907 Test against the South Africans, when there was general press concern after the game about his condition but no newspaper cited epilepsy in terms. It is significant, however, that these two Test matches in which his physical and mental condition were so widely discussed just happened to be the ones in which he achieved his greatest performances.

For the great enigma of Blythe's international career was his apparent under-achievement at this level. In part it was the effect of under-selection, a handicap that all slow bowlers have to face, but particularly Blythe who had always to compete with the doughty Wilfred Rhodes. It is noteworthy that Blythe often got his chance to play in Tests when Rhodes was indisposed or unable to travel. More significant in his career after 1907 was the physical and mental toll that Test matches clearly took upon him, and even more important the perception among selectors and public alike of the threat of nervous breakdown. George White, the South African batsman, once said that Blythe hated Test cricket, and this may have been no exaggeration.

His first two tours, with MacLaren's team to Australia in 1901/2 and the MCC to South Africa in 1905/6, were as we have seen relatively successful. He played in all 10 Test matches and took 39 Test wickets, his best innings performance the 6 for 68 he took in the fourth Test at Cape Town in March 1906. In both these tours, the standard of English play was below par and the tourists were soundly beaten by their hosts.

Yet, quiet and shy a man as he could be, his cockney sociability was always fired by social occasions and he seems to have entered fully into the conviviality of these tours away from the disciplines of life at home. One of his social assets on tedious shipboard journeys was his violin. On the first tour to Australia, Gilbert Jessop praised his performances with the ship's band: "your selection at the concert was quite one of the features of the voyage".

It became a cliché of later commentaries on Blythe that the long fingers that could cover the strings so fluently were the same that, wrapped round a cricket ball, could produce that prodigious spin. This was not so far-fetched as it sounds, since with both violinists and left-arm spin bowlers, it is the left hand that does the work. For, as Gerry Weigall noted, Blythe had a most delicate and artistically shaped hand, "more like that of a young girl than a professional cricketer." When Blythe's left arm came over at the crease, it was the final flick of the fingers that made the ball spin and bite, and he always maintained that it was violin practice that gave his fingers such strength and pliability.

But it was not common for a professional sportsman to play a musical instrument – it did not always go with the macho style – and Blythe's violin, that gave so much pleasure to his colleagues on these winter tours, must be seen above all as one other facet of that sensitivity that turned some of his Test matches into nightmares. Indeed, the two were linked. It was said that after a particularly nerve-tingling match when he needed to relax, he went home to play on the violin.

It seems likely he learned the instrument from childhood, for by all accounts he was appearing as a youthful musician at village concerts long before he had shot to cricketing fame. Evidence in this area is sparse. All we have is a bill for a Lorenzo Carcassi violin that he bought at Alfred Tubbs emporium in Wardour Street early in 1903 for £35, a serious price for a violin at this time. He seems to have had trouble with his eight guinea bow with the silver mounts, purchased at the same time, for he returned to buy a sturdier one for twelve guineas just three months later. And in his last will he left to his father two violins, a sure sign that music still played an important part in his life right up to the end.

He was a really good player and, as with his cricket and his engineering, always single-mindedly keen to improve his technique. While he lived in the parental home at New Cross he played regularly in a London music hall orchestra, but he much preferred classical music. When he moved permanently to Tonbridge in 1907, he became for some years one of the first violins in the Tonbridge Orchestra, playing Brahms and Mozart with the best of them. His violin teacher recalled the conductor, Dr Stewart, a former Kent player himself, once remarking in relation to a Mozart symphony that Blythe had been "the nimblest player in the orchestra". He was much sought after as a violinist and performed in other local concerts given by the choral and orchestral societies of that part of Kent. He had a particularly close relationship with the Rochester Orchestral Society and played regularly too with them.

The move to Tonbridge altered his traditional winter habits. In his early career, when not off on winter tours, he would return to his engineering work, either at the Woolwich Arsenal or Maxim's, but after his marriage he would treat his winters as domestic rest periods when he could concentrate on his beloved violin. It was from this time that he received regular tuition from Leonard Furnivall, a master at the Judd School in Tonbridge, and between October and March he practised regularly for two hours a day. He had now graduated to a more expensive Italian violin worth about £80, once again from Alf Tubbs in Wardour Street.

Tubbs himself was a cricket enthusiast and was so pleased by the performance at the Leeds Test in 1907 that he invited Blythe down to his shop to be given the best bow in stock. It was a generous and symbolic present from which he would not be parted. When that winter in Australia he bumped into a violinist from the Clara Butt concert party, he refused an offer of an identical bow plus £7 for it. The violin became as powerful a part of his public image as the havoc he could wreak on wet wickets. After the Northampton match in 1907, the correspondent of the *Daily Mail* warned the Yorkshire team who were next in line to beware of "Blythe the Fiddler".

By the start of the 1907 season, the prowess of the epileptic violinist had scarcely been tested at the highest level of cricket. Though ten Tests overseas were under his belt, he had been selected for only one at home, the third Test against the Australians at Headingley in 1905, and this only because Wilfred Rhodes had a damaged finger. The match was drawn, and Blythe bowled uncommonly well in the second innings, though had he held on to a fairly simple return catch from Noble his little flurry of wickets towards the end might have given England victory.

Blythe was selected for all three Tests against South Africa in 1907, primarily because Rhodes' form as a bowler had declined precipitately the previous season. The first Test at Lord's was ruined by rain and petered out in a draw with England in a winning position. Blythe took only two wickets in each innings and suffered the misfortune of splitting his hand between the knuckles of the second and third finger when he dropped a hard catch from Faulkner at mid-off. He came back, however, and managed to continue bowling with his hand strapped up. Fortunately, there was a break of a week before Kent's next match, by which time he had completely recovered.

The third Test at the Oval was a much tighter match, but also a draw because of rain interruption. Blythe was surprisingly out of form in the South African first innings, being totally inaccurate in his length. He finished the second day of the match with figures of 1 for 47, and it seemed as if the Test match bug had got at him again. But on the third morning he returned to brilliant form, being instrumental in a South African collapse in which they lost their last five wickets in 50 minutes for 29 runs. Blythe's haul that morning was 4 for 14.

But it was the second Test at Headingley, the only one of the series to be decided, which was to prove Blythe's greatest Test triumph. The wicket was soft before the start and was refreshed by constant showers of rain, particularly on the stop-start second day. On such a wicket England clearly needed to maximise their spin attack, but the selectors left out Crawford, the only other spin bowler in the squad, in favour of the pace of Knox who, in the event, bowled only four overs in the match. Blythe's support, therefore, came from one fast bowler and two medium-pacers; he might as well have bowled alone from both ends.

Only 40 minutes play was possible on the first morning and England started well in the conditions, scoring 34 for 1. After lunch, however, came a disastrous collapse, nine wickets going down in an hour and a quarter for a further 42 runs. Only Hayward, Tyldesley and Hirst made it into double figures, but Blythe, who added 13 runs with Knox for the last wicket, the most productive partnership after lunch, finished on 5 not out.

The defence of this paltry total of 76 was now left to Blythe alone. Test match nerves seem to have got to him from the start, for he lost his normally impeccable length, and towards the close of the innings was constantly overpitching, but he did so much with the ball off the wicket that this did not seem to matter. After an hour and a half South Africa were 59 for 7, with six of those wickets falling to Blythe. They then made a partial recovery and were all out by ten to six for 110, a first innings lead of 34. Even this lead might not have materialised had England held their four missed catches, two of which were dropped off Blythe. He finished with his best ever Test figures of 8 for 59.

In the 25 minutes remaining, and in poor light, the England openers managed to hold on and at close of play were 25 without loss, just nine runs behind. Next morning constant showers of rain had the players racing from the field on four occasions, but they were nevertheless able to take the score at lunch time to 110 for 4. Fry, masterful and confident from the first, played an almost faultless innings for his 54 and Tyldesley, as the second string, made 30. It rained after lunch and at half past four play was finally abandoned for the day.

Following a fine night and a bright windy morning, to everyone's surprise play started on the final morning on time. Batting proved very difficult and between further showers of rain England were able to take their total on only to 162 all out. Foster made an invaluable score of 22, and Blythe and Knox again made a mini last wicket stand, the former finishing this time on 4 not out.

The South Africans now needed 129 to win and, in spite of the pitch, this seemed by no means impossible. After his superb feat of bowling on the first day, the responsibility passed once again to Colin Blythe – only he could prevent South Africa from winning. The tourists made a bad start. Sherwell hit the ball to the left of Jessop at cover point and called Tancred for a run; a fatal error against the smartest fielder on the side and Tancred was easily run out. Sherwell, disconcerted by the incident, hit what seemed like a slow half-volley from Blythe on the leg-side up in the air and was easily caught by Foster for 1. When rain stopped play just before lunch, South Africa were 10 for 2.

On the resumption at five minutes to three and with no further addition to the score, Nourse played back to a well-pitched up ball from Blythe, failed to hit it and was out lbw. Six runs later, Hathorn hit a ball from Arnold hard on to his leg and it rebounded into his wicket. Then in the following over Blythe deceived White with the flight of a slower ball and the batsman in trying to drive it was easily caught by Arnold at third man. South Africa were now 18 for 5 and defeat seemed certain.

Sinclair then decided on attack and hit Blythe for 12 in one over, which can not have done much for the Kent man's confidence. But he kept his head, and proceeded with his policy of maintaining a perfect length, while cleverly changing his pace without any discernible change of action. It paid off. Soon after, he sent down a rather faster ball which so deceived Sinclair with its pace that he chopped it straight into Braund's hands at slip. The tourists were now 38 for 6. There followed a tense passage of play in which Faulkner and Snooke hunkered down to try and save the match; they defended well and the wicket now seemed to play a trifle easier than before, though every now and then Blythe made the ball get up awkwardly. He kept up the pressure and the batsmen were unable to get the ball away. Finally, Blythe tempted Faulkner to make a big drive outside the off-stump and he skied the ball to Foster at point.

After that the result was never in doubt. Shalders was ill at ease and Hirst soon had him lbw. Vogler made two big hits and then Blythe induced him to go for another, Tyldesley making a fine catch in the deep, falling over as he made it. The next ball Blythe had Snooke caught by Hirst and the innings ended at a quarter to five with South Africa all out for 75.

Blythe had clearly won the game for England with a second innings analysis of 7 for 40; it had been a devastating display of how to deceive batsmen by the pace and flight of the ball through the air. Throughout the game he did not once hit the stumps, but altogether had taken 15 wickets for 99, then a record for England Tests at home; only Wilfred Rhodes had ever taken 15 before, back in Australia in 1904, and they had cost him 25 runs more. But records apart, Blythe had been left alone with the crucial responsibility in both innings of getting the South Africans out, and ironically he was the man whose nerves were least fitted for the job. Apart from one over, he had bowled unchanged throughout the match – a total of 38.3 overs, while Hirst, the next highest, had bowled only 18. And this followed on from a week in which he had bowled Kent to two brilliant victories against Surrey and Leicestershire, a further 96 overs and 23 wickets.

Little wonder, then, that the press all commented that he had bowled himself almost to a standstill, a euphemism for what he had really suffered. C B Fry, whose 54 had been the other signal contribution to the game, spoke of Blythe under the exceptional strain of the match as being "completely knocked up". In the second innings he had proved quite unplayable, and from first to last had never bowled a single ball except of impeccable length. In Fry's assessment, just three bad overs could have lost the match.

This then was the measure of the strain that Blythe came under in this match, and what makes it likely that this too was the Headingley occasion on which he had the epileptic fit, though all were silent at the time. There had been a bad precedent on that ground. In 1899 against the Australians, that other slow left-arm legend, the Lancastrian Johnny Briggs, bowled 30 overs on the first day, then had an epileptic fit and subsequent illness which put him into Cheadle Asylum. In two years he was dead at the age of 39.

Briggs' epilepsy was clearly of a much more serious nature than that of Colin Blythe, but the strain of this Test match was to remain with him the following week. The next day he was at Worcester bowling another 38 overs for Kent on a good batting wicket and having 143 runs taken off him. He then broke down entirely and was forced to sit out the next match against Sussex at Canterbury. When he returned for the second match of the Canterbury Week, his bowling was so well below par that his 57 overs in the match produced only three wickets.

It was the second time he had broken down that summer, missing two matches after the supreme effort at Northampton. But the Leeds Test this year was both a clear vindication of his stature and potential as a Test player and a warning of the dire effects wrought by the pressure of Test cricket. It was to be another two years before the issue would finally come to a head.

Noting his performance in the three Tests this summer, and turning a blind eye to the strains of Headingley from which he had eventually recovered, the England selectors made Blythe an automatic choice for the 1907/8 MCC winter tour of Australia. It was in some respects a surprising choice, since Wilfred Rhodes was also selected and two left-arm slow bowlers seemed something of a luxury in Australian conditions. It meant that Blythe would be in constant competition for the top slot and a Test place; but nonetheless he and his violin, together with Arthur Fielder, his bosom friend from the Nursery days, set off for their second tour of the Antipodes.

It proved the most disappointing of all his foreign excursions. In the match against Queensland at the end of November he took 11 for 83, but he was to take only a further 30 wickets in the other 10 matches he played. This relative failure seemed inexplicable given his commanding performances in the last two English seasons, but since his greatest weapon was always his flighting of the ball through the air, it seems that the Australian atmosphere just did not suit him. There he rarely managed to get the ball to swing.

He was selected for the first Test as principal spin bowler along with Rhodes and Crawford, but managed to take only one wicket in his 31 overs. It was not so great a personal disaster, for Rhodes also took just one wicket, and Crawford two, in the English defeat. Nonetheless, they were both selected for the second Test while Blythe was left out – and England won. He played in no further Tests that tour.

Since Rhodes took only seven wickets in all five Tests, it seems likely he was picked for his superior batting skills, though he was far from the brilliant opening bat he was later to become. Crawford topped the Test bowling figures that winter and was therefore almost self-selecting. But it may be that Blythe's known dislike for Test cricket and his problems at Headingley the previous summer weighed in the selectors' minds. The first Test had, in any case, ended in a nail-biting finish with the English bowlers under extreme pressure, and they were generally felt not to have taken full advantage of the wicket. It was the kind of situation in which the Blythe nerves would be the first to suffer.

He also had his share of physical illness and injury. He caught a chill during a match at Bendigo and had not completely recovered by the start of the second Test, which may partly explain why he was left out. By the end of the tour, a number of English players were laid up with illness or injury. On the last afternoon of the final match against South Australia, Blythe split his left hand very badly in attempting to catch a hit from Clem Hill. This had now become his standard occupational injury; the local doctor ruled him out of playing for at least a month. His reaction in the light of the current spate of injuries, as reported by Philip Trevor, the tour manager, was typical Blythe low-key irony: "Blythe took the accident philosophically. So far he had only suffered from illness. It was apparently his turn to be hurt".

Both Blythe and his Kent colleague Arthur Fielder, who had had a most successful tour, received £200 each for their pains. It had been the habit on previous tours for the Kent authorities to swoop upon these windfalls that professional cricketers could not be trusted to manage on their own. They did so again on this occasion. The club sought investment advice and in June 1908 the two players finally agreed the money should be invested in River Plate Trust 4% Debentures. But Blythe at this point had paid in only £100 of his remuneration, with the promise of the balance shortly. It was perhaps the first sign that he was growing impatient with the club's presumption of control over his money, now that he had someone other than himself to support. The ground was well prepared for the conflicts that lay ahead.

1908 was a blank year for Test cricket in England, the only touring team to visit being the Philadelphians whose substandard performances were scarcely enough to provide proper competition for county sides. All were looking forward to the arrival of the Australians in 1909, a tour that had almost been aborted because of Australian opposition to the half-baked proposal of a triangular competition with England and South Africa, which did not reach its disastrous fruition until the summer of 1912.

Having taken no less than 38 wickets in his previous three county matches, Blythe was on fire and a certain choice for the first Test against Australia at Edgbaston at the end of May 1909. Like Headingley in 1907, it was a wet wicket match and Blythe once more acquitted himself brilliantly, but with the same dire consequences.

The Australians came into the game under the cloud of two early defeats by Surrey and the MCC, with many of the side not yet played into form. They won the toss but, because of constant showers following a day and night of rain, were not able to bat until the late evening of the first day. In Blythe's first over, Cotter hit the ball hard to Hirst at mid-off and was promptly caught for 2. Then Hirst had Bardsley caught by MacLaren, also for 2. By close of play, batting in poor light on a soft wet wicket, the Australians had made 22 for 2.

The wicket was very slow the following morning, but not a real bowlers' one. Straightway, Trumper misjudged a ball from Blythe and was caught by Hirst at mid-off. This was the start of a devastating spell in which Blythe and Hirst, with scarcely a loose ball bowled, took the remaining eight wickets in an hour-and-a-half for 52 runs. Both made the ball swing in the air and occasionally come back off the pitch in the other direction. Hirst finished with figures of 4 for 28 and Blythe 6 for 44.

Facing so low a score as 74, it seemed England would swiftly reap the advantage; but the wicket proved equally difficult for them, and by lunch they were 17 for 3. Tyldesley and Jones temporarily made up for this bad start, putting on 41 runs together in less than an hour, but England were soon in trouble again at 61 for 5. Jessop made 22 in twenty minutes, but no-one else did much of value and England were all out at a quarter to five for 121. It was a first innings lead of only 47, but at that stage of the match seemed likely to be decisive.

Australia started badly in their second innings. In the fourth over, Blythe had Macartney lbw with only four runs on the board, and at 16 Jones made a brilliant catch at forward short leg to dismiss Noble. By late afternoon the wicket had begun to improve and Ransford and Gregory now made a stand which took the score to 67 for 2 when bad light stopped play for the day. In the first half hour of the next day's play, with Hirst and Blythe struggling to find their length, they put on a further 30 runs, and with a 50 run lead and 8 wickets in hand the Australians now looked well set for victory.

There then followed an astounding reversal in which the next five wickets went down in half an hour for just nine runs. Inevitably it was Blythe who produced the turning point of the match. The *Kent Messenger* reported in some awe

> He was invidious and tempted men to their doom.
> The Australians would not at first attempt to hit him
> but he tried out their patience by sending down mix-
> tures of full tosses and half-volleys.

Full of confidence from hitting consecutive fours off the first two balls of a Blythe over, Gregory attempted to pull the third, a sharply turning ball, and Thompson running from mid-on to short leg made a beautifully judged catch. The wickets then went down like ninepins. Trumper was neatly taken at short leg, Ransford bowled by Blythe off his pads, Armstrong misjudged the next Blythe delivery and made a feeble hit to Jessop at cover point, and Carter was then caught by Hobbs at long leg.

Warwick Armstrong's dismissal was widely discussed in the press, where he was accused of just throwing his wicket away, together with the match. But, as Edward Sewell saw it, the real villain of the piece, tempting him to hit out off his first ball, was the Blythe half-volley.

> A Blythe half-volley is not even half so innocent a thing as the look on the face of the man who bowls it. The one which secured Armstrong's wicket was a snare and a delusion. It was a half-volley right enough but it rose a bit more than normal and went away right into the hands of Jessop.

With seven wickets down the Australians were only 59 runs ahead. Cotter hit out for two or three overs and O'Connor and Whitty put on 26 for the last wicket, but at twenty to one the innings closed on 151, leaving England 105 for victory.

In such a low-scoring match the outcome was still in doubt, particularly since the opening pair, Hobbs and Fry, now walking to the wicket, had both been out first ball in the previous innings. In a typically touching gesture, Blythe had presented Hobbs, after this failure in his first home Test, with a little statuette of a boy holding a bat and bearing the inscription "The Hope of the Side". He told him to cheer up; this would bring him luck. And it did. Never was there such a turn-round in batting fortunes. Hobbs set off at once on a superlative knock, which Fry, playing strangely nervously at the other end, believed was the greatest Test innings he had ever seen. The two openers hit off the runs in an hour and a half, Hobbs finishing with 62 not out to Fry's anxious 35. The crowd rushed to the pavilion and cheered for MacLaren, Hobbs, Hirst and Blythe.

For remarkable though the *dénouement* was, the real victors were Hirst and Blythe who, apart from five overs on the second afternoon, bowled unchanged throughout the match, finishing in the second innings with identical figures of 5 for 58 each. In that innings Blythe, with his deceptive flight through the air and occasional break-back off the ground, varied his length bravely and was always difficult to play. His match figures of 11 for 102 ran close the stunning performance in the Headingley Test two years before. This was another taut low-scoring match in which a few loose overs would have thrown the game away, and the mental pressures had much the same effect on him.

Superficially all seemed well for the moment, but the next county match was to show just how fragile his mental state was. Two days later, as he went out to bat against Middlesex at Lord's, the Whit bank holiday crowd of 16,000 rose as one man and cheered him all the way to the wicket for his rout of the Australians the previous week. It was a spontaneous demonstration that took him completely by surprise. He survived the first ball from Patsy Hendren, and then spooned the second back down the wicket for a simple caught and bowled. When he got back to the pavilion, he was clearly overcome with emotion.

By the start of the Middlesex innings, the effects had not worn off. He bowled the second over of the innings to Tarrant and was hit for three off the last ball. He complained of feeling faint and was immediately taken off. It was the tension of bowling once more that had produced the effect; he was still well enough to keep his place in the field while Woolley took over from him. But later he felt better and came back on when Middlesex had reached 62 for 1, clean bowling Payne with his second ball. His next six overs produced just four runs; he was back to normal once more. So normal in fact that the next eight produced 21 runs and five wickets, and by the close of the innings he had shredded the Middlesex batting with figures of 6 for 37.

He may still have been feeling unwell at the start of the next match with Lancashire at Old Trafford, for Dillon, the Kent captain, took the precaution of holding him back until the eighth over, off which he was promptly hit for seven runs.

In his fifth over, he had Tyldesley caught and bowled, but after nine was taken off with figures of 1 for 19. For his second spell, however, he came back like a whirlwind, taking a wicket off the last ball of his first over and first ball of his third. Back to normal again. By varying his pace and keeping the usual excellent length, he caused panic among the Lancashire batsmen, taking 6 for 44 in this second spell and finishing the innings with a very creditable 7 for 57.

So whatever the problem was, it seemed to be instantly triggered by the act of bowling itself, with recovery coming eventually once he had settled back into the routine of the game. Then he would play as superbly as ever. The Kent authorities were naturally worried by the apparent breakdown at Lord's and slow start at Old Trafford, and sent him to a specialist for a check-up. The conclusion was that the Edgbaston Test had badly shaken him up, and he should not play in the next one at Lord's, due to start on 14 June. Lord Harris sent a telegram to the chairman of selectors in Bournemouth: "Specialist strongly advises Blythe ought not to play on Monday, but is quite hopeful he will be fit for remaining Tests if wanted". It was as well that he was not selected, for on the evening of 15 June, in the middle of a match against Worcestershire, he had a fit and was taken back to the hotel, and then sent home. Up to that point in the game, he had bowled 65 overs and taken nine wickets.

It was perhaps unfortunate that Blythe's indisposition at this time should have become caught up in a major controversy over the selection of the English team for the Lord's Test. *Wisden* fulminated "Never in the history of Test matches in England has there been such blundering in the selection of an England eleven". The press was dumbstruck when Jessop and Walter Brearley were axed in favour of the Leicestershire professionals King and Jayes. It became even more incredulous when it learned that Fry, tied up in a court case, and Blythe would also not play, and Hayward had been selected, though unfit.

In defending themselves against this uproar, the selectors felt obliged to justify their decisions, in some cases with all the evidence to counterbalance the general incredulity. Thus it was that the specialist's opinion on Blythe, though strictly a matter of medical confidentiality, was made public. The report to the Kent authorities ran as follows

> C. Blythe, whom I have seen this morning, suffers severely in a peculiar way from the strain on his nervous system caused by playing in a Test match, and the effect lasts for a week afterwards. It is desirable that he should have a temporary rest from this work, and should not play in the coming match at Lord's. If this can be arranged there is good hope that with treatment his difficulty will pass away. It does not exist in the case of county matches.

There could not have been a more telling endorsement of the dire effects of Test matches, particularly as they impact on slow bowlers with their knife-edge precision skills – the strains that had killed Johnny Briggs seven years before.

But the publication of this text had an important impact on Blythe's reputation and his future in Test cricket. The collapse after Headingley two years before was known on the inside, but had been kept from the general public. Now he had a public reputation for being "flakey", future decisions on his selection would always be made with that at the back of selectors' minds – or even at the front. Nevertheless, he played in the fourth Test that summer at Old Trafford and acquitted himself well in the first innings with 5 for 63, though he seemed quite out of form in the second, returning 2 for 77 off 24 overs. Any falling off in his Test performances was now looked on with a more critical and knowing eye. This Test match seems to have had the same predictable effect, for he had to be rested from the next Kent match against Essex to ensure he was fit for his benefit week coming up at Canterbury.

He was selected for the tour to South Africa the following winter, but played in only the final two Tests. He was unimpressive in the fourth, which South Africa won and with it the series, but, perhaps not surprisingly with the pressure now off, bowled brilliantly in the final Test, taking 7 for 46 in the first innings and ensuring an England victory. But the events of 1909 were to have a lasting effect on his career. He was now less well disposed towards Test matches even than he had been before, and the selectors were more wary. Though for the next five years he continued to produce wondrous and consistent feats in county cricket, he was never selected for England again.

Putting aside the epilepsy, which made Blythe a special case, his reaction to the pressures of the game was not all that extraordinary, except that it was success that caused the problem rather than the more usual cause of failure. What is perhaps more difficult to understand is why someone always so cool and collected in the county game, where pressures were also at times intense, should have buckled so completely after a tense Test Match. Perhaps the key lies in the word *after*. For in those great performances of 1907 and 1909, he still maintained his warm and cheery demeanour on the field, with time, as we have seen, to give support to others, like the neophyte Jack Hobbs. But the intense pressures, which he rode so well throughout the game, were to get him at the end as soon as he was free to relax.

And though the cricket world of today has changed beyond recognition, the pressures remain much the same in Test cricket, where the slow bowler is faced by great batsmen of high consistency, where the slightest deviation of delivery is heavily punished and one loose over can lose a match. And what is worse the critical eye of millions is over one's shoulder. Ashley Giles, our modern Colin Blythe, took a hammering recently from the New Zealanders at Lord's and an even worse hammering from the neandertal press in the weeks that followed. In the dressing room that match, he told his captain "I'm not sure how much longer I can do this". He is also reported as saying "my mind was about to explode". The difference with Blythe was that his did.

It is another cliché of Blythe's career to contrast his brilliant county record with his relative lack of success in Test cricket. But this is to be influenced too much by the infrequency of his selection and the severe personal traumas he went through. One need only look at the raw figures to gain the true perspective. Altogether in his Test career, he played in just 19 matches and took exactly one hundred wickets at an

Colin Blythe

average of just over 18. Wilfred Rhodes, his great contemporary rival, played in 58 matches (three times as many) and took 127 wickets at an average of 27. Derek Underwood, a very different style bowler but his modern successor in most other respects, took 297 wickets in 86 matches at an average just under 26. Only Bobby Peel, his distinguished Yorkshire predecessor, comes close with 102 wickets in 20 matches at a cost of nearly 17. Simply by making these few comparisons, we can clearly see that Blythe carried his greatness into Test cricket as he carried it everywhere else.

Chapter 8

Benefit

Back in the gentler world of county cricket the performance of Colin Blythe, much as his doctor had predicted, seemed untouched by the traumas of the Tests. True, he may have had to take the odd game off after a particularly gruelling Test match, but he would soon be back to his natural rhythm of perfect length and puzzling flight which had most county batsmen quaking in their heavily studded boots.

After the disappointing season of 1907, Kent came flying back in 1908 as runners-up to Yorkshire, who nonetheless proved worthy champions. In all Kent lost only three matches this season, being routed by Yorkshire at Bradford and Surrey at the Oval, and just pipped at the post by Hampshire at Canterbury, a game in which Blythe's own problems cost them victory.

The Surrey match was little short of a disaster with Kent losing on a good wicket by an innings and 318, thanks to a superb 155 by Jack Hobbs and 167 by the Australian Alan Marshal, whose career like Blythe's was ended by war. But the game is famous in the Blythe canon, not for his remarkable analysis of 2 for 181, but for spawning the incident in which he managed to take the whole side off the field for bad light and a well-needed rest, while the sun was yet blazing down from a clear blue sky. Once again, it is Edward Sewell who has the story.

> In Blythe's record is a quite unique appeal. On a blazing afternoon he was bowling at the Oval to Marshal of Surrey, who was smashing up a matter of 160 odd. The 5pm sun caused the awning in the front of the pavilion to throw a jet-black shadow. "If he hits one straight

back I shan't see it", said Blythe to the umpire, "what about it?" So, without a cloud in the sky, play ceased for a quarter of an hour or more, the players retiring. I often think of that when I see them coming in since the last War when the faintest of drizzles has begun.

Three years later Blythe himself was to face an appeal "against the sun" and with much more untoward consequences.

On mostly good batting wickets this summer, Blythe could not hope to return the spectacular analyses of previous wet seasons, but he nevertheless managed to take 13 wickets in both home matches against Northamptonshire and Leicestershire. His strength as ever was his consistent wicket-taking, even when runs were being hit freely off him, and he finished the season with 167 county championship wickets, 26 more than his previous best.

In a season where no Test matches were played, Blythe's persistent injury problems were physical rather than mental. After the hammering at Bradford in May, Kent invited Yorkshire back on 6 July to play in the beautiful man-made amphitheatre of the Crabble Ground in the Downs outside Dover. A first class match had been held there for the first time the previous season and the Kent authorities had now decided, following the precedent of Canterbury, Tonbridge and Tunbridge Wells, to inaugurate a Dover Week. This first match of the new Week was a resounding success, with as many as 10,000 spectators turning up on the second day.

Yorkshire won the toss and batted, and affairs seemed to be following their natural course when Blythe bowled Hardisty with the last ball of his first over for 4. But this proved a false dawn as the Yorkshire batsmen hit out on a good wicket, and were still there at close of play on 331 for 8. Blythe tried his leg-theory with eight men posted on the leg-side, but secured only one further wicket. It was a gruelling day as he bowled on, over after over, and just before tea, when he had already bowled 25, he twisted his knee and had to go off. In the tea interval it was found to be a serious injury, which developed into water on the knee, and he was packed off to see a specialist in London, taking no further part in the game.

Benefit

With the help of rain, Kent eventually managed to save the match, but their bowling problems were made worse in the next game against Somerset when Fielder, who had already bowled 72 overs in the Week, renewed an old strain in his leg and had to be packed off too to see the same specialist as Blythe. They were worrying injuries – the doctors' final bill came in at over £7 – and Blythe was paid £5 in compensation for time lost and travelling expenses. But, rather surprisingly, both returned the following week for the match against Lancashire at Tunbridge Wells, ruined by rain but not before Blythe, in a brilliant spell of bowling, had taken 7 for 69.

This apparent return to Blythean health was borne out by the next five matches, all of which Kent won, with Blythe taking 40 wickets at a cost of 15 runs each. But the injury to his knee caught up with him in the second match of the Canterbury Week, which was to provide the most thrilling finish of the season. He must have aggravated the earlier strain in the latest matches for, by the start of this game, the water on the knee had returned. Despite the pain in his swollen leg, he was determined to play. As the game progressed, he grew noticeably lamer and lamer, but nonetheless turned in one of the bravest performances of his career.

Kent batted first and, thanks to some stolid performances by the middle order, managed to reach an unconvincing 203. Hampshire then demonstrated the ease of the wicket by putting on 65 for 1 by close of play. They carried on in similar style the following morning and when Blythe came on for his fourth stint from the pavilion end they had taken the score to 167 for 4, just 36 short of a first innings lead. At this stage Blythe, suffering pain from every delivery, had bowled 33 overs and taken 3 for 76. It looked like a long and painful day ahead.

But in a devastating spell, he had the remaining Hampshire batsmen caught in a hopeless trap, unable to judge the constantly varying flight of the ball. He took a stream of wickets by inducing the batsmen to play out to the pitch of the ball, which turned so quickly they could do nothing but spoon up simple catches to the off-side field. Of this final spell, the first two overs went for two runs apiece, and then in the remaining 25 balls he took five wickets for three runs, Hampshire losing their last six wickets for twenty five. As he limped off to the pavilion and rest, he had produced his best analysis of the season – 8 for 83.

Kent fared little better in their second innings and had it not been for brave knocks by the Day brothers, who scored half the Kent runs, they would have been in dire straits. As it was, by close on the second day they had scored 165 for 8, just 190 ahead. Thanks to some bold hitting by Fairservice, the last two wickets put on a further 75 runs the next morning, leaving Hampshire the substantial task of 266 in five hours to win.

Having bowled 39 overs in the first innings with an injured knee, Blythe would not, in the normal course, have been fit to field in the second, but for one painful fact – it was absolutely essential he should bowl. Thus despite his leg, he opened as usual from the pavilion end and took up his traditional fielding position at mid-off. And true to form, he immediately took a wicket, yorking Llewellyn for 1. Bowell was then badly missed by Woolley at mid-off off Blythe's bowling, and this seemed to set the pattern for the innings. Bowell went on to make 57 while Kent continued to drop several easy chances. So it was that by five o'clock Hampshire needed only 72 to win with four wickets in hand, and the game was poised for an exciting finish. But three wickets fell in the next twenty minutes and, when Newman joined Stone at the crease, Hampshire were 215 for 9, still 51 short of the win.

Victory for Kent now seemed assured, with 55 minutes left to capture the last wicket. But the batsmen kept their cool and, despite a flurry of bowling changes, began to score steadily. As the total mounted, a one-day atmosphere invaded the ground and the spectators buzzed with the excitement. The poor Kent fielding, which had been a feature of the innings, finally cost them the match. With 11 still needed to win, Newman was dropped at slip.

Then came the most dramatic moment of the whole game. Three runs were still wanted, when the same batsman spooned the ball up just short of Blythe at mid-off. The fielder needed to make just a few yards to turn it into a simple catch; on that depended the victory, and perhaps even the championship. But he had been bowling all day, was already up to his 50th over of the innings, and had an injured leg that would scarcely carry him. He made a gallant effort to reach the ball, but just failed. Five minutes from time, off the third ball of his 52nd over, Hampshire made the winning hit, and Kent were effectively out of the running for the championship.

It was one of the closest finishes he had taken part in, and one of his most heroic performances which, ironically enough, had left him personally with the harsh responsibility for defeat. He had bowled 90 overs in the match and his courage became a talking point for some weeks. One journalist wrote:

> Blythe had an injured knee which must have caused him much pain whenever he bowled: the fact that he sent down as many overs as he did is eloquent testimony to his pluck.

A week later, they were still discussing sympathetically the more philosophical aspects of the dropped catch.

> If a player meets with an injury and pluckily fields instead of enlisting the services of a substitute, why is it that any chance which is offered is almost certain to go to him? Near the close of the memorable Kent v Hampshire match at Canterbury, Blythe, had he not been lame, would probably have succeeded in running-in from mid-off and catching Newman when Hampshire required only three runs to win and with one wicket to fall.

Blythe missed only one match after these heroics at Canterbury, but the problem of the knee in 1908 was a timely reminder that he was not perhaps so young as he was and, though still only 29, was fast becoming a veteran member of this newly successful Kent side. In June he put in a request to the Kent authorities that 1909, his tenth full season, should be made his benefit year.

The request was deferred to a meeting on 24 July when

Colin Blythe

it was finally agreed subject, as always, to the controlling condition felt essential for professionals whatever their age – that any proceeds should be invested on the advice of the Committee. In August Blythe wrote back to the Committee thanking them for their decision and stating that he was willing for the proceeds to be held in trust for him so long as he played for the county. He also, perhaps a little cheekily, invited the Committee to become involved in the collection arrangements, the distribution of collecting cards and books. But this would have been a step too far. The Committee, while promising to do everything to help as individuals, decided that to become formally involved in the collection process would set an awkward precedent. So the beneficiary himself had to set up his own arrangements for circulating the little red subscription booklets, with the proud emblem on the front "C. Blythe's Benefit" and the quiet injunction on the final page "Kindly return at end of Season to C. Blythe, 40, St Mary's Road, Tonbridge".

The club did its best, however, to support its leading professional in public by suitable praise, even if to modern ears the plaudits sound at times a little back-handed. At the general meeting of the club that launched Blythe's benefit year, the best compliment that Lord Harris could find was that he had bridged the class barriers that were cricket's most prominent feature. "I do not remember any professional, not even the Hearnes, who so completely contracted the confidence and friendship of the amateurs with whom he has played than Colin Blythe".

The *Kentish Express* paid glowing tributes too, in a rather less patronising vein, to speed him on his way:

> In all times, in periods of adversity or in periods of success, Blythe has proved himself a thorough sportsman – genial in defeat, modest in victory. There is no "side" about him; but he does not lack confidence in himself. On a bowler's wicket he goes to work pretty confident that he will shake up the nerves of his adversaries, on a plumb wicket he still hopes to do damage. He never gives in. With patience and

exhaustive manoeuvring he tries to circumvent the tactics of the batsman.

Patience and perseverance contribute to Colin Blythe's success. He never gives up – you never see him finishing an over in a flurry, or in a temper, even if he has been severely trounced. In early days he was slower; this season he is mixing them up more than usual. On broken wickets he is the most deadly of modern bowlers; on a hard pitch that would break the heart of the average slow bowler he manages to take wickets.

Yet the threat posed by the armoury of weapons is even more deadly because subtly concealed beneath a façade of fragile innocence.

Physically he is not very strong; his action makes one think that he is sometimes too languid to bowl. But it's only his style. Last week a writer in a Lancashire paper described how the Manchester crowd "laughed at his comical, mincing little steps as he started his quaint run to the wicket". It is this innocent method that makes the batsman serious; it makes him think; and in the thinking he is undone. For Blythe, behind that smile, is thinking too.

By the opening of the 1909 season, the arrangements for his benefit were in place. He had had printed all the little red booklets and obtained the agreement of the Committee for collections to be made at each match of the county Cricket Weeks, a promising total of eight collections in all. Despite the persistently wet weather at the start of the season, the Kent authorities decided, wisely as it turned out, not to insure for the amount of his benefit. For it was the wet weather that itself ensured that this was to be Blythe's greatest season, and that where cricketing excellence prevailed, money was certain to follow.

He took more wickets this benefit season – 215 – than he was ever to take again, and 18 of those were in the two exhausting Test matches against the Australians. In the county championship, he also achieved his highest tally of

Colin Blythe

178 wickets at an average of 14. He swept all before him in the first three months of the season, taking 60 wickets between 13 and 31 May, a new record; but by August he had already bowled over 900 overs, and the heavy toil had left him exhausted. Nonetheless, he managed to take five wickets in an innings 23 times and 10 wickets in a match on seven occasions. Once again he was the linchpin in Kent's remarkable success.

But it was not just his bowling performance for which this benefit year will always be remembered. In August, he earned himself his one lasting place in the Kent *batting* records. Altogether it was a good year for such records. In the match against Worcestershire at Stourbridge in July, Blythe had come in when Kent were 320 for 8 and was caught first ball. He was followed by his friend Arthur Fielder who, with Frank Woolley, now achieved such mastery of the bowling that they hit 119 off the last hour of the day. Quite remarkably, they continued next morning with a further 116 in 80 minutes, before Woolley was caught for 185. Fielder batted faultlessly for his 112 not out in a partnership of 235, which still remains the tenth wicket record in county cricket today.

If Blythe could not quite emulate his friend's prodigious feat, he did at least put his name up in the Kent batting lights just behind him. On 17 August Kent were struggling against Surrey at the Oval. They had dismissed the home side for 191 the day before, and now found themselves in trouble on 146 for 7. But Jack Mason, in the midst of a run of three consecutive centuries, was in sparkling form and with Douglas Carr put together 56 for the eighth wicket. When Blythe came in in late morning the score was 214 for 9, and the Surrey members were looking to an early lunch.

But they were forced to wait. After hitting three runs off his first scoring stroke, as if to prove once more the old McCanlis dictum that Blythe could bat if he put his mind to it, he got his head down and played slowly and steadily for six more singles. Meanwhile Mason was blasting on all guns at the other end. The two held on for more than half an hour, defying the increasingly desperate changes in the bowling attack, and when the Surrey members finally got their lunch at the official time, the score had leapt to 280, with Mason 102 and Blythe on 9.

It must have been a suitably liquid lunch, for Mason and Blythe were given a stirring reception when they walked out to resume their innings. Blythe immediately caused a sensation by flashing at two balls outside the off stump, which sped through the slips for a two and a four. Then Mason sent one racing through between wicketkeeper and slip. Excitement ran higher and higher, as the partnership continued and the score quietly rose. Mason took no further chances, his drives and strokes to leg passing all along the ground; and Blythe kept his head down in stubborn defence. On 22 he should have been caught at the wicket, but this chance life seemed to galvanise the pair, who put on another 30 runs in double quick time.

All manner of bowling changes were tried by Surrey without success until, rather late in the day, they called up "Razor" Smith who soon deceived Blythe with a slow ball that kept low, and had him clean bowled for 29. Jack Mason came through with 152 not out, and the pair had together put on an incredible 141 in just 70 minutes, which remains still today the second highest partnership for a Kent tenth wicket. And discounting his lesser ninth wicket partnerships, the only appearance of Colin Blythe in the Kent batting records.

But it was, of course, for his bowling record that 1909 will be mainly remembered. The first county match of the season was played at Leicester in the middle of May when both Blythe and Kent gave notice to their opponents of what the season might bring. The game started with a shock and ended with a shock. Kent, batting first, lost Hardinge and Seymour for ducks with the score on 0 for 2. Dillon, now captaining the side, with Day and Humphreys in support commandeered a stern recovery which took the score to a respectable 247 for 6 by close of play. Some rain had fallen this opening Monday, which was to have some influence on the proceedings next day.

For it was to be another one of Blythe's extraordinary days. Kent batted on with a swish of the tail to make a total of 334 by mid morning. The Leicestershire openers, Wood and Knight, batted steadily to lunch time and looked set for a big score. At that time, after seven overs, Blythe's analysis was an unpromising 0 for 20. Then with the score on 49 Fairservice had Wood lbw, and this seemed to bring Colin Blythe to life. In a typically devastating spell after lunch, he took a wicket in each of his first three overs and by the end of the fifth had taken 4 wickets for 3 runs. He continued to demolish the Leicestershire batting, taking in this one spell of 14.1 overs 9 wickets for 22 runs. His final innings analysis of 9 for 42 was the third best of his career.

Leicestershire followed on 230 behind and immediately found themselves in trouble. Though not quite so deadly as in the first innings, Blythe took the first three wickets for 14 runs and Leicestershire were soon 26 for 3. The middle order held up for a while, but at close of play the home side were eight wickets down with a Kent victory certain. Play was even extended for a quarter of an hour to see if the game could be polished off in two days, but Hazlerigg and Astill stood firm. Ironically, after this late evening effort, Blythe bowled the first over next morning and took the two remaining wickets with his fifth and sixth balls, the game concluding, as it started, on a two wicket shock. He finished with 7 for 60 in the second innings and 16 for 102 in the match. Furthermore, he had taken 14 for 101 in a single day, an achievement which harked back to the Northampton triumph of two seasons before.

This superlative start was no flash in the pan. He took eight wickets in the two day victory over Derbyshire at the end of the week, and then the team moved on at the weekend to their favourite hunting ground – yes, Northampton again. Once again the weather conspired to assist the stronger side. The wicket was fast and hard, and the outfield cracking and in need of rain. In spite of this, the early Kent batsmen were slow to take advantage, and by lunch were five wickets down for 121. Then Arthur Day played a brilliant innings, scoring his 133 out of 199 in a little over two hours, with some hard cutting and driving – one six and twenty fours. He was ably supported by the lower order, putting on 85 runs in fifty minutes with Fairservice for the seventh wicket, and 69 in forty minutes for the eighth with that promising batsman, Colin Blythe, who made 24.

Benefit

Northamptonshire had the misfortune to follow Kent's total of 326 after a heavy day in the field and in defective light. By close of play they had lost half their wickets for 58, three of them falling to Blythe. In good Northampton tradition, it rained all the second day and, at the restart on the third, it became quickly apparent that Blythe would never be mastered on the damaged pitch. Throughout the day, the sun rarely shone for more than a few minutes at a time, which prevented the pitch from ever drying out completely. The first Northamptonshire innings was quickly polished off for an additional 30 runs with Blythe bowling unchanged and taking 5 for 31 off 17 overs.

Funnily enough, he started rather shakily when the home side followed on, sending down some loose deliveries which were peremptorily punished. He was hit for 3 and 1 off his first over, two boundaries off his second, and one boundary off his third. But in this over he happened also to take his first wicket, and then the old mastery supervened. On the slowly drying pitch, he had every batsman in great difficulty. A local correspondent wrote to the *Kentish Express:*

> It reminded me of the best days of Bobby Peel. The ball was breaking both ways and I should think the batsmen's hearts were breaking too.

The next ten overs produced five more wickets at a cost of 18 runs. He nearly repeated his clean sweep of two years before, but finished with 9 for 44 as Northants were dismissed for 78. He had again bowled unchanged throughout the match with total figures of 14 for 75. It seemed that the Northampton gods were always on Kent's side since, just like two years before, as soon as the last ball was bowled, rain began to fall and continued for some time.

It was a remarkable start to his benefit season – two hauls of 9 for 42 and 9 for 44 in just over a week – and 38 wickets in his last three county matches at an average of 7.1. But Blythe took it all in his stride. He was off next day to the Test match at Edgbaston where his 11 wickets put paid to the Australians. These fine performances on foreign fields were all very well, of course, but what mattered most in his benefit year was success in the four Cricket Weeks, and more than that – good weather!

The Tonbridge Week in mid June was fine for weather and crowds, but disastrous for cricket. Kent went into the week as championship favourites, undefeated as yet in seven games, but were soundly beaten in both matches. Against Worcestershire they were set 217 to win and were coasting to victory on 78 for 1 when they suffered an extraordinary collapse, the last eight wickets going down for 30 runs. They were comprehensively beaten by Lancashire by 312 runs, and although Blythe had much bad luck, beating both bat and wicket, his figures of 2 for 111 and 2 for 115 attest to a long slog on an essentially batsman's wicket.

They won their next four matches and looked set for another championship when the Tunbridge Wells week opened in mid July. The first match against Derbyshire was signed and sealed on the first morning. Blythe took the first three wickets and by lunch Derbyshire were 71 for 5. After lunch Blythe carried all before him, taking the last five wickets (including two hit wickets) for 17 runs in 7 overs, and finishing with 8 for 49. Kent quickly overtook the visitors' score of 98 and were 242 for 2 at close of play. They completed their total of 360 next morning, and the game was over by the afternoon as Derbyshire struggled to a second innings total of 128. By this time the pitch was, if anything, rather too slow for Blythe, who finished with 11 wickets in the match.

In the second match against Sussex, the Kent beneficiary distinguished himself as much for his batting as his bowling. A cautious Kent batting side had crawled to 208 for 8 when Blythe came in to join Mason. Blythe hit out boldly and helped to put on 63 for the ninth wicket, his score of 38, including four fours, being his highest of the season. But this was not to be the highest stand of the season for these two players, merely a gentle dress rehearsal for the fireworks at the Oval in August. After rain on the second day, Sussex were skittled for 97 on the morning of the third, Blythe taking 5 for 30. They batted better in the second innings and just managed to save the match, having two wickets still in hand when stumps were drawn.

Benefit

As we have seen, Blythe was rested after the Old Trafford Test against Australia so that he would be in good form for the Canterbury Week – the fitting culmination of any benefit season. In a predominantly wet summer, the gods smiled brightly this week on Kent and its most famous bowler. On the opening Monday, however, the omens were not good. In a day of constant short showers, play was limited to just over two hours, in which Kent pressed on as fast as they could to make 186 for 4 at the close, Hutchings hitting a dazzling 74 in 55 minutes. In a flurry of run-getting the following morning, Kent pushed the total on to 278, and Middlesex went in to bat on a wicket now drying rapidly under a strong sun.

Colin Blythe took full advantage of the conditions and, varying his flight and spin with wonderful precision, proved insuperable. The batsmen in desperation attempted to force the game against him, and all failed. They were bowled out for 78 in just over an hour and a half, Blythe taking 6 for 26 off 17 overs, his last seven overs producing four wickets for six runs. Following on, they fared slightly better in the second innings, but just after six o'clock were bowled out again, losing the match by an innings and 37 runs and shooting Kent to the top of the championship table. It was the first time in many years that the opening match had been concluded in two days, and Kent paid for their achievement with the loss of one day's gate money. But there had been time enough to make the vital collection for the beneficiary, who had been so instrumental in the speedy victory. The 7,000 spectators who attended that Tuesday put their hands in their pockets and fished out a splendid £71. 7s. 3d.

The second match of the Week had been allotted to Blythe's benefit, and all the proceeds would accrue to him. If Kent were to win, they must do it in three days, not two. Thursday was Ladies' Day and the high point of any Canterbury Week. It was also the crucial collection day of any benefit season, when the Kent public would be at their most teeming. What mattered most was not the cricket, though Kent were now at the top of the championship table, but good weather to bring out the crowds in their thousands.

It turned out, in fact, to be one of those perfect summer

days so beloved of Edwardian mythology – bright sun, a large crowd of 13,000, a high population of ladies in long white dresses and parasols over the shoulder. This was not a sight that many Edwardians had actually seen that cold wet summer, nor for many summers past, as the *Times* correspondent, slumped in his deckchair and basking in irony, was quick to point out.

> The skies and sun are positively old-fashioned in colour and brightness, the blue and gold of the days before the flood. The St Lawrence ground, except that the hopfield behind the line of tents is gone, is looking its very best, and, for a day that is not a Bank Holiday, the crowd looks likely to beat all records before the end of the day. It took almost as long to clear the ground when play began after lunch as it does at Lord's during an Eton and Harrow match; and, because of the splendid old trees that surround it, the scene looking from the pavilion past the tents to the brown plough-lands, or from the other side down to the distant grey spires of the Cathedral and the red roofs of the town, makes a far more effective background for the constantly-moving picture of summer frocks and shady hats (too shady, some of them for the happiness of the people doomed to sit behind them) than the dull dark surroundings of the Marylebone ground. The crowd of motors and motor-omnibuses and carriages is astonishing. Though in places they stand four deep behind the spectators round the ropes, there is not nearly room enough for them all to be placed so as to command a view of play, and they huddle in groups under the trees or stretch in long rows against the fence in the full blaze of the sun, while their owners sit or stand in the various tents or search high and low, not always with success, for seats from which they can watch the cricket.
>
> Just now, half an hour after the luncheon interval, things are not going particularly well for Kent.
>
> Blythe, who ought to get a fine benefit as the result of

the match, has been on and off, and on and off again, and has taken only one wicket... .

Indeed, as these things often turn out, it was a relatively poor match for the hero of the hour. In a wicketless morning for Kent, he contrived to drop a sitter at cover point off the bowling of Woolley. Both he and the crowd were quick to see the irony of it all, as the *Kentish Express* reported.

> Would a batsman fall before lunch? Yes. For up goes a miss-hit straight to Blythe at point. The crowd is ready to cheer. But they change the tone to a groan. For Blythe has dropped the ball and Llewellyn smiles and Woolley strokes his chin to see yet another catch missed off his bowling, and Blythe – well, Blythe looked as if he would like to smother himself. But that would have been a pity just when he was raking in his hundreds of pounds.

Of all the Kent bowlers, he was the most hit and when Hampshire were finally bowled out in the last hour of the day, his figures were a cool 1 for 71. But there was some consolation in the thought that this was a day to celebrate not this performance, but the dazzling performances of the last ten years. The collection that afternoon on the ground produced a magnificent £78 4s. 2d., a true signal of his worth to the public of Kent.

Meanwhile the rest of the team did well. Kent began the Friday morning on 33 for 0 and by late afternoon were 406 all out, 170 runs ahead. In the middle order, Hutchings, Woolley, Mason and Day all hit 50s, and Mason and Day in particular thrilled the crowd with a partnership of 129 in 90 minutes. Blythe was cheered all the way to the wicket, but was caught for 5. Hampshire seemed certain to save the match, as Fry and Mead made a faultless start, and by close of play had put on 79 for no wicket. That evening at the Friday theatricals, during the mock cricket match that had become a traditional feature, when the boyish figure of this year's beneficiary was led reluctantly onto the stage by one of the prettiest actresses, the house came down.

Colin Blythe

Fry and Mead continued steadily the last morning, taking the score to 133 for 0, before the new Kent bowler, Douglas Carr, produced an astonishing breakthrough. Carr had come into the Kent side, and into first class cricket, that season at the age of 37, a time when most cricketers were thinking of retiring, on the strength of his prowess with the new-fangled googly bowling which wrought havoc among batsmen. An amateur, he did not join the team until late July, but in seven matches took 51 wickets and ended up second in the Kent averages behind Blythe. Even the England selectors were dazzled by his performances and, with scarcely any first class games behind him, he was picked in place of Blythe for the final Test against Australia, where he made a dramatic start, dismissing Gregory, Noble and Armstrong for a mere 18 runs.

When he came on in this match no wicket had fallen for almost two hours, but he got rid of Mead and White in his second over, Fry in his third and McDonell in his fourth. Five Hampshire wickets went down for five runs in less than half an hour. They managed to limp on to 199 all out, leaving Kent with 30 to win. Blythe had bowled 24 overs in this second innings, but had taken only three more wickets.

Ted Dillon, the Kent captain, now played an inspired hand. He sent in Blythe together with his trusty partner, the wicket-keeper Fred Huish, to knock off the runs. It was not without risk, for the two had made five and nought respectively in the first innings. Charles Fry, not normally the most popular opponent on Kent grounds, as events two years later were to show, nevertheless entered fully into the spirit of the occasion and, recapturing the skills of his youth, bowled the first over. Huish promptly hit him for 4 off the first ball, 2 off the third, 4 off the fifth and a single off the last, whereupon Fry just as promptly took himself off.

To the chagrin of the crowd, Blythe did not face strike until the third over, off which he took two, and then in the fifth hit Newman to the boundary. At the start of the sixth over, Kent on 22 for 0 needed 8 to win. Blythe hit the first ball for 4 and the second for 2, and all seemed set for an heroic finale. But it was not to be. He hit the next for a paltry single, leaving his colleague the honour of the winning run. In just ten minutes, the two tail-enders had cemented victory in some style, Huish finishing with 16 not out and Blythe 14.

With Kent still on course for championship success, this was still a dream ending to a benefit match. As the shy beneficiary was cheered all the way to the pavilion, it seemed as if the clock had turned back to his first match in Canterbury Week nine years before, when he had pulverised the Lancashire batting and likewise been given a cash collection, though then an informal spontaneous one. This time, the gate money he pocketed for the three days of the match came to a handsome £518.

The final Dover Week of the year was disappointing for a benefit season, with three days in succession completely washed out. In the first match against Yorkshire, play was possible for only the first morning in which the visitors knocked up 100 for 1. Blythe bowled only 8 overs and did not take a wicket. Interestingly, the previous match against the Australians at Canterbury he had also failed to take a wicket, and this had been the first time since August 1902 that he had been wicketless in a match – an extraordinary seven year spell of bowling!

No play was possible until the second day of the match against Leicester, when the wicket was drying and becoming deadly. The visitors took advantage of the early conditions, and were 50 for 3 when Blythe and Carr struck. Coming on for his second spell, Blythe conceded six runs off his first over, but in the next four overs took 4 for 4. The last seven wickets went down for 18 runs, with Carr taking 3 for 8 in the innings and Blythe 6 for 30. The Kent openers, Humphreys and Arthur Day, then made a determined start, putting on 62 for the first wicket, but soon the pitch caught up with the Kent batting too, and they were all out for 193.

Two Leicestershire wickets fell that night and it took only two more hours on the following morning for Kent to polish them off. Blythe bowled less well in the second innings, and by the end of his first spell of 19 overs had taken 3 for 32. But his hand was fittingly in the final act, which was to secure victory and also the championship. Facing 124 to save the follow on, Leicestershire were 79 for 8 when Shipman joined King for the ninth wicket. Both batted carefully, steadily building up the runs, and when they had taken the score to 114 seemed certain to make Kent bat again. At which point Blythe was called up to try and break the partnership. Off his third ball he had King, who had batted for two hours and a quarter, caught behind, and Sturman caught at slip the very next ball.

This then was the ball that finally clinched the championship for Kent, their second in four years. There was less general excitement than on that first occasion in 1906, which had caught the cricketing world so by surprise, but the players were rewarded by a banquet at Canterbury on 23 October, when each member of the team was presented again with a memento, this time a commemorative inkstand. They were an ingenious design, lozenge-shaped in silver, with two wickets at the front facing each other, and a cricket bat leant nonchalantly against each. At the back between the wickets was a silver cricket ball on a stand, whose top opened as a lid to reveal the inkwell inside. One was engraved *Presented to C Blythe Champion Eleven 1909 by the Kent County Cricket Club.*

The staggering Blythe success in the first eleven was not, unfortunately, replicated among the Kent colts. For it was in the previous year that Colin's younger brother Charlie, another slow left-armer, had first come to light on the cricket field, and now in this championship year of 1909 his career was just as quickly extinguished. In 1908 he had marked his debut for Club and Ground by coming top of their bowling averages with 17 wickets at 8.64, albeit the same number in a season that his brother had secured in a day.

In May 1909, perhaps attracted by the name as much as this performance, Essex put out feelers for him but were soon seen off by the Kent Committee, who immediately signed him up for the Tonbridge nursery at the princely salary of 35 shillings a week. But there the mercurial rise abruptly ended. He played in only a handful of matches for Club and Ground this second summer and with no success. Against the Band of Brothers on 1 September he took one wicket for 35 runs, and that seems to have been his positively last appearance.

Like many before and since, early promise was not enough to persuade him to persevere in the hope of eventual promotion. He did not, in any event, seem to have the commitment and staying power of his elder brother. He went back to civvy street where he later played a continuing role in his father's bookmaking business. Maybe it was the burden of the name that was too much for him. It certainly has an odd ring on the scorecard, where he appears under the shadow of his remarkable brother as simply "C.Blythe junr.".

Blythe's friend Claud Woolley, the younger brother of Frank, also left the old Tonbridge nursery this year to go and qualify for Gloucestershire, ending up eventually with Northamptonshire. A gentle kindly man, obsessed with cricket, he had much the same temperament as Blythe. They were to become close again in 1914 when they joined the Kent Fortress Engineers both on the same day. Claud saw his friend die on that fateful day in 1917 and later suffered a complete breakdown.

Blythe's benefit fund remained open until the end of June the following year and produced the magnificent sum of £1,519. 13s. 8d., about three times the average for the period. His personal assiduity in pursuit of the collection arrangements was not, however, without its critics. An aggrieved correspondent from Maidstone wrote to the *Kentish Express* at the close of Canterbury Week.

> I do not wish to check Blythe's benefit, but I think it is being overdone. I was asked to contribute by one of his friends, in May, and gave my half-crown (all I could afford) but at every match I have attended during the season a collection has been made on the ground and a collecting bag thrust under my nose. Nothing is more awkward than to refuse. When you say you have already given, your neighbours grin and look upon you as a humbug. I have also been asked by nine men for contributions to their collecting cards. I do not object to see Blythe getting a bumper, but I think the committee are setting a bad precedent for future benefits.

But the pressing concern of the Kent Committee just now was getting its hands on Blythe's bumper. At its instance and that of its financial advisers, the money was invested in three equal amounts in the Army and Navy Investment Trust, the Bankers Investment Trust and the Grand Trunk Railway of Canada. From these it produced a return of £60 a year, the average wage of a poor labourer and, as security for the future, not to be sniffed at.

Blythe gave full consent to tying up his capital in this way, just as he had in the past to the freezing of his winter tour money, but he was now a married man, no longer a teenager, and consequently less inclined to be treated like a schoolboy. Before long he would want to entrench his domestic security in the purchase of a house, and his smouldering disgruntlement with the Committee's usurpation of the role of banker would be drawn out into open conflict.

Chapter 9

Controversy

The sun is beating down on the few hundred of us as we lounge in our seats at Wantage Road, watching Andrew Symonds, fearlessly and clinically, take the Northamptonshire bowling apart, after a morning which has seen Kent very much on the back foot. I am sitting at the Indoor Schools end (what romantic names we conjure up these days) staring into the face of the old pavilion, the self-same view that the Northamptonshire batsmen of 1907 would have had as Colin Blythe's deadly left arm came over.

The square box-like pavilion, with its pattern of rectangles pieced out in brown and white, and the tiny belfry at its summit, looks pretty much the same one hundred years later, though not enhanced by the yellow Weetabix advertisement stretching balefully across its façade. But the atmosphere of the ground itself seems very different from that of my imagination, with more stands and a new pavilion, and a protective girdle of trees concealing the mile upon mile of workers' housing with which it is surrounded. A comfy country cricket ground, in fact, in place of the bleak industrial desert that peers out from the old Edwardian sepia prints.

I have spent a couple of hours in the library this morning, looking at local newspaper accounts of the battle of 1 June 1907, the Glorious First, and have realised for the first time that for the Northampton spectators that day this was not so much a shameful rout as a Dunkirk "victory". The Northants batsmen who, from a total of 4 for 7, put on 20 for the eighth wicket and 34 for the tenth were heroes indeed. And the biggest cheers of the afternoon in both innings were for saving their team from the ignominy of the lowest score of the season.

Ironically, the only reason I can come here today to rekindle the atmosphere of 1907 is because last season Northamptonshire did well enough to win promotion from the second division, and Kent are back here after a two year break. Perhaps not so different from 1907, when Northants had won a less formal promotion from second class cricket only two years before. But the irony lies in the fact that this new-fangled concept of two divisions, which has outraged some parts of humanity, was first mooted in the Edwardian years and has taken another century to implement.

For it was at the end of the 1909 season that, with Yorkshire on a downward slope, Lord Hawke announced that to assist those first class counties threatened financially "something is needed to stimulate public interest in first class cricket". He put forward a proposal for a two division championship, ten clubs in Division A and six plus two minor counties in B. More spectator money would flow into the B clubs since every match would affect their chances of promotion. At the end of the season, the bottom club in A would fight it out with the top club in B, a variation on the play-off system adopted in soccer today. The Kent Committee, looking at it in February 1910, were predictably cool in their reaction, and Lord Harris was instrumental in binning the attempts to revive it in subsequent years. Now we have it, and it's not so painful after all.

I realised also today, with something of a shock, that this is the first cricket match I have attended since the bicentenary Test sixteen years ago and the dismal tour of New Zealand that came after, where draw followed pointless draw in remorseless attrition. My favourite memory of that time was one afternoon at Auckland when the England captain sat inside the boundary board, legs stretched out in front, part sunbathing, part watching his colleagues at the crease, for all the world as though enjoying a picnic on the village green. He didn't, in fact, take a snooze, but I wouldn't have blamed him if he had.

Controversy

What is striking about this match, nearly twenty years later, is how the lack of noise we few helpless spectators can generate is fully made up for by the players themselves, as they shout to each other from boundary line to boundary line, cheer or gasp at every delivery, race menacingly across between overs and generally give the impression more of attendance at a boxing match than at one of those genteel encounters of my youth. It is probably part sledging, with the aim of destroying the batsman's concentration, and part genuflection to those twin modern gods of fitness and bonding. But since they have only for company the "three men and a thermos" of Lord MacLaurin's immortal phrase, it may be to prevent themselves, like Mike Gatting at Eden Park, from falling asleep.

In 1910, the year of the old King's death and the technical (but only technical) end of the Edwardian age, the Northampton match brought no great spectaculars for Blythe to equal the 17 wickets of 1907 or the 14 of 1909. He had to wait till 1914 for that. But there were spectaculars enough that year of a very novel kind for him. In his ten full seasons of first class cricket, Blythe had not yet succeeded in taking a hat-trick. This year, in just two weeks at the end of June and beginning of July, he did it twice. He was never to do it again.

In the winter of 1909/10 he had been on his last overseas tour, the relatively successful one to South Africa in which he had finished top of the MCC averages but played in only two of the Tests. As had now become traditional, the tour produced a sharp little spat over money. In November 1909, before the tour had even started, the Kent Committee asked Blythe and Woolley (who had also been selected) to hand over £100 of their tour money for safe investment by the club. Woolley, not yet of an age to dispute with his elders and betters, concurred at once. But after ten years of such treatment, Blythe was now more worldly wise. He wrote back to ask that he should be allowed to retain all the tour money because he still had to pay the printing and postage expenses of his benefit, and would have to pay about £70 income tax on the proceeds. The Committee decided to appeal against the demand for income tax and await the result, before settling the fate of his South African money.

But the issue had to come to a head some time, and by the beginning of the 1910 season the Kent Committee had decided to exert its muscle. At a meeting on 17 May, while Blythe was playing the opening county match of the season at Lord's, the Committee "ordered" (yes, ordered) that he and Woolley be asked to pay over the £100, and that Blythe be told they would pay his income tax out of the money, if that proved necessary. It is clear that the Kent authorities were getting a little wound up on the matter. At the same meeting they also "ordered" that in future an authority be obtained from professionals taking part in overseas tours empowering the Secretary to the MCC to pay over part of their remuneration to the club. In other words, they were not to be trusted with the money passing through their own hands.

But Blythe's polite resistance to this paternalism was having its impact on the confidence of the Committee. He was now a mature player and linchpin of the recent Kent supremacy, one whom it might be foolhardy to press too closely. Also at this May meeting, the Committee decided finally to wind up his benefit collection, but instead of investing the balance that remained decided it should be paid over to him in cash.

And he was to win too the battle over the South African money. In June he wrote to the Committee to say that he now had only £70 left of the tour money and that that sum was already spoken for. The Committee gave in, but with a bad grace. The formal minute of its decision, like all minutes an understatement of the true sense of the discussion, said briefly but sharply: "It was decided to accept the excuse".

While the Committee on 17 May was pondering how to get their hands on Blythe's money, the subject of their attention was wreaking havoc among the Middlesex batsmen at Lord's and setting Kent, in this first match of the season, on the road to their third championship in five years. Kent had won the toss the previous day before a good Whit Monday crowd and, since the weather was warm and the pitch good, had decided to bat. The first wicket put on 116 in no time at all and by the close of play Kent were 412 for 4, with Dillon making 115 and Woolley 116 not out. They batted on briskly next morning and declared on 500 for 8.

The wicket was still very good and only occasionally would a ball do anything odd, so a competitive response seemed likely. But this was to take no account of the psychological effect of Blythe's bowling on a Middlesex team just coming to grips with the new season. He and Morfee, a new and promising fast bowler, continued unchanged throughout the innings with wickets tumbling regularly. In 36 overs the fragile Middlesex batting was routed for 105, Blythe's last nine overs producing 5 for 18. The *Times* correspondent waxed lyrical once more at the fresh sighting of Kent's best bowler straight back to his superlative form.

> Blythe, who bowled from the Pavilion end, came out with the wonderful analysis, for such a wicket, of six for 27. He was no doubt flattered by weak batting, but the tricks of flight, the changes of pace, and the ball that comes with the arm bowled at the right moment were as good as ever. There is no more fascinating bowler to watch.

Middlesex battled more conscientiously in the second innings, and by the end of the second day had scraped to 160 for 5, still 235 behind. It took only an hour the next morning to polish off the remaining batsmen and hand Kent their first victory of the season by an innings and 198 runs.

Blythe continued in this rich vein through May and June. In the next match against Lancashire he took 5 for 48 in the first innings and against Cambridge at Fenner's 6 for 19 in the second. He took 6 for 36 against Derbyshire, 5 for 51 against Sussex, and 5 for 70 against Leicestershire. These tended to be single innings triumphs; he saved his 11 wicket matches for later in the season.

When he joined the Kent team on 23 June for the match against Surrey on his "home" ground at Blackheath, he had already taken 60 first class wickets. As it turned out, it was a game ruined by rain in which only one and a bit innings were played, but it was nonetheless a most important match in the Blythe canon. A heavy shower stopped play soon after the start, and with heavy showers through the afternoon no further play was possible until twenty to five. A late evening burst was something at which Blythe was adept; many of his greatest performances were saved to the end of the day.

The wicket played easily at first, but as the ball dried and the pitch started to bite, Blythe began to get among them. He quickly disposed of Bush and Bird, the first playing back to be caught by Huish behind the stumps, the second hitting out at the pitch of the ball and being caught by Day in the deep. This neatly illustrated the dilemma of the Surrey batsmen, who found that if they played forward and hit out they could not keep the ball down, but if they played back, the stroke had to be of great accuracy if they were not to be caught behind.

The second wicket pair, Hayward and Hobbs, wisely decided that whatever they did they would hit the ball hard and, with a bit of luck on their side (both were missed once and hit up a number of catches that fell just short of the fielder), they managed to put on 62 runs. This was a fine performance in the light of what was to come. By the time the score had reached 98 for 2 the wicket had become ideal from Blythe's point of view, and he proceeded to take full advantage of the opportunity. He had the Surrey batsmen absolutely at his mercy, and he showed them none.

Hayward was finally out on the first ball of Blythe's next over. Ducat, who replaced him, knew very little of the next four balls and from the last ball was finely caught at second slip. At the other end, Woolley was causing no problems at all; off his next over Hobbs and Strudwick scored six runs. The latter now faced up to Blythe in an atmosphere electric with expectancy. Off the first ball of the over, there was a general appeal for a catch at the wicket which the umpire turned down. With the second came a similar appeal, and he was given out. Off the third Abel was stumped; and off the fourth Smith was well caught at point.

The Kent crowd went wild in celebration of this first Blythe hat-trick on the ground where, thirteen years before, he had bowled in the nets to Walter Wright and been given his big break. But the manner of the hat-trick was truly sensational. He had taken four wickets in five balls, and five wickets in ten balls, all for no runs; and the five balls where no wicket fell were all either failed appeals or close calls. It seemed as though Blythe could take a wicket on any ball at will.

The game itself petered out in a rain-sodden draw, but with Kent top of the county table and their prime bowler in such form, another championship looked well on the cards. In the next match at Gravesend the Essex batsmen were comprehensively trounced by Woolley and Blythe, who finished with figures of 11 for 98. One match later, he took a further 11 wickets against Derbyshire at Gravesend and in the first innings did the hat-trick again, the second time in just 17 days, dismissing Lawton and Howcroft off the last two balls of one over and Beet off the first ball of the next. He strained his back in this match and was sent to a specialist, Dr King, for treatment. He managed to recoup £2 for expenses while being treated, and later successfully claimed half match pay for the two games he had missed.

He took 11 wickets in two more matches that season. The match against Yorkshire at Maidstone towards the end of July was a concerted triumph for the now accepted combination of Woolley and Blythe, the "terrible twins", who bowled unchanged throughout the match. There had been rain overnight before the game and the pitch became more difficult towards the end of the day when Kent, under pressure from Wilfred Rhodes, slumped to 203 all out. But this was the time of day for Blythe too, and he had two Yorkshire batsmen snapped up at short leg before the close.

On the second day Woolley, in particular, was turning the ball prodigiously and Yorkshire declined to 120 all out, Blythe taking 5 for 64. Kent batted well but lost their second wicket just before the close with the score on 105. Blythe, who scored a record 400 runs this season, came in as night-watchman successfully to guard against further mishap. Kent went into the final day on 107 for 2, 190 runs on, but lost two further wickets at the same score and were swiftly demolished by the off-breaks of Haigh, who took six of the remaining wickets for 31 runs. Some really fine hitting by Blythe himself was the out-standing feature of the morning's play. He started with three fours in his first five scoring strokes and then hit Haigh mag-nificently to the boundary for six. His 28 was instrumental in pushing the Kent score on to a respectable 173.

Yorkshire now faced a target of 257 to win, which seemed well within their sights as Rhodes hit off the first twenty runs with some fine forcing strokes. But the rest of the Yorkshire batsmen had been frightened by the success of Haigh that morning into thinking the wicket was playing more quickly than it was, and Blythe and Woolley were well able to exploit this psychological advantage. The Yorkshiremen attempted to force the game when they should have played a more ortho-dox one. The bowlers showed splendid skill in working on their weaknesses and the majority of wickets fell to rash or half-hearted strokes.

Typical of Blythe's skill was the dismissal of Haigh. Blythe took a wicket in his fourth, fifth and seventh overs and on the third ball of his eighth faced Haigh for the first time. The latter, remembering Blythe's stroke of the morning, by way of com-pensation promptly hit the bowler for six himself. Two balls later Blythe tempted him down the wicket again for a repeat performance and Huish had him easily stumped. Yorkshire were dismissed in an hour for 78 runs and Blythe in his 11 overs had taken 6 for 31.

It was fitting in this third championship year that Blythe's last triumph should be – where else? – at Canterbury. For the second year running in Canterbury Week Kent polished off Middlesex in two days, this time by an innings and 150 runs. The second opponents of the Week were Gloucestershire, and on a rather damp Ladies' Day Kent had struggled on a per-fectly good wicket to reach 163 for 5.

When rain came late in the afternoon the score was 240 for 9 as Carr, the last man in, joined Blythe at the wicket. He immediately hit the Gloucestershire bowler, Dennett, past cover point as a signal of good intent. There was another brief interval for rain at 265, and then with the ball wet from a constant fine drizzle, the batsmen continued to dominate the bowling and brought up the fifty partnership. One run later,

Blythe offered a low return catch to Brownlee who just managed to take it rolling over. Typical of his batting form this year, he had hit four fours in his 38 and taken the Kent score on to 291.

The following day was a complete wash-out, and when Gloucestershire began their first innings on the Saturday a draw seemed certain. But since Northampton in 1907, wet Saturdays were something of a Blythe speciality. Despite several missed catches by Kent, including by the usually safe hands of Huish behind the stumps, in next to no time Gloucestershire were 19 for 5, and managed somehow to limp on to a total of 55. Blythe took a wicket in his first over and 4 for 4 in his last 18 balls, finishing with a healthy return of 6 for 23.

The Gloucestershire batsmen fared little better in the second innings, apart from a courageous knock by Brownlee who in the space of three overs hit three sixes and four fours, making 39 altogether out of a partnership of 46. But Blythe proved devastating once more, taking five wickets for 51, and before four o'clock Gloucestershire were dismissed for 140. In less than five hours Blythe had taken 11 wickets for 74 runs, and had won another match for Kent.

Kent won their next three matches to make sure of their second championship in consecutive years. Though Blythe's total of 175 wickets was down on the record 215 of the previous year, there was no doubting the significance of his contribution, along with Frank Woolley, to the Kent success. Championships were now becoming almost a commonplace of the Kent dressing-room, and in celebration Blythe was given the standard bonus of £10, together with a pair of silver candlesticks. In another ingenious design, the stem of each candlestick was formed by three bats intertwined above a wicket – perfect companions for the inkstand of the previous year.

1911 was the one summer that lived up to the historical image of what a fine Edwardian summer should be. It was, without doubt, the most difficult season that Blythe was to face with hard, true, fast wickets providing little scope for the skills of a left-arm slow bowler. The inexperienced Woolley found life in these conditions really difficult, but Blythe, with eleven full seasons behind him, fell back on his accumulated craft and skill, and ended up with 138 wickets in the season for an average of 19, a very creditable performance in the circumstances.

There was that summer the usual cluster of Blythe spectaculars. In the second county game of the season at Leicester, he toiled the whole of the first day as the home side crawled to a total of 270 just before the close. He had taken 4 for 100 off 24 overs. The second day was curtailed to 80 minutes play because of that rare 1911 commodity – rain. By the third day, the combination of sun and rain had made the wicket difficult. Kent were finally dismissed for 197, 73 behind on first innings.

The Leicestershire second innings was little short of sensational. It started well enough, with 3 taken off Blythe's first over and 6 off that of Woolley. The batting then collapsed from 9 for 0 to 11 for 6. Blythe took a wicket in each of his next three overs and three in the fourth; Woolley kept up the pressure with a further four wickets. Leicestershire were dismissed in 50 minutes and 9.3 overs for the grand total of 26. Six batsmen made ducks and two, Wood and King, made 21 of the total. Woolley took 4 for 16 in 4.3 overs and Blythe 6 for 10 in 5 overs. To Leicestershire's embarrassment, Kent knocked off the hundred runs needed for victory in 70 minutes for the loss of only one wicket.

In the match against Gloucestershire at Cheltenham in August, Blythe produced another of his one day specials. Kent hit up 334 on the first day, thanks to a brilliant 148 by Frank Woolley, who had been dropped at long-off when only 36. On the second day, 18 August (Blythe's favoured date for major triumphs), the pitch had begun to crumble at one end and in face of some superb bowling by Blythe the Gloucestershire batting broke down entirely. It was another of those occasions when wonderful bowling produced such anxiety in the batsmen that they were psychologically beaten before taking guard.

Controversy

The real devastation occurred in the second half of the first innings as Gloucestershire plummeted from 91 for 4 to 104 for 9. Blythe's first eight overs produced 18 runs and no wickets; his last ten 8 for 27. And the second innings was no better. By twenty to four, Gloucestershire had been dismissed twice for 115 and 125. Blythe took 8 for 45 in the first innings and 6 for 39 in the second, another day's haul of 14 wickets.

In the last home match of the season at Canterbury, he wrought similar havoc among the Yorkshire batsmen on a rare wet wicket. On the first day, with the wicket still affected by rain from the day before, Yorkshire batted carefully to 66 for 4 when Blythe pounced. He took three wickets in his fourteenth over, as the last six fell for nine more runs. Blythe and Woolley bowled unchanged, the latter taking 5 for 39 and Blythe 5 for 35. Kent hit up a total of 151, Blythe making 12 and Woolley 57, the best innings of the day.

It rained in the night, and showers and sun continued for most of the second day. Play could not start until 5 o'clock, and on such a wicket Yorkshire were saved from the ignominy of dismissal in the hour and a quarter remaining only by the batting of Rhodes and Hirst. They came together when the score was 9 for 3, and added 48 in 40 minutes, a most remarkable display of how to play first class bowling on a very bad pitch. By close of play at 6.15, however, Yorkshire had slumped yet again to 59 for 7. It took only a further half hour next morning to dismiss them for 79 and for Kent to make the four runs for victory. Blythe had bowled unchanged again and taken 6 for 28.

It was towards the end of the season that the incident occurred which, perhaps more than any other, defined Blythe's attitude to the game and the cricket world's attitude to him. Blythe had always had an unparalleled reputation for sportsmanship; as Plum Warner once said of him, he would never ever appeal against a batsman without very good cause, a self-denial it would be hard to find on any cricket field today. Now for the first and only time in his life he was accused of unfair play; hundreds were outraged and sprang to his defence. In itself it was a minor incident, but since it involved the player with the best sporting credentials in the game, it gave rise to a bitter controversy that was to last for more than forty years. C B Fry, the arch-protagonist of it all, was still wittering on about it in the early 1950s. And of all places, it happened at Canterbury, Blythe's spiritual home, and right in the middle of The Week.

There were two contributory factors that helped to blow it out of all proportion – one was the weather, the other Kent's position in the county championship. The summer of 1911 was the hottest in England since 1868. At the beginning of August the shade temperature in London was regularly over 90 degrees and on the ninth, the day after the incident, it hit 97. Tempers were boiling over in the political world as the Government, forfeiting its holidays, strove to confront a wave of industrial unrest that seemed to threaten revolution.

Little wonder, then, that tempers should rise too at the end of a long hard day in the cricket field, even down at the sea-cooled Canterbury. And Kent, with 13 wins already under their belt, were top of the county table and pressing hard for a third championship in a row. Hampshire were their opponents, and Kent could not afford the game to develop once more into the rather tedious draw that the teams had played out at Southampton in June. Anything short of a win would see them overtaken at the top.

But whether it was the hot weather, or the easy-going nature of the pitch, this never turned into a scintillating game of cricket. The ground was in perfect condition, fresher and greener than one would have expected after the long drought. It was a good fast wicket, with no ball getting up awkwardly, and anything hit in the middle of the bat shot like a rocket to the boundary. In the first over of the match, Fry hit Fielder for 12 runs, and his batting was to prove the feature of the innings. Though never at his fluent best, he made only one mistake, being very nearly bowled when attempting a big hit off Blythe. He batted on and reached his hundred after lunch, but after tea, when the Hampshire score was 266, Blythe had him brilliantly stumped by Fred Huish for 123.

The Kent crowd had never loved Fry. A few years before they had barracked him at Canterbury for two misfields, and more generally for his swaggering walk and his unconventional apparel – a voluminous pair of trousers and a white linen hat with the front of the brim turned up. It was much the same treatment given to the Hampshire captain, Desmond Eager, in the 1950s when he too swaggered to the wicket in his flashy Harlequin cap. On the earlier occasion, Fry had been incensed and threatened to take his players off the field, while the Kent captain was despatched to calm down the spectators.

It was probably for his general demeanour as much as for his slow scoring that the Kent crowd booed him during this long hot day in 1911. There was jubilation, of course, when Blythe finally got him, so much so that the *Times* correspondent felt moved to comment, rather defensively it would seem, on the good nature of his reception: "The large crowd, whether judges of cricket or not, must have appreciated his innings, and expressed their approval at the end of it with no uncertain voice".

Hampshire were all out before the close for 339 and on 8 August, the second day, Kent batted rather faster. When Blythe came to the wicket, they were 57 runs behind and, after one or two good hits, one dropping just short of the press box, he was caught in the slips for 14. Nevertheless, his contribution helped Kent to a total of 324 all out by mid-afternoon. Honours were even on first innings and everything set for an exciting finish.

Hampshire went in at twenty to five and plodded steadily on to add to their small lead. Carr had Bowell caught at backward point by Hardinge when the score was 38, but this was the only wicket to fall that evening. When Johnston came in, the scoring became even slower as he and Fry struggled with the googly bowling of Carr and were beaten on several occasions. As Blythe prepared to bowl the last over from the pavilion end, Hampshire were 80 for 1 and Fry 41 not out, looking to his fifty.

The circumstances that gave rise to the incident were simple enough. Blythe saw that Fry had been playing his careful safety-first game and decided to use this last over of the day, always a time of high psychological pressure, to entice him and shake him up a bit. To catch his opponent by surprise, he put up a high full toss which Fry immediately despatched to the long leg boundary for four. Blythe, as we have seen, was never one to be intimidated by a hitter; he always acted on the philosophy that after a big hit a batsman was at his most vulnerable. He put up a second ball in similar fashion which Fry likewise despatched to the same boundary, but this time Jack Mason was just able to cut it off and save two. Coming back down the pitch, the batsman said some words to Blythe and then complained to the umpire. There was an altercation in which it appeared that Fry was unwilling to bat on, but he eventually returned to the crease and Blythe finished the over by trundling each ball down the off-side where no damage could be done.

What was happening out on the square was a puzzle to most of those looking on, not least the *Times* correspondent who seemed to exonerate the players while roundly castigating the spectators.

> Right at the end of a long day's cricket came one of those unfortunate incidents which occasionally happen at cricket. Blythe bowled the last over of the day from the pavilion end to Mr Fry. He had bowled one high full-pitch to him before; he bowled two more in succession in this over. Mr Fry after the second came out of his ground and apparently either appealed against the light, which was no doubt awkward, owing to the shadows, or else protested heatedly against Blythe's tactics. Some discussion followed, and a few of the crowd most reprehensibly began to jeer. The umpire, sole judge of fair and unfair play, pointed to the wicket, Mr Fry went back and the over was finished. Such was the course of events as it appeared from the enclosure. Whatever may be thought of the tactics of Blythe in bowling the full-pitches, they are within the rules of the game. No doubt it was unfortunate that Mr Fry should have showed his displeasure so obviously, but for those who jeered there was no excuse whatever. They surely had no right to show their feelings in the matter. It is greatly to be deplored that anything should have occurred, especially at Canterbury, to detract one whit from the dignity of the game.

Controversy

But the poor spectators had been as puzzled as the correspondent. All they had seen was Charles Fry, who all match had seemed to be playing for a draw, now holding up the game in the last over, apparently to appeal against the light. It was only with reluctance that he had agreed to play on. Inevitably, when he returned to the pavilion, he was greeted with a hostile reception from a section of the crowd, derisive cheers mixed with groans. What happened next is uncertain, as fantasy took the place of reality when the controversy exploded in the press. In one version, Fry challenged a spectator to a boxing match behind the pavilion, but this was later denied by all parties. What seems incontrovertible, however, was that he addressed the crowd from the pavilion steps and vowed to bat out the whole of the next day's play to ensure a draw.

Apart from the attack on Blythe, it was this vow that raised the temperature from the Kent side. Fry did bat on the following day to make a second century, and deprived the Kent batsmen of sufficient time to get the runs needed for victory. His progress the next morning was painfully and deliberately slow, only 75 runs coming between 11.15 and lunch. Kent were set the impossible total of 335 to win in two-and-a-half hours, and the match was drawn. Despite winning five of their next six matches, Kent just failed by 0.16 of a percentage point to carry off their third championship in succession. As the controversy deepened, it seemed as though it was only the behaviour of Fry that had deprived them of this record.

After the match, the atmosphere became even sourer. When Fry took the matter up in the press – he was too incensed to let it rest – it at last became clear what the incident had all been about. He was accusing Blythe, a player with an immaculate reputation for fairness on the field, of cheating by throwing the ball up into the sun. Fry wrote to *The Sportsman* and to the editor of the *Athletic News*. As the correspondence built up, new accusations were spawned as to what had actually happened on the field: that Ted Dillon, the Kent captain, had ordered Blythe to bowl the full tosses; that the umpire had ordered Blythe to bowl down the off-side, but Dillon had told him to bowl as he liked; that Blythe had bowled deliberately at Fry's head and at breakneck speed.

Colin Blythe

When the *Kentish Express* went to press four days later, the allegation of using the sun was now out in the open but, perhaps predictably, the Kent correspondent supported such tactics as fair and castigated Fry for his petulant conduct.

> The painful incident of Tuesday evening has dwarfed all other interest in the Week. People talk of nothing else. The facts are these: Blythe, either at his own instigation or acting upon his captain's instructions, sent two high tosses to Fry. His hand was almost in a line with the sun. Fry got both away and then walked up the pitch and appealed against the light. The umpire appealed to Dillon and the latter left it to the umpire, and Street ordered that the over should be completed – there were only three (*sic*) more balls to come before the drawing of stumps.
>
> So far it was plain sailing. But Fry showed his annoyance by behaviour that reminded one of a petulant schoolboy. He gesticulated and after going back to his crease returned once more in the direction of the umpire, and banged his bat on the ground in evident annoyance. Then the public groaned. Blythe, in a sporting manner, finished his over by bowling from the edge of the crease away from the sun and keeping his delivery as low as possible. Thus ended the over, but not the fussation, for Fry was hissed and hooted as he came back to the pavilion.
>
> … Of course, it was bad form for the crowd to hoot a visitor. But I must contradict my contemporaries who say that the public groaned when Fry appealed. This was not so. They did not groan till he showed his annoyance by a remarkable display and by apparently starting to leave the pitch.

The question on everyone's lips was: who was to blame? The local paper felt Fry was within his rights to appeal against the light but when the umpire decided against him he was wrong to show his annoyance in such an open way – "the most elementary code of cricket tells us to accept the umpire's

144

decision without demur. By his conduct rather than his action Fry lost the respect of a large section of the crowd".

But was Blythe right to take advantage of the sun in this way? The local correspondent thought he undoubtedly was.

> Whether it was in good taste is another matter. But there is no rule against it. A bowler takes advantage of a wind blowing in his favour; he tries to pitch the ball in a hole on the turf, and there is not a man who has played cricket that does not remember a time when a bowler has done the very same thing as Blythe – bowled in the sun.

In such a sensitive climate, this well-intentioned public justification of the tactic now got under the skin of the noble lord, Lord Harris, for he was adamant that it had *not* been used. He wrote to the local paper with historical experience to pray in aid.

> Blythe's hand was nowhere near in line with the sun. I have played till 6.30 instead of 6.15 in Canterbury Week against W G Grace bowling right hand round the wicket and even then his hand was not "in line with the sun", but the light was unquestionably dazzling in the case of a right hand bowler with a high parabola, and therefore the time of drawing stumps was then, or shortly after, altered; but Blythe's hand must have been near the outside of the canvas and almost into the pavilion.
> Secondly, Blythe had not, I know, given a thought to the position of the sun. He does bowl the high full pitch occasionally, when a long stand has been made, in the chance of getting a catch. E M Grace frequently did so; but that there was any design of taking advantage of the position of the sun I emphatically contradict. Mr Dillon and Blythe are too good cricketers to think of such sharp practice.

The whole issue had so stung his Lordship that he went to the ground in person to measure up the case for himself.

Colin Blythe

Since writing the above, I have personally checked on the Hampshire wicket my statements and I find that Blythe's hand was well into the pavilion; whilst the sun, a week later than the Hampshire match, was at 6.15 over the southern end of the one shilling stand, ie a difference I should guess of about 25 degrees.

In general the Kent authorities did what they could to patch up the affair, without admitting any liability. On the evening of the incident, Dillon expressed his regret to Sprot, the Hampshire captain, that any unpleasantness should have arisen in a game between the two sides, and Lord Harris followed this up with a letter in similar vein. The Old Stagers were quick to respond to the controversy with good naive Edwardian humour. At the Friday night's performance, they mounted a tableau in which a batsman, played by the son of Lord Harris, was clean bowled while a spotlight was shining in his eyes. When the batsman complained, he was given to console him a bar of Fry's chocolate.

But these Kentish efforts to defuse the situation were of no avail. When Fry returned to the fray, attacking both Blythe and Dillon for unfair play, the Kent Committee decided on a robust response which they sent to *The Sportsman, The Times* and the Press Association. The Kent letter set out clearly the tactical background to the incident.

Blythe occasionally tries a high full pitch when a long stand is being made, and on his own responsibility, ie. without any instruction from Mr Dillon, and did so on this occasion. He had no intention of taking advantage of the sun, and had no idea that the sun would embarrass the batsman, in which he was perfectly justified, as his hand was on the extreme north end of the canvas about three parts into the Pavilion, whilst the sun was over the south corner of the shilling stand, a difference of about 25 degrees. These positions were checked by Lord Harris a week later at 6.15 pm. He bowled two full pitches, and Mr Fry hit the first for four and the second for two, and then

146

crossed over to Blythe and suggested that it was not good cricket. That was the first intimation Blythe had that Mr Fry considered that that particular ball was made specially awkward by the position of the sun, and he did not bowl another.

The incident had clearly been blown up out of all proportion, primarily because of the character of Charles Fry. He was by nature a *prima donna*, certain to respond in over-sensitive fashion to the hostility of the Kent crowd; and he was also a journalist, who felt happiest fighting his battles in the press. All of which gave to the affair a solidity and importance it did not deserve.

But it was an important affair in the career of Colin Blythe, who was a simple man who played his cricket hard but, quite unlike Fry, was not obsessed with his own self-importance. It was the only time he was ever charged with unsporting behaviour and, given his personality and reputation, it was little surprise that the press and his county colleagues should all have leapt to his defence. For Blythe's sensitivity was in a different class from that of Fry. What comes out most clearly from the internal accounts of the episode was the genuine upset that it caused him – not just because his reputation for sportsmanship had been challenged, but because he had done something on the field that had, quite unintentionally, given such hurt to another human being. If this sounds idealistic, it is because in such matters Blythe was a genuine idealist.

The most telling documentation of his personal reaction to the affair comes from a chance revival of it that took place thirteen years later. In 1924 the retired Hampshire bowler, H C McDonell, produced a pamphlet entitled *What is Cricket?*, intended as a serious discussion of what constituted fair and unfair play in the game. In it he analysed a number of incidents, starting with the "ball in the sun" affair of 1911. His description of what had occurred was taken almost entirely from Fry's own distorted accounts in the press. Blythe was bowling "leg theory" under express instruction from his captain, aiming fast full tosses at Fry's head with three men out on the long leg boundary. When Fry appealed against the tactic, the umpire agreed it constituted unfair play and ordered Blythe to stop. At which point, everyone lost their temper.

It was seven years since Blythe's death, and the Kent Committee was, quite naturally, even more jealous now of Blythe's unblemished reputation than it had been in his lifetime. It went to great pains in drawing up a detailed memorandum refuting all the contentions in the pamphlet, on the grounds that "the Kent Committee cannot allow the distinguished record of an extremely capable and honourable cricketer, viz. Charlie Blythe, to be attacked without presenting the other side of the story".

The memorandum set out the tactical background much as in the letter of 1911. "Blythe was in the habit, when batsmen were fast set, of trying every method to effect a dismissal; amongst others, what was termed by the Kent XI his 'leg theory'. He put a large majority of the field on the leg side and bowled more on the on side of the wicket to a right hand batsman than he customarily did, and also would give the ball a higher trajectory than usual."

Then in a quite extraordinary exercise in protective zeal, the Committee took individual statements from those of the protagonists who were still around, as though embarked on a quasi-judicial process. Inevitably after a lapse of so many years, there was not complete agreement on every aspect of the story; for example, whereas Fred Huish, Blythe's close colleague from behind the stumps, was adamant that the bowler was not engaged on his leg theory, but bowling on the off, Jack Mason, Blythe's first captain, clearly remembered him changing from round to over the wicket and packing the leg side. But all agreed that, given the angle from which Blythe was bowling, the sun did not enter into the equation at all.

The memorandum is worth quoting in detail, if only because it gives a unique insight into the on pitch behaviour at the time and the great respect, bordering on love, in which Blythe was held by both professional and amateur colleagues, expressing themselves in their two quite different modes. What stands out above all is the emotional effect the incident and its aftermath had on Blythe himself.

Controversy

Fred Huish: "Before Charlie started this over he came up to me as I was starting for the other end and said 'What about trying a swinging full toss at the off bail?' I said 'Yes! I should'. He said 'All right then, the first one', but unfortunately he did not bowl it wide enough and it swung on to C B Fry's body, who promptly hit it to long leg for four. As this one was unsatisfactory, he tried another a little wider, which the batsman again hit well and in the same direction, but as Mr Mason anticipated this ball he started running to the boundary and was able to just save the boundary and two runs. Fry then started appealing to our Captain, accusing Charlie of all manner of things. Charlie was bowling round the wicket and the sun was setting somewhere over the scorer's box, ie. over mid-on and at the time I know I considered the complaint of 'bowling in the sun' absurd.

Jack Mason: "Blythe on his own initiative changed from bowling round to over the wicket with two or three deep legs and three or four short legs (a method which I had frequently seen him adopt). I am sure Blythe had no intention of bowling 'out of the sun' and Mr McDonell's statement that it was done reluctantly under his captain's orders is quite untrue.

Douglas Carr (the new googly bowler): "Charlie was very much upset by Fry's accusation which was, in my opinion, quite unjustified. I am quite sure that Charlie tried the experiment entirely on his own and not at the suggestion of anyone else."

Ted Dillon (captain on the day): "As you well know, it was quite customary for Blythe to bowl a fast full pitch, especially to a batsman who was showing little initiative in trying to make runs, or to a batsman trying to play out a time. So far as I myself am concerned, I repudiate, and take great exception to, what Mr McDonell implies when he states 'Acting somewhat reluctantly on instructions from his captain', as I gave no instructions whatsoever to Blythe; had I issued any instructions and wished to take any advantage as Mr McDonell implies, I should have had a right-handed bowler on at that end, instead of a left-handed one."

Stanley Christopherson (the retired fast bowler and future President of the MCC): "I saw Charlie Blythe the morning after the incident with Fry at Canterbury. I had left the ground just previous to the happening of it and Charlie told me of it, and was much distressed at the imputation which had been made against him. He told me that Fry was playing in his normal correct and painstaking style and that he (Charlie) tossed up a full pitch or two to see whether Fry would change his tactics. He told me very emphatically, and with considerable feeling, that he had not realised for one moment that the sun was behind his arm, and indeed, he rather suggested that it was not so, but added that if there was any doubt as to this, nothing would have induced him to take advantage of it in this manner."

Questions of fair play, and imputations as to a player's honesty and integrity, were matters of high seriousness in the Edwardian age. Fry came so badly out of this adventure that he continued to complain about it for another forty years. On the whole, it served to enhance Blythe's well-earned reputation for impeccable sportsmanship, since no-one who knew him well believed him capable of anything underhand.

But for the moment, as Christopherson attests, it shook him up badly. He was off form, having taken only eight wickets in the last four matches. The incident added to the pressures and, whether it was at his own request or not, he was rested for the next game against Lancashire. It was only the second time in his career that he was to miss a match in Canterbury Week.

22 *Poised for the camera.*

23 *The team that beat Northants at Dover to win the 1913 championship. (standing) Wally Hardinge, Arthur Fielder, Arthur Day, Frank Woolley, Jack Hubble, Ted Humphreys (seated) Fred Huish, Douglas Carr, Ted Dillon, Jim Seymour, CB (on ground) Dave Jennings (twelfth man).*

24   *Canterbury Cricket Week 1913. Framed in the pavilion – Ted Dillon, Frank Woolley,*
Wally Hardinge, Fred Huish, CB …

… Douglas Carr, Bill Fairservice, Ted Humphreys (partly obscured),
Arthur Fielder, Jim Seymour.

25　*England in South Africa 1905-06. (standing) CB, David Denton, Albert Relf, Walter Lees, Jack Board (seated) Jack Crawford, Frederick Fane, Plum Warner, Schofield Haigh, Leonard Moon, Teddy Wynyard.*

26　*England in South Africa 1909-10. (standing) George Thompson, Wilfred Rhodes, Frank Woolley, Jack Hobbs, Herbert Strudwick (seated) George Simpson-Hayward, Teddy Wynyard, H D G Leveson-Gower, David Denton, Claude Buckenham, Morice Bird (on ground) Neville Tufnell, Frederick Fane, CB.*

27 *Blythe, Huish and Hubble lead Kent onto the field while the back-markers pause for a chat.*

28   *Claud Woolley and CB outside the Constitutional Club in Tonbridge
the day they joined the KFRE.*

29 *Sergeant Blythe of the Kent Fortress Royal Engineers, about 1915.*

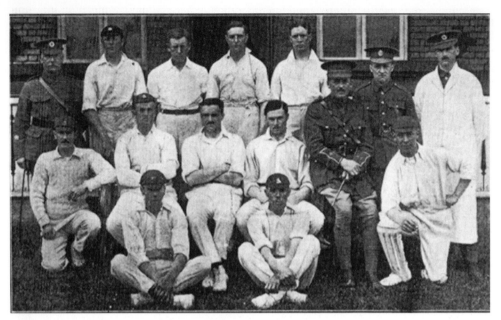

30 *The Kent Fortress Engineers regimental team, 1916. CB is seated left, with Claud Woolley behind and Bill Fairservice kneeling to his right. Ted and Dave Jennings sit cross-legged in front.*

31 *Linden Park CC v Kent Fortress Engineers, Saturday 5 August 1916 at Tunbridge Wells. CB stands second from right. Arthur Fielder, who bowled him, stands third from left, holding pipe.*

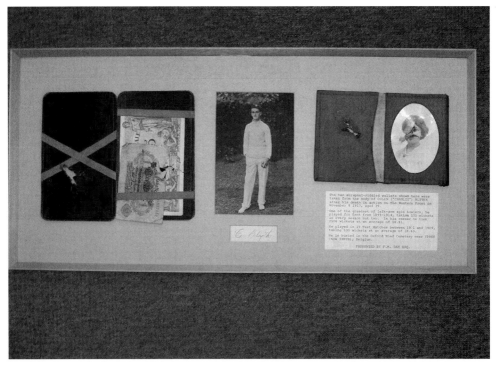

32   The two wallets in the pavilion at Canterbury.

*33   Canterbury Cricket Week, 1926. The captain of Hampshire, Lionel Tennyson, lays a wreath on
the drinking fountain complete with taps and dog troughs.*

34 The grave at Oxford Road cemetery, near Ieper.

35 Janet Blythe in later years at Tunbridge Wells.

36 *The memorial at the St Lawrence Ground with the Bat and Ball behind.*

37 *The left-arm legend in his prime.*

Chapter 10

Swansong

By the opening of the 1912 season Colin Blythe had reached the ripe old cricketing age of 33. He looks an older, quieter man in the team photos now, standing at the back with his hands in his pockets, or promoted rather self-consciously to an exposed seat on the front row, gazing out of the picture instead of at the camera, present as required, but not really a part of it all. Still shy and detached, as in his youth, but greyer and gaunter in these days of his maturity.

An older man, then, but still young enough to play a full season. For despite a career that had had its fair share of short-term illness and injury, his general levels of fitness remained high. One of his greatest assets, apart from his equable temperament, had always been his relaxed and easy action which, despite the apparently frail physique, enabled him to bowl for hours unchanged without undue physical strain.

> To look at Blythe from a distance a spectator would hardly think that he would be likely to last for he does not give one the idea of being a powerful man. As a matter of fact he can do a great deal of bowling without becoming tired and without losing his accuracy.

Where there was strain, as in the Leeds Test of 1907, it was more of the mental variety. Thus he wore well as a bowler and his later years were coloured by as much brilliance as in the nursery days. In fact, his success now seemed even more remarkable for its apparent natural effortlessness, the product of the instinctive wisdom that comes with long experience. The constant variation in length, flight, pace had now become second nature.

The season got off to a bomb-like start. In their first county match, Kent slaughtered Somerset at Gravesend by 280 runs, Blythe's contribution being a mere 7 for 78 in the first innings and 6 for 31 in the second. But this was nothing to the destruction he wrought at Leicester in early June. The wicket was treacherous when Leicestershire went into bat and Blythe and Woolley bowled supremely well. In just under 15 overs, the terrible twins had dismissed their opponents for a total of 25. Blythe kicked off with two maidens and then took a wicket in each of his next six overs, two in the penultimate one. Overall, Woolley took 3 for 15 and Blythe an astonishing 7 for 9. Kent themselves struggled in the conditions and it was only thanks to a bold knock of 45 by the reserve wicketkeeper, Jack Hubble, that they managed to get to 110.

At the start of the Leicester second innings, an incident occurred which was to demonstrate beyond doubt Blythe's physical resilience. He had already taken one wicket in his first over, when on the last ball of his second the opening batsman, Mounteney, made a full-blooded drive back down the wicket which caught him full on the leg. Such was the force behind the stroke that it rebounded to mid-off where Humphreys made the catch. Blythe was badly hurt and had to leave the field, while Leicestershire finished this extraordinary day on 66 for 3, 19 runs behind.

When Blythe came on next morning, it was apparent that he was in pain and badly handicapped by the blow of the previous evening. Nonetheless, he continued undaunted, and immediately took a wicket in his first over. In his third over he was hit for 8 runs and taken off to rest; but despite the injury came bouncing back for a third spell, in the last 12 balls of which he took 4 wickets for 7 runs, nearly all of which were accounted for by a single hit for six. He finished with figures of 8 for 36, a remarkable analysis for a man still carrying a painful injury. His even more remarkable haul for the match was 15 for 45 – shades again of that great day at Northampton in 1907.

By chance the match at Northampton was next up, but there was to be no repeat this time of the familiar annual rout. Blythe took eight wickets in the game but it was not enough to prevent a Northants victory by four wickets. Worse was to come when, two matches later, Northants themselves routed Kent by 240 runs at Tonbridge. At this stage Kent had won only three of their first nine matches, and these two surprise defeats by their own traditional whipping-boy had almost certainly put them out of championship contention. In fact, a rally in August led by Blythe took Kent to a final placing of third behind Yorkshire and, most surprisingly of all, Northamptonshire. The world was surely turning upside down.

Blythe nevertheless produced a number of performances this season that came close to rivalling that at Leicester. On a treacherous pitch at Dudley in late June the Worcestershire batsmen were totally defeated by him, and his tally of 8 for 55 in the first innings set Kent on the road to an innings victory. It was a victory perhaps over-celebrated by an excited team, for a few days later a letter arrived at Canterbury from a hotel keeper of Dudley complaining about the behaviour of the Kent professionals. We do not know what boisterous antics were in question here, but it is comforting at least to know that such behaviour has never been just the province of the modern footballer. Nor was there much point in singling out the professional players for opprobrium; by this time almost the whole Kent team were professional. In any event, the incident cannot have been all that serious for the Kent Committee decided to allow it quietly to drop.

Against Lancashire at Tunbridge Wells in early July, the combination of bright sunshine after overnight rain produced another pitch so treacherous that all the batsmen, save Tyldesley, were helpless against Blythe, who took 7 for 40 in the second innings. Against Surrey in late July he took 4 for 10 in the first innings and 6 for 60 in the second to give Kent victory in two days by an innings and 76 runs. Much of this success, of course, could be put down to an appallingly wet summer, making up for the glorious weather of the year before, but there were few bowlers who could take such compelling advantage of favourable conditions as Blythe.

It was one striking aspect of Blythe's career that his records tended often to arrive in clusters. We have seen already how the only two hat-tricks he performed took place in the space of two weeks in 1910. On five occasions in his career he shared an unchanged bowling partnership throughout a completed match, and two of these occurred in two weeks of August this year. The most startling of these was, true to usual form, in Canterbury Week.

1912 was in fact the worst Week in living memory. There was a full day's play on the Monday, but the Tuesday and Wednesday of the drawn match with Hampshire were entirely rained off. On the Thursday and Friday only two thirds of playing time was possible each day, but this was enough for Blythe and Woolley to polish off Nottinghamshire. After two days of solid rain, it was a surprise to see clear weather on the Thursday, though the sky remained threatening. The rain in fact held off till four o'clock, long enough to enable the normal rites of Ladies' Day to be fulfilled with the studied perambulation of new dresses round the field in the lunch hour.

Kent started badly and were 24 for 2 when Seymour (73) and Woolley (66) came together to put on 112 for the third wicket. When rain stopped play for the day Kent were 201 for 8, a satisfactory total in the conditions. Play was delayed till twelve on the following morning when Kent, thanks to a sterling innings by Sammy Day and a contribution of seven by Blythe himself, took the score on to 236 all out. The wicket then was soft, but as soon as the last Kent wicket fell it began to dry out.

When Nottinghamshire went in, Blythe and Woolley took full advantage of these conditions. In no time the visitors were 6 for 3, and then 18 for 4. They then decided to concentrate on defence, and an interesting battle ensued between bat and ball. Woolley and Blythe bowled unchanged – Blythe from the pavilion end was judged the cleverer of the two, but Woolley bowling down the hill with his height and spin made the ball climb and proved very awkward to play. In 32 overs, Nottinghamshire were all out for 58.

Swansong

By the second innings the wicket was even worse, and the batsmen, believing all resistance hopeless, reversed their tactics and proceeded to hit out. Blythe was unplayable, and in his last six overs took 5 for 11. Only 20 overs from Woolley and Blythe were needed to dismiss the visitors a second time, and by half past four Kent had won the match by an innings and 120 runs. As sometimes happens in cricket, the game itself, apart from the unchanged bowling, produced a statistical oddity. Nottinghamshire made identical scores of 58 in each innings, and the same number of runs were taken off each bowler, Woolley having 5 for 29 in the first innings and 4 for 29 in the second, while Blythe's figures were 5 for 28 and 6 for 28. There was to be an even more remarkable convergence of their figures when the terrible twins took on Warwickshire the following year.

The second unchanged bowling partnership that Blythe enjoyed that August was against Gloucestershire in Dover Week. His partner on this occasion was the googly bowler, Douglas Carr, whose career had burst like a new comet on the scene in 1909, and was just as quickly extinguished by the onset of the First World War. He had topped the Kent bowling averages in 1910 and was to do so again this year. On another difficult wicket, he and Blythe dismissed the visitors in 32 overs for 67, Blythe taking 5 for 27.

Kent were then decimated in their turn by the exceptional skills of the Gloucestershire left-armer, George Dennett, who had vied with Blythe back in 1907 for the best destruction of Northamptonshire that year, taking eight wickets for nine runs in the Northants record total of 12. With his varied flight and pace, he now broke the futile Kent resistance and at one time had six Kent wickets for 0 runs. Kent managed nonetheless a first innings lead of 39, before Blythe and Carr went to work again, dismissing Gloucestershire once more just before the close for 95, Carr taking the laurels on this occasion with 8 for 36.

After coming so close to a third consecutive championship the previous year, it was disappointing for the Kent team to drop as low as third. Despite it all, Blythe had taken 170 county wickets this year, his second best total and only eight

Colin Blythe

short of his benefit year record of 1909. He had earned his winter's rest.

It seems that in 1911 Blythe bought his first house, the some-what delayed consequence of his marriage four years before. Since 1907 the couple had happily rented the little semi-detached in St Mary's Road, Tonbridge, built in the early years of the century, and here he had played out the most illustrious days of his cricketing career, returning home on days off to relax with his violin.

Now, in the spring of 1911 they decided to branch out. They moved half a mile away to the more expansive envi-ronment of Goldsmid Road – a broader street with fine views over the town, boasting a more up-market development, with some detached houses, even three storeys high. Just a two-minute walk down the hill would take you right into the old Angel Ground. The fact that the new house was purchased made it somehow more their own; they named it *Emohruo*, which is simply "our home" backwards.

They were to stay there until late in the War when, prob-ably because of Colin's absences in the army, they eventually moved to another small house, much like St Mary's Road, in his wife's home town of Tunbridge Wells, where she could be nearer her mother. It was there at 100, St James' Road that she received the news of Colin's death.

This bold expansion of the Blythe domestic economy was to lead to his final confrontation with the Kent authorities over money, and once again it was his persistence and refusal to be overborne that carried the day. The house appears to have cost eight hundred pounds, which would have bought a size-able property in the Edwardian housing market. To finance it, he had taken out a mortgage of £400 and borrowed the same amount from his father, Walter. But all the time he was con-scious of sitting on £1500 worth of assets from his benefit year, still closely guarded by the Kent authorities.

In November 1912 he wrote to the Managing Committee asking for permission to draw out £500 of his benefit money to pay off his father for the purchase of the house. Still driving on in paternalistic mode, the Committee could not just take

156

his word and give him the money; they told off the general manager to "ascertain Blythe's true position". At a further meeting a fortnight later the Blythe finances were laid bare: the hundred pounds he sought after paying off his father were to meet "other liabilities" unspecified. The Committee was in generous mood that day and recommended that the General Committee sanction the withdrawal of the full £500; there was even some talk of inviting him to clear off the mortgage as well, though this suggestion was kept out of the official minutes. But it was also decided that, as part of the deal, he should be treated to a lecture on the principles of depreciation of securities, implying perhaps that their investments on his behalf had not done quite as well as they had hoped.

His father was paid off, but the senior committee would not let go of the question of the "other liabilities". Three months later, in February 1913, Blythe was still explaining to them the make-up of these – part mortgage interest, part taxes – and that he needed the £93 now remaining from the £500 to pay them off. Whether the Committee members felt that the additional money was about to be squandered on high living, it is not clear, but certainly they were still not satisfied. They decided that Blythe should be recommended to invest £60, to take care of the depreciation of his securities, and make do with £33 for his other expenses.

Professionals were now the backbone of the Kent county side. In fact, for the 1913 season coming up, the only full-time amateur was the captain, Ted Dillon, five part-timers making the occasional appearance. And yet the Kent Committee had not caught up with the full implications of its own policy: it still insisted on treating its professionals like children, as though they were the marginal contributors to the side they had once been when Blythe first joined.

His confrontation with the Committee followed its accustomed pattern; that is, he stood his ground. On 10 March, four months after the initial request, the Committee considered a polite letter from its most senior professional stating that "he would prefer" to receive the whole sum of £93 rather than reinvest a part of it for depreciation. As in the wrangle over the South African tour money three years before, the Committee gave way, but the official record of its decision has a similarly dismissive and exasperated tone, as though conniving in a bank raid: "It was decided to let Blythe have the money".

1913 was the last of the great run of triumphant seasons for Kent which had begun in 1906. Leading the attack were the terrible twins of Woolley and Blythe: whenever Colin Blythe was making mayhem with the scorebooks, his younger protégé was, like as not, wreaking similar havoc at the other end. From the batsmen's perspective, there was never any let-up; the two left-arm slow bowlers had become one personality – a diabolic spinning juggernaut.

Their performances seemed to reciprocate each other, the success of one in a first innings being matched by the dominance of the other in the second. A good example was the match against Worcestershire at Stourbridge in early June. Worcestershire were first in and the openers, Bowley and Pearson, put on 95 in 80 minutes for the first wicket. Then Woolley and Blythe got to work, all the Worcestershire wickets falling for a further 61 runs. Woolley was supreme with figures of 6 for 31 while Blythe, bowling more than twice the overs, had 3 for 56.

In the second innings the tables were turned. After a poor start, Kent managed on the second morning to reach a total of 254, thanks to a splendid innings of 99 by Woolley and a minor tail-end contribution of 12 by Blythe. Worcester went in again 98 behind and were expected to make a game of it. They had, after all, made 529 for 4 in the match against Gloucestershire the previous week, albeit on a good true wicket. But this was not a good true wicket, and Blythe and Woolley had another field day. By lunch the home team had crawled to 25 for 2, but after the interval lost their last 8 wickets for just 18 runs, in another devastating burst from Blythe. In eight overs after lunch he took 6 wickets for 7 runs, 4 for 4 in his last two overs, finishing with an analysis for the innings of 7 for 21. In their match analyses, the terrible twins achieved their accustomed symmetry – Blythe had 10 for 77 and Woolley 9 for 52.

An even more startling symmetry was evident in the final day of the match against Warwickshire at Tonbridge on

Swansong

21 June. On the first day Warwickshire had made a respectable 262 all out, but only one hour was possible on the second because of rain, at the end of which Kent had replied with 104 for 4. By the start of the final day, a draw seemed inevitable.

It was altogether a sensational day. In the first three-quarters of an hour, the last six Kent batsmen were dismissed for a further 28 runs, leaving Warwickshire a first innings lead of 130. On such a wicket, that seemed enough to ensure victory. But, as the *Times* reporter commented, "on sticky wickets, Blythe and Woolley are a terrible proposition. Blythe is probably as clever a bowler of his type as has ever been seen. No one, it is said, makes the batsman think more, and Woolley, with his height and spin, on such wickets is almost as formidable. The batsman gets no rest at either end, and with the slips standing almost in reach of the bat, they are indeed terrors to face".

Warwickshire went in to bat at twenty past twelve. The first wicket fell at 5, the second and third at six, the next five went down when the score was on 12. By five past one they were all out for 16 and a rapturous reception awaited the two bowlers as they returned to the pavilion. It was one of the most spectacular 45 minutes of Blythe's bowling career, and the lowest total for which he (or Kent) had ever dismissed an opposing side. Even more remarkable was the fearful symmetry.

	overs	maidens	runs	wickets
Blythe	5.2	1	8	5
Woolley	5	1	8	5

Needless to say, it was Woolley, driving and hitting to leg with great power, who was instrumental in knocking off the 147 runs needed for victory. He hit 76 not out in 80 minutes and the game was all over by twenty to four.

There was another such astonishing day against Middlesex at Maidstone in July, when in just over four-and-a-half hours play 32 wickets fell for 227 runs. The weather was sunny and delightful, but the wicket treacherous following heavy rain the day before. Sensing the danger, when Middlesex went out to bat, they hit out recklessly and were soon 53 for 5. Then in a sudden collapse their last five wickets fell for just three runs, Blythe taking 5 for 9 in his last seven overs and 5 for 17 in the innings overall.

Colin Blythe

Kent fared little better in their first innings and by lunch were 12 for 3. Then Frank Woolley took charge with some hard driving and one enormous six; his 33 not out was the highest score of the day. At 49 for 8, he was joined by Fairservice, and with the help of their ninth wicket stand, Kent managed to reach an invaluable 79. In Kent's innings, there was a similarly brilliant bowling performance by J T Hearne who took 6 for 21.

There followed a dreadful afternoon for Middlesex who by ten to five had made 49 for 5, only 26 ahead, and it looked as if the game might be all over in the day. But Kidd, Mann and Hendren stood firm and helped their side to a relatively respectable 86 all out. In the last ten minutes of the day, Kent had another scare on 6 for 2, but Hardinge and Seymour polished off the 41 needed for victory in 40 minutes the following day. In the second innings Blythe had taken 6 for 48, and 11 for 65 in the match. The thrills of the afternoon produced what was to be the last major milestone in his career – he took his 2000th wicket for Kent, the only player to do so until Tich Freeman in 1930. There have been no others, nor will there be.

By 18 August 1913, Kent had 16 wins to their name and were rightfully head of the county championship. But with two draws and one defeat in their last three matches they were beginning to grow jittery, as they remembered the tiny margin by which they had been pipped at the post two years before. They were playing Leicestershire in the last match at Canterbury that year, after which there were only three more games to go. If they were defeated in any two of them, there was still an outside chance that Yorkshire would be champions.

Despite the good championship prospects, only a few hundred people had gathered at the St Lawrence Ground, in dismal contrast to the thousands who had thronged there a fortnight before for The Week. They saw Kent sprint to 140 for 2, and then in a nervy collapse lose the next four wickets for six runs. By four o'clock, and with less than three hours batting, they were all out for 201. Leicestershire themselves were soon on the hop, Blythe taking two wickets in his first over, but in an evening disrupted by murky light managed to reach 79 for 4 by the close.

Swansong

The omens the following morning were bad enough to perpetuate the Kentish jitters. There had been a few light showers earlier but the wicket was still firm and the clover in the outfield made the ball retain the moisture, which seemed set to handicap the bowlers. But Blythe as ever came to the rescue of his team, varying the pace and flight of the ball with all his old skill. He took the last five wickets in the visitors' total of 192, and finished with 7 for 54. Thanks to a lively innings by Hardinge, who eventually made 154 not out, Kent raced to 272 for 6 by the end of the day, and stood well poised 281 ahead.

There was a heavy thunderstorm overnight. That was all Blythe needed. When he was stumped for a duck the next morning, his captain, Dillon, deciding he would rather watch him bowl than bat, immediately declared, leaving Leicestershire 358 to win. Woolley was handicapped that day by an injury to his hand received three weeks before, but Kent this time could manage without him. Blythe summed the situation up at once and through the morning kept the batsmen hard at work, varying the flight of the ball and turning it a mile. By lunch, the visitors were 81 for 4, and Blythe had taken 2 for 35.

During the lunch interval the sun now became very powerful, as if planning the inevitable *coup de grâce* on another brilliant Blythe season. On return to the field, he carried all before him, aided by the silly point and array of short slips which were the usual decorative accompaniments to Blythe on the rampage. After lunch he started with a maiden, and then in the next four overs took 4 wickets for 5 runs as Leicester were bowled out for 94. His analysis was 6 for 40, 13 for 94 in the match. Who could have asked for more from an ageing veteran?

It was not enough to button up the championship that day, but it certainly put an end to the team's fit of nerves. They won their next match against Hampshire at Dover, and it was there in the gentle amphitheatre of the Crabble Ground, cut out of the beautiful tail of the North Downs, that the championship was finally sealed. On 27 August Kent found themselves, in a relatively low-scoring match against Northants, chasing a total of 262 to win. After lunch a magisterial partnership between Jim Seymour (114 not out) and Arthur Day (54) took Kent to an unexpected victory. It was Kent's fourth championship in eight years. It would be 57 years before the next.

There was a touching, almost modern, scene to mark the end of the match. A crowd of 3,000 spectators clustered round the little pavilion set in the tiered banks of grass reaching up to the sky. They called for the players individually, and each was greeted with delighted cheers as they stepped forward to take a bow. And there was one special cheer for the tall, slim figure who came forward shyly, in his large crumpled blazer with the white horse, reluctantly to acknowledge his own special contribution to these novel years of unimagined success.

Chapter 11

War

Early summer and fledglings are squawking in the roadside hedges along the pilgrim paths that all lead to Canterbury. There is a timeless quality about the Old Dover Road as I trudge up it in the dusty morning heat and the occasional office worker comes rushing past me, late for her daily nine o'clock tryst with some demanding boss in St Margaret's Street or Best Lane. I myself am early for my appointment and under no pressure, except that generated internally by an overactive mind.

I can almost smell the wafts of hot air rising from the pavement, in a world where June has become August and there is little seemingly we can do about it. For me once again it is August 1950, and I feel the press of the crowds pushing forward expectantly up the road to see the West Indies open the batting. Or again that fateful August bank holiday of 1914 when shirt-sleeved crowds, unmindful of the cauldron that was stirring just across the water, watched Colin Blythe on top form take ten wickets against Sussex in the very last of his Canterbury Weeks.

As I reach the top of the road and the turning for the cricket ground, I see straight ahead an old man, sitting on the wall outside the Bat and Ball, his face turned towards the sun, basking in its incandescence. He is dressed in an old dark suit, a once white shirt open to the neck, and, most becomingly of all, a grey cloth cap – the Kentish insignia. His presence and his dress complement my mood. He could certainly have been sitting here in 1950, and perhaps even 1914 – in the same posture and the same attire.

I wait behind the Frank Woolley stand till the time of my appointment. Three official-looking men are in a huddle a few yards away, complaining that someone has taken the committee room for the day, so preventing their *ad hoc* meeting. I know that I am the interloper of which they have cause to complain. At last I greet the curator, my helpful minder for the past two years, like a long lost friend and we go on a reconnoitre of the pavilion, that building whose distance and untouchability had held its almost mystic sway over my childhood.

We wait at the back for the caterers to come with a voluminous bunch of keys and let us in the back way through the shining metallic kitchens. For in this day and age, it is the caterers that hold the key – to the pavilion and the club's finances. In the off season, and even in the season itself when no matches are playing, the pavilion does not rest, as in the past, on its historic laurels, gathering dust like some ancient museum. I enter from the kitchen doorway what appears at first glance an open ballroom, bristling with small round tables and their clusters of chairs. The large alcove to the right, set on a low dais, seems tailor-made for a 1950s dance band. So here they have dinners and conferences, and who with the slightest instinct for cricket and its past would not want to bring their club or company along to this prestigious building. And out of this income, cricket can live on in the present.

It is all very different from the dark, enclosed, holy of holies atmosphere when I last set foot here as a small boy. Yet high on the far wall I spot a familiar object, the 1906 picture that also played its part in my childhood imaginings. It is only a copy, of course, and the colours are faded and inaccurate beside its gaudy cousin up the stairs at Lord's. But it is perhaps fitting that it should be here – it carries its age rather better than does the original. In the glass case to its right are assorted mementoes of those now inimitable Edwardian championships – the gold cufflinks of 1906, donated by Frank Woolley, the silver candlesticks of 1910, entwined by stumps and bats, and the menacing dagger-like paper knife presented to mark the championship of 1913, all donated by Bill Fairservice.

War

And there, tucked away in the right hand corner, is what I have come to see. A small display, it is true, but holding a power in inverse proportion to its size. To the left is a thin open leather wallet securing under green elasticated straps a couple of foreign bank notes; they have been punctured by a single hole the shape of an arrow head which is symmetrically repeated in laterally inverted form on the wallet's other side. A foreign body has passed through when the wallet was closed.

In the middle, a touching photo of a slim youthful figure, looking typically unassuming as he stands in the corner of a field with Invicta cap perched on the back of his head, his right hand in his trouser pocket and a cricket ball resting in his left, grasped in the deadliest of grips. And finally, to the right, another open leather wallet, thicker and more substantial than the first, holding in an oval window a small greying photo of a woman. The leather has been shattered by the same spear-like thrust, jagged at the edges; the entire woman's face has been shot away by the same evil object that has pierced the wallet. You cannot reform her image, let alone look into the cool greyness of her eyes. It is a frozen portrayal of unspeakable violence.

Below is a typed card which aims to explain the provenance.

> The two shrapnel-riddled wallets shown here were taken from the body of Colin (Charlie) Blythe after his death in action on the Western Front on November 8 1917, aged 39.

It was the matter-of-factness of this explanation and the physicality of the words "taken from the body" which put the fears into me as a small boy. It seemed somehow even more brutal than the objects on display. Until then my second-hand meetings with death, in book or picture, had always been camouflaged by the comforting words of religion that hid the horror; and this was a novel shock. But today the sun is pouring through this open hall and the horrors of death and the past seem a long way off. Today only one thought strikes me – they have got the date right at last but, oh dear, the age wrong.

Colin Blythe

In the furthest corner of the showcase, away from the horrors of war, stands a more cheering link with the personal past. A silver rosebowl presented by members of the Kent Eleven to Captain McCanlis to mark his retirement in 1913. On it are engraved the signatures of them all, including one C. Blythe whom the Captain had discovered so fortuitously outside the pavilion at Blackheath that July day in 1897. The beginning of a great cricketing career.

So here on the same spot we find reunited the beginning and the end, the high and low points of the past shaken out into one continuum, which in time we come to comprehend, both intellectually and emotionally. The new perspective of a life made whole.

For Blythe, as for Kenneth Hutchings and many others, 1914 was the last season of first class cricket. No-one knew it, of course, either at the beginning or the end. The current county champions set off in May to add further laurels to the distinction of four championships in eight years. They finished a disappointing third, a result that would have been acclaimed with joy when Blythe first joined them in 1899.

It was a fine summer of good firm wickets, difficult for bowlers, but on which he continued to perform as well as ever. His 170 wickets at 15 apiece was fully in line with the average of the latter half of his career. It may have been the firm wickets, it may have been the wisdom of maturity, but the consistency of his batting now began to stand out. In the first county game of the season, on a splendid wicket at Taunton, Kent made 305 in their first innings in less than four hours, and the last three batsmen, Fairservice, Blythe and Fielder, put together 79 between them. Of these, Blythe finished with 35 not out.

He took 17 not out off Oxford University in the next match, and two matches later made his highest score of the season against Sussex at Hove. Sussex had made 323 in their first innings when the Kent batsmen in reply began to crumble against the medium pace of Albert Relf. They were soon

27 for 3 and, despite a strong rearguard action by Hardinge and Seymour, 95 for 5. Then Frank Woolley took charge, hitting 60 runs in an hour and a quarter. When Blythe joined Troughton, his captain, at the wicket Kent were still in dire trouble at 189 for 8. The two proceeded to put on 38 in half an hour for the ninth wicket, and Blythe and Fielder 59 for the tenth, before the latter was caught by Relf with the score on 286, just 37 behind. The match was eventually drawn, but Blythe's 61 which had kept Kent in contention was his highest innings since 1905. What is more, he had made Kent's top score of the innings for only the third time in his career.

Whereas in the past his big scores had come from very occasional bouts of hard hitting, on good wickets he was now capable of holding his own in both innings of a match, with quite reputable totals for a tail-ender. In June, for example, he made 14 and 19 not out in Kent's victory over Leicestershire, and in the high scoring match against Lancashire in August, transferred from Dover to Canterbury, his 27 and 39 played their part in helping Kent save the game. His 382 runs for the season was the best aggregate since the 400 he had scored in 1904 and 1910, but while in 1904 almost half the runs had come from three big innings, now as in 1910 they were more evenly spread. As McCanlis had predicted so many years before, he could have been a more prolific batsman if he had really had the will.

But as always the real triumphs were with the ball. In a hard fought Kent victory at Sheffield in July, he caught the Yorkshiremen in their second innings on a wet wicket drying fast under a powerful sun. The result was an analysis of 8 for 55. When Middlesex faced Kent at Maidstone towards the end of that month before a record 8,000 crowd, the visitors were top of the county table and the only unbeaten team in the championship. *The Times*, which had not yet caught up with the times, still thought Kent's disadvantage lay with its reliance upon the very professionals that had brought all the success of recent years.

> Middlesex had a fine side, but Kent had none of their amateurs except their captain, Mr L H W Troughton, to assist them.

Colin Blythe

The handicapped professionals of Kent knocked up 265 in their first innings; then Blythe, with 7 for 26, bowled out their undefeated opponents for 88 in their first innings and Woolley, with 7 for 54, for 132 in their second.

The wicket had not been easy, but not very difficult either. What had counted most on the first day was Blythe's subtle variation of pace that gave him the edge even on good wickets.

> Blythe's bowling on the previous day had been splendid – he hardly sent down a bad-length ball. He is commonly supposed to be a slow bowler, but he has the great faculty of altering his pace and spin according to the pace of the wicket he is bowling on. At times yesterday he was more than a medium-paced bowler, and seldom bowled the ball with a really slow flight, which he reserves for very fast wickets. Woolley, too, kept a capital length and yesterday probably made the ball spin even more than Blythe did, although he had not the latter's variety of delivery.

One week after the declaration of war, Kent faced Surrey at the unaccustomed venue of Lord's, since the Oval was now given over to military occupation. It was the benefit match for Jack Hobbs and 7,000 spectators turned up on the first day. The £24 that was collected for him on that day makes the £72 and £78 gathered in for Blythe at Canterbury five years before stand out for the remarkable sums they were. Kent were soundly beaten in this match, making precisely 140 runs in each innings. In Surrey's first innings of 234, Blythe with immense patience and stamina bowled 25 overs and took 9 for 97. These were the best figures of his last year in the game, and the sixth and last time in his career that he would take nine or more wickets in an innings.

It was in 1914 that he said farewell to the two cricket grounds in England most closely associated with his name – Canterbury and Northampton – and on both he continued to work his marvels. There was some astonishing cricket at Northampton on 4 June when the Kent match began on a very fast wicket. Humphreys and Hardinge, the Kent openers, started confidently enough and put on 45 in the first half hour. Then Hardinge was dismissed and the batting side went to pieces, losing its last nine wickets for 41 runs in an hour and a quarter. Wells did the damage with 7 for 39, bowling unchanged with the slow-medium of Claud Woolley, Frank's younger brother who was also a friend of Blythe. Kent were used to an average score of 350 or more at Northampton; their total of 86 was a profound shock.

As was perhaps to be expected, the Northants batsmen did not fare much better. They soon found themselves on 73 for 5, but managed to steer on to 141 all out, a lead of 55 that seemed significant in the circumstances. Blythe himself took only one wicket while Fairservice, bowling finely, took 6 for 24. On the second day, it rained till an hour after lunch, the rain taking all the fire out of the wicket. Nonetheless, Kent looked vulnerable again when Hardinge was out with the score only 20. At the same total, Seymour was missed by the wicketkeeper standing back, a fatal error since he then went on to score 110. Seymour and Woolley put on 138 in 80 minutes for the third wicket and by close of play Kent were 237 for 3, a substantial lead of 182.

Fittingly, the final Northampton day belonged to Blythe. On a drying wicket, the remaining Kent batsmen chose to hit out, adding in quick time 102 to the overnight score. Blythe himself was caught by Claud Woolley for six. Northants were left to score the improbable total of 285 to win; once again, it was Blythe and Frank Woolley that stood in their way. In 45 minutes Northamptonshire lost their first five wickets for 19 runs, Blythe taking four of them. In another half hour, the whole side were dismissed for 57. Only Wells, who hit a short ball from Woolley for six, and Thompson managed to make double figures. In this, his last appearance on the ground where he had made his record-breaking performance seven years before, Blythe finished his 9.4 overs with figures of 7 for 15. In the eight games he played on the ground he had taken 73 wickets at an average of 9.50. He needed just 27 balls to take a wicket there.

He played four matches at Canterbury this season, a combination of the Canterbury and Dover Weeks. On the

Colin Blythe

Bank Holiday Monday, the day before war was formally declared, Canterbury Cricket Week opened with a match against Sussex. He scored 22 runs and took ten wickets in a closely fought game which the visitors won by just 34 runs. In the second match of Canterbury Week, he worked his old magic against his friends from Northamptonshire. Kent knocked up 301 on the first day when Claud Woolley had the pleasure of bowling Blythe for a duck. On a wicket giving considerable assistance to the bowlers, Northants were bowled out twice on the second day for 70 and 179, Blythe taking 5 for 24 and 3 for 56.

By the time Dover Week was due to open on 17 August, the tentacles of war had reached out to the cricket field, despite the brave attempts of the Kent authorities to maintain business as usual. The Crabble Ground had become a military camp and the Week was transferred to Canterbury. In the first match against Lancashire, as we have seen, it was Blythe's solid batting performance in both innings that helped save Kent from an innings defeat.

It seemed only right that his last match at Canterbury should have been a typical Blythean triumph. On the first day Kent tore the Worcestershire bowling apart with a total of 461, mainly due to a superb partnership of 200 between Sammy Day and Frank Woolley. Day took 100 minutes for his 109 in which he hit 18 fours; Woolley 200 minutes for his 160 not out containing 24 fours. The last six batsmen managed only 54, but Blythe was the best of them, staying long enough with Woolley to score 23.

Only two hours was possible on the second day; rain fell at lunchtime and play was abandoned at four o'clock. In this time, Worcestershire carried their overnight score of 5 for 1 to a fairly creditable 164 for 4, due to a fourth wicket stand of 111 from Pearson and Chester. The last day was one of those Saturdays in which Blythe revelled, strong sun following a day of heavy rain. Worcestershire managed to limp to 245 in their first innings with Blythe taking 4 for 63. But by the time they followed on, the pitch was drying so fast that Blythe and Woolley excelled in the conditions. With the exception of Cuffe, who made 20, none of the batsmen could do anything against them. Worcestershire were soon bowled out for 62, and in his seven overs Blythe had taken 7 for 20. It was the most wickets for fewest runs he had taken there, on this his most prolific wicket-taking ground.

Since his debut there in 1900, he had played at Canterbury 43 times and taken 281 wickets, almost twice as many as at any other ground, at an average of 15. He had taken ten wickets in a match there 13 times, and five wickets in an innings no less than thirty. What could be more fitting, therefore, than a haul of seven wickets in his last seven overs from the pavilion end he had made his own.

––––––––––––––

The declaration of war on the second day of Canterbury Week this year, while passing apparently unnoticed by the sun-soaked crowds at the Nackington Road end, had an immediate impact on the usual celebrations. The strong military contingent were already absent following the early mobilisation, and the balls and theatricals were cancelled out of patriotic duty. The loss of the final Saturday's play as a result of the quick win over Northamptonshire, when added to the international developments, posed a serious financial setback for the club.

It is difficult now to view the cricket season of 1914 separately from the shadow thrown over it by the events of the first week of August. But apart from these reflex reactions of the first few days and the loss of some grounds like Dover to the military, county cricket creaked on to the end of the season, despite the competing patriotic fervour. And the apocalyptic future, so clear in hindsight, was nowhere to be seen. Like the Franco-Prussian war, the last time armies had come head to head in western Europe, this conflict would be sorted in a matter of weeks or months, but definitely all over by Christmas. Planning for the 1915 season continued through the autumn and winter, and was not finally abandoned until January.

A similar distortion by hindsight has been applied to the career of Colin Blythe at this time. In the few very patchy accounts in cricket histories, he is often supposed to have announced his retirement at the end of the season, as if he himself knew there would be no more first class cricket for five years to come. But the reality was somewhat different. In August 1914, a time when cricketers, especially slow bowlers, played on into their forties or fifties, he was a young 35 and, with 170 wickets in the latest (batsmen's) season, still at the height of his powers. Far from retiring, he remained on the Kent payroll for the period of the war, and continued to play in the frequent services and charity matches to keep his eye in and his spinning finger tough. It was, as we shall see, not until the summer of 1917, when he was 38, that he began to wonder whether there was enough left in his bowling to contribute to the first class game, and retirement became a real issue.

After the last match at Canterbury, Blythe played in the two day victory over Warwickshire at Gravesend, and then the two day defeat by Middlesex at Lord's. In this, his very last first class match, he took 5 for 77 in the first innings and 2 for 48 in the second. But like many of his compatriots, he was chafing at the bit. He had determined to enlist, and in the last two matches at Canterbury, transferred from Dover, he was constantly to be seen climbing the steps to the press box to glean the latest news from France. He stood out from the last game of the season, against Hampshire at Bournemouth, for he had already enlisted with the Kent Fortress Royal Engineers, joining the No. 1 Reserve Company at Tonbridge at the end of August.

The onset of war posed a dilemma for most clubs – they wanted for economic reasons to continue to the end of the season, but were at the same time sensitive to the charge that permitting idlers to play and watch cricket, while their brothers were signing up for the Front, was wholly unpatriotic. In defensive mood, the Kent Committee met at Canterbury on 4 August, the day war was formally declared, and decided to send a message to the press that, while not indifferent to the war crisis, they had to keep the matches going because the livelihood of their large staff depended on it.

But the press were not convinced. The cricket correspondent of the *Kentish Express* ran a strong campaign for abandoning the season, pointing to the pathetically small crowds now attending matches as a counter to the economic arguments. And he felt he had support from the people.

> It will be a relief to everyone when this fiasco called county cricket comes to an end. The people don't want cricket, won't have cricket. I know of one newspaper office where they put cricket scores and war news in the windows. Hundreds look at the latter, practically no-one at the former. Indeed, there was hissing when a cricket score was put in the window the other evening.

A fortnight later the Committee took stock of the longer term consequences of war, accepting the inevitability of troops being stationed on the Canterbury ground. They decided to stand down the watchman who slept overnight in the pavilion, while retaining the services of the dog. They also agreed not to put pressure on their professionals to enlist and to continue with winter money, but worried, nonetheless, how their players would survive once matches had ended for good.

Some of the professionals, like Blythe, joined up within weeks of the declaration of war; Bill Fairservice, Wally Hardinge and the irregular batsman, David Jennings, all signed up along with him for the Fortress Engineers, as did Northamptonshire's Claud Woolley, the brother of Frank, who now became an even closer friend. But by December, when the war was patently not to be over by Christmas, the Committee had hardened its line. A letter was received from a Major D'Aeth drawing attention to the fact that many professionals appeared to be avoiding service to their country. The Committee decided to write to eight of the professionals of military age to tell them their inaction was now the source of public criticism, and to ask why they had not enlisted so far.

The eight replies were closely studied at a meeting in March 1915, and four were allowed to pass. As for the remaining players whose replies were unsatisfactory, the Committee now thought it was time to wave the white feather. "It was decided to write again to four of them and warn them that in the event of a Benefit being granted to any one of them their

Colin Blythe

popularity with the public might be adversely affected if they did not come forward." The quickest way, seemingly, to a professional cricketer's conscience was through his wallet.

But to be fair to the Committee, they were still very exercised about the financial well-being of those who had joined up, and it was at the same meeting that they decided to supplement the pay of those in the Army during the cricket season, to bring it up to the level of normal ground pay. Thus in May 1915, Blythe's pay in the KFRE of 24 shillings a week, plus 15 shillings separation allowance, was raised until 31 August by 11 shillings to bring it up to his standard ground pay of 50 shillings a week.

This decision, which applied to five other players, was renewed for the summer of 1916, when the Committee agreed in addition to pay the contribution that Blythe had to make towards the separation allowance. The policy was not, of course, purely altruistic. Kent was now almost wholly dependent on its professional players, and these supplements, like the winter payments introduced in the 1890s, were designed to ensure that most returned to the fold once the war was over. But the Committee was still keen to see that the payments went only to those who had offered themselves of their own volition for King and Country. As for those enlisted under the Military Services Act: "it was considered inappropriate that those who have been forced, or all but forced, to join HM Forces should receive the same consideration from the Club as those who volunteered readily early in the day".

Colin Blythe was one of the earliest to join this latter deserving category. As an epileptic since his youth, he should never have been recruited, but he used all of his traditional ingenuity somehow to avoid, or deceive, the medical inspection. As someone who had earned his bread for the last fifteen years by sweated physical labour, that might not have been too difficult. Through September, he was given his elementary training in the reserve company in Tonbridge, but he did not lose sight of the wider picture. Like the majority of the country, he was caught up in the early war fever and was determined to use his celebrity in the national cause. He embarked on a recruiting tour of Kent and enlisted 25 men in the process. It was October when his own call-up came and, with five cricketers enlisting together, including Claud Woolley and Dave and Ted Jennings, he rang up a journalist friend from the *Tunbridge Wells Advertiser* to see them off by train for Chatham.

Such publicity was common in those weeks as the sight of celebrities going off to war would, it was hoped, inspire others to follow suit. He arrived at Tonbridge station in the afternoon of 12 October, a rather dark and gloomy Monday. The news photo shows him standing legs apart at the centre of the group of five cricketers, impeccably dressed in dark suit and tie, a wide flat tweed cap on his head, a dark haversack over his right shoulder, and a broad smile on his face. The newspaper headline read "Charlie Blythe in Great Form" and he was clearly out to milk the maximum publicity. For the crowd that had gathered to see them off, he put on all of his usual cockney jocularity, and we catch first-hand a rare glimpse of the personality that had played such an important role in knitting together the Kent teams of the past decade, and killing the seaboard boredom of winter touring sides.

> As might have been expected, Blythe was the life and soul of the party. He arrived at the Constitutional Club with a great haversack which he could scarcely carry, and when a friend told him his kit must not weigh more than 28lbs. he drew a very wry face, and said "Why, it weighs half a hundredweight, and now I haven't got all I want. I shall have my fiddle down there before long. I shall start a band, and then you chaps" (turning to his fellow recruits) "will have to pay a penny a day towards the upkeep".

And then Blythe the clothes dandy comes to the fore.

> "Yes, you can laugh at the size of my bag, but I'm going to make myself as comfortable as they'll let me. I've got five shirts, two dozen collars, another suit, and a blanket or two. Ought to be all right, hadn't it?"

Colin Blythe

It continued non-stop.

> After a photograph had been taken, a move was made
> to the station. On the way Blythe caused much amuse-
> ment by suggesting that the five recruits should have
> a sweepstake to be given to the one who secured a
> stripe first.... Right up to the last moment Blythe kept
> the little party in high spirits, and he was the last to
> clamber in the carriage just as the train was on the
> move.

The Kent Fortress Engineers had grown up gradually in the
pre-war period following a decision in 1908 to raise six companies of Royal Engineers as part of the local territorial force.
By 1914 three such companies had been established, based in
the Medway Towns, Tonbridge and Ashford, with their headquarters at Gillingham. As the war progressed, extra companies were raised when the three original ones were turned
into field companies and despatched for action abroad, some
of the first members of the KFRE ending up at Gallipoli.

Defence from the sea was, of course, the most vital part of
homeland defence. Batteries had been set up to guard ports,
harbours and estuaries, and schemes of field defences established in the intervals between batteries and at any likely landing places. These defences were put on alert a week before war
was declared and continued to operate much as planned until
the end of the war. They were never seriously attacked, apart
from a raid by two cruisers on Hartlepool in November 1914.

The job of the Fortress Engineers up and down the country was to man these coastal defences and protect the harbours, ports and estuaries. Their major active tasks were construction work and military engineering; but the most typical
duties were long nights of monotonous watching and waiting
for the attacks that never came. The greatest enemy was not
the Germans, but boredom. The heaviest workload fell upon
the Kent Fortress Engineers who, in guarding the coast closest to the continent, were naturally seen as most vulnerable to
attack. Control of the Straits of Dover was as ever the key to
homeland security.

With his twenty years of engineering experience and his natural practical ability, Blythe proved a valuable recruit. He was posted with his colleagues to Woodlands Camp, Gillingham, the permanent base from which they were sent out on detachment. He was appointed to 2/7th Company, one of the companies newly formed in 1915 out of the temporary reserve company to which he had been recruited. His contribution was soon recognised and he was quickly promoted to corporal in the autumn and then in 1915 to sergeant, the rank he retained to the end of his service. Had he taken that bet on speed of promotion, he would undoubtedly have won it.

Though the hours were long, work on the coastal defences was a relatively safe occupation, as the armies bogged down in France and threat of invasion grew more and more remote. Blythe's only "wounds" were self-inflicted, as he began to prove just as accident prone on the training ground as he had seemed on the cricket field. In October 1915, just a year after joining up, he broke a small bone in his ankle and had to be laid off for several weeks. It cannot have been that much of a hardship to spend a few weeks at home. But in any case, he was no stranger to family life. Unlike so many others serving in the army, wherever he was stationed in Kent was always within touching distance of his home, in Tonbridge and later Tunbridge Wells, and he was always able to maintain his links with his wife and the wider family.

And just as important for a man who had lived and breathed cricket for the past fifteen years, he was able to keep in close touch with his colleagues on the cricket field, many of whom had joined the KFRE along with him. Whatever the workload, there was always time for the relaxation provided by a game As the war became part of everyday life, cricket began to be seen as a means of boosting morale rather than the specious indulgence it had appeared in 1914. In the last three years of the conflict, the Kent authorities were among the first to recognise this change of outlook. In 1917 no less than 119 services and school games (mostly one-dayers) were played at Canterbury alone.

Football was the primary game of the KFRE, and in the winter of 1915-16 each company set up its own team to compete in a cup competition whose progress was followed avidly by all the men. Blythe's company were the eventual winners, but he did not play, saving his breath for the summer. He participated, however, in the regimental sports for 1916, gamely entering the blindfold driving competition and piloting his horses equally gamely into the water trench. Following the example of the football fanatics, the companies now set up their own cricket teams to engage in internal competition.

Blythe and Claud Woolley were elected to the cricket committee and a regimental team was established. It was a talented grouping for a small army unit, with the Jennings brothers, Claud Woolley, Bill Fairservice and Blythe himself. Its chief handicap was that it was too talented to find local clubs that could give it a competitive game. In the first match in May 1916, it thrashed the Royal Engineers by an innings, Blythe taking 3 for 33 in the first innings, and 4 for 3 in the second.

By the end of August, the regimental team was playing two or three games a week and Blythe was back in the world he knew best. Despite the lack of consistent practice he could still produce the odd miraculous performance. In June against a South African XI at the Bat and Ball Ground at Gravesend he took a match-winning 7 for 36; and against the Chatham Garrison in August he had match figures of 14 for 85. He played at Lord's and the Oval this summer, but the most nostalgic occasions were saved for Kent.

On 5 August, the KFRE team were beaten by Linden Park, the most powerful of the Tunbridge Wells clubs who boasted among their company no less than four top-class Kent players – Fred Huish, Jim Seymour, Gerry Weigall and Arthur Fielder. Blythe took only three wickets, but the moment of the match came when Fielder bowled him for a duck. They had been the closest of friends throughout the Kent glory years, and Fielder could not repress a smile as he sent his old comrade's middle stump cartwheeling out of the ground.

But if the public mood were softening as regards the playing of cricket, the war on the Western Front, post the battle of the Somme, was hardening and becoming more of a life-threat for all those under arms. As the slaughter intensified, manpower became the central critical concern of both governments and generals alike. Following the Somme, Royal Engineer units throughout the country were combed for men of good physical fitness to make up the numbers. In early 1917, 5000 men of the RE Territorials were drafted to France, not necessarily to join other RE units. It was their bodies, rather than their technical expertise, that was required. By August 1917, a further 8000 men of the RE were available for posting to units in need of replacements – and one of these men was Colin Blythe. He spent most of that summer in the Royal Engineers camp at Marlow.

Eventually he was drafted into the 12th battalion of the King's Own Yorkshire Light Infantry (12/KOYLI in its military abbreviation). The one thing to be said for this arrangement was that he had not been recruited merely as cannon fodder; the 12th was a pioneer battalion and his knowledge as an engineer was needed. Engineers were integral to the war on the western front, building the emplacements for the heavy artillery, the accommodation for the increasing number of troops, the physical means of communication from roads, railways and trenches to simple trackways. Almost 300 members of the KFRE were transferred that year, along with Blythe and Claud Woolley, to pioneer battalions up and down the country; they went as individuals, not as a militarily attached unit of the KFRE.

That summer, despite the threat that lay ahead, there was still time for cricket, and many matches were played at Marlow. In June he went up to Lord's, still with the same spirit of the old days at Canterbury – in one innings he took 7 for 26. An even bigger game was planned for August between the Army and Navy and the Australian and South African forces, a charity match organised by the indefatigable Plum Warner for the benefit of Lady Lansdowne's Officers' Families' Fund.

This one day match was played at Lord's on Saturday 18 August (fittingly the date of many of Blythe's past triumphs) before a crowd of about five thousand. The title of the visiting side turned out something of a misnomer; it contained ten Australians and only one South African. The home side fielded some big names – Ernest Tyldesley, Plum Warner,

Colin Blythe

Patsy Hendren and Percy Fender – and two of Blythe's Kent colleagues, Wally Hardinge and Dave Jennings.

The English were caught on the wrong end of a rapidly changing wicket. It was damp to begin with when they went in, but by the time of the visitors' innings had dried out completely and was playing easily. The Army and Navy were dismissed for 106 shortly before three o'clock, when Blythe was bowled by Massie for a duck. Blythe opened the bowling and took the wicket of Macartney for 1. With the visitors on 11 for 2, an exciting finish seemed in prospect, but Barbour and Bell put on 101 in an hour and the colonial team batted on to 242 all out.

It was a wearisome farewell to cricket for Colin Blythe, who took 1 for 54 off 14 overs. Was he losing his ability to turn the ball, as he apparently thought, or was it just the misfortune of being caught on an easy wicket? The final *coup de grâce* was delivered when Barbour hit him for six just in front of square leg to win the match. And he was then hit for six again, twice in the same over. A solemn end to his last match for England against Australia and, in truth, his last match ever. A month later he was on his way to France to support these Australian forces on the same side in the mire of Passchendaele.

No-one could know what the future might bring, but it was at about this time that he took the decision to retire from the world of cricket. Lord Harris recalled a conversation with him before his departure for France: "One of the last things Charley Blythe said to me, before he left for the Front never to return, was that he would not be fit for the County Eleven when the War was over; he knew what there was of spin left in his bowling, and that without that he would not be good enough". His retirement was formally announced to the press in the middle of September, just a couple of weeks before his departure for France. There was another bit of positive news as well. He had signed up with Eton to become the cricket coach there, and feed the post-war county game with brilliant young bowlers raised in his own subtle, unassuming image.

But it was not to be. With the move to France beckoning, he had to take care of a quite different future. On 24 August he wrote his will. He left all his estate to his wife, including an insurance policy for five hundred pounds, and twelve hundred

180

pounds in shares that were still being held for him by the Kent authorities, that same money that had provoked all the battles of the past. He left to his father to distribute among friends and family a number of personal items: most especially, the mementoes of the four championships – the gold cufflinks of 1906, the silver inkstand of 1909, the matching candlesticks of 1910 and the silver paper knife of 1913. And two violins.

Having made his farewells, on 25 September he sailed for France. The 12th battalion of the King's Own Yorkshire Light Infantry that he was now joining, made up mostly of tough Yorkshire miners, had had a long war. It had been raised at Leeds in early September 1914 by the West Yorkshire Coalowners Association, which had spent the large sum of £10,000 on equipping it, most of which went on refurbishing its camp at Farnley Park, Otley. In May 1915 it had been reconstituted as one of the new-fangled pioneer battalions, who fought more with pickaxe and shovel than with rifle, an appropriate role for a battalion swarming with miners. After a short period of service in Egypt, learning how to dig in the desert, it had arrived in France in March 1916 as pioneer battalion of the 31st Division, ready to play its crucial supporting role for those in the front line at the Somme, at Arras and at Vimy Ridge.

With a complement of 27 officers and 880 men, it had spent the early months of 1917 at various camps about 30 kilometres south west of Arras, working on roads and then, under a Canadian construction company, on building railways. In April it had moved its headquarters to Bray for work on the Fond du Vase railway, from where it had been called briefly into the line at the beginning of May for pioneer trench making and close support of the advancing line of the 31st Division. It then returned to its work on the railways. At the end of June it joined an operation by the 94th Brigade, and was tasked with digging a new communications trench in the front line. It was a reminder that these "backroom" jobs, though much safer than the infantry, were not without their dangers. The trench was built but at the cost of three dead and 33 wounded.

In July, the 12th battalion was called up to join the troops massing in the Ypres salient for the long planned disaster that was to become the third battle of Ypres. In a new bold thrust, the Germans were to be pushed off the Passchendaele ridge overlooking the salient and, with a sea-borne invasion from Ostend, the allied forces would join up to sweep the fleeing enemy all the way back to Berlin. But it didn't quite work out like that. The conception was always too ambitious for the execution, and this campaign of mud and mire became the archetypal image of the First World War – thousands slaughtered for the gain of a few hundred yards of useless territory.

Pioneer battalions were called on occasion to swap shovel for gun when infantry resources were running low. Indeed Blythe's battalion distinguished itself in the engagement near Vieux Berquin in April 1918; it was reported to have "held part of the line most determinedly, as well as the best fighting battalion could have done", and thereby acquired the nickname of "the Yorkshire Guards". But the price it paid was heavy: 13 officers and 275 other ranks killed, wounded or missing. Had Blythe managed to live through 1917, he might well not have survived this encounter.

Some infantry battalions of the KOYLI saw action at Third Ypres, if only for a few days at a time. The 6th and 7th battalions were in the front line at Langemarck and Inverness Copse in July and August, while the 9th and 10th fought in the bitter engagement at Polygon Wood in September. But the 12th battalion retained its pioneer role and was attached to the Fifth Army on active service throughout the campaign, from the first offensive of 31 July to the securing of Passchendaele Ridge on 10 November. Blythe was there for the thrusts of early October.

The main tasks of the engineers the year before, at the Somme and Arras, had been the construction of strong points. In the mud and constant shelling of the Ypres salient, the overriding emphasis was now on communications. The principal task for the pioneer battalions was the organisation of men and materials to make and maintain the roads and tracks to the front – roads for serving the batteries and ammunition dumps, duck board tracks for the infantry. In addition they bridged streams and cleared blocked ones, built advanced

182

dressing stations and cover for field guns, screened roads in exposed positions, removed and destroyed bogged down tanks, laid tapes at night to guide the infantry to their assault positions.

But the unending task of the infantry tracks was one of the most onerous and dangerous. Trenches were no use in the mire of Ypres and the narrow duckboards were laid upon the surface of the earth. Their repair was a constant task. The engineers would go out at night in working parties, with the infantry carrying the loads of duckboards behind them, to repair the tracks. In places a careless step off the track might lead to instant death; in crucial sectors the continual shelling took its toll. In the case of the 5th Army, the duckboard tracks to reach the front line stretched from Ypres for five miles.

While the frontline divisions were relieved in turn, the field companies and pioneer battalions worked on in the danger zone on roads, tracks and railways without a break. They found their sleeping quarters where they could – the lucky ones in the honeycomb of dugout shelters along the banks of the Yser canal, those less fortunate nearer to the front line in shattered farm buildings, old German pill boxes, and even old shell holes. Work went on day and night on maintaining communications in the nightmare of mud. The input of labour was immense. For the 2nd Army alone, the average daily labour force devoted to roads in the forward area amounted to two infantry battalions, seven pioneer battalions, ten field companies, seven tunnelling companies, four army troops, and two labour companies.

This then was the world joined by Colin Blythe in the first week of October 1917, and in which he was to live for the next five breathless weeks. An exhausting life of unending toil, in the short run less dangerous than that at the front, but in the long run perhaps equally dangerous with so much greater exposure over time. The 12/KOYLI had a much more clearly defined role than many of the other pioneer battalions. As a result of its work in the first half of 1917, it had become expert in the building and maintenance of light, medium and standard gauge railways, and so was assigned to this task almost exclusively throughout the four months of the Third Ypres campaign.

Colin Blythe

The major problem facing the railway builders round Ypres was the nature of the ground. In the rear areas, shelling had done much to destroy the drainage systems and, even if the water were still retained within the dykes, there were so many ditches crossing the fields that the tracks had to be laid on numerous bridges and rafts of brushwood. Considerable engineering skill was needed here as well as bare brawn.

The 12/KOYLI was called north to Poperinghe, east of Ypres and well behind the front line, on 2 July 1917. There it spent a month under the 2nd Battalion Canadian Railway Troops in beautiful sunny weather practising the rapid laying of light railways. On 29 July, in the shadow of the coming attack, it began the real work, laying actual railways to selected tactical points, and then to ammunition and food dumps in the wake of the advance – all of this under constant fire, sometimes intense. Roads were rare luxuries in the environment of the salient; it was only through railways that food and ammunition could be got to the front, without which the fighting would have ground to a halt.

Throughout the campaign, the battalion carried on laying down a regular network to batteries and dumps, over which many tons of ammunition and supplies were transported, as much as 18,000 tons in a single week. In the four months of the campaign, a total of 29 miles of light railways were laid by the battalion, in the course of which it sustained some 200 casualties. The actual laying was only half the job; keeping those miles of track in working order was the more difficult, since much of it was under direct enemy observation and shelled to bits, day and night. When these endless breaks in the track occurred, volunteer parties would go out under cover of darkness, and under very heavy shell fire, to make the necessary repairs. They lived in bivouacs and temporary shacks, improvised from any materials found lying about, and these so-called camps were, like the railways, subject themselves to shelling and bombing by day and by night.

Like many pioneering duties, railway work was relatively safe and even considered by some quite enjoyable. But this depended on your personal fortune and viewpoint. In September before Blythe's arrival, the battalion lost seven men killed and 18 wounded while working on the main line, the Bedlington Loop and the Cambridge Spur; but many of these casualties were in fact sustained not on a working shift but by direct shelling of their camp.

As the momentum of the early attacks of the campaign declined, so the call on the pioneers grew less, and other pioneer battalions were gradually withdrawn from the field. But the expert feats performed by the 12/KOYLI were so admired and had become so essential to the campaign that they alone were kept on, together with half the Canadian Railway Troops. As their Commanding Officer remarked, if you do a superlative job in the army, more and dirtier work is your reward. To perform this increased workload, the battalion was heavily reinforced from the Royal Engineers in September and October of 1917, until at one point it had expanded to 40 officers and 1300 men.

Blythe must have been among the fresh drafts of 277 untrained men that arrived from base on 2 and 3 October, and were sent immediately to Watou for training. B Company, to which he was apparently assigned, was itself formally moved to Watou on 11 October for rest and training, and did not return to active duties until the 28th, when it moved to the Labrique Road camp and started work on the Wieltje (Forest Hall) line, one of the little tangle of lines to the north east of Ypres, running out to the village of Wieltje.

So for most of October, Blythe appears to have seen no action; meanwhile his new colleagues in the three remaining companies had suffered that month eight killed and 33 wounded. Of course, the casualties sustained by the pioneer battalions were small by comparison with the infantry, and the historian of the 12/KOYLI, commenting on these October figures, felt moved to remark that the battalion was under "the special protection of Providence". But when it came to Sergeant Blythe, starting work now in earnest, Providence had gone absent without leave.

For the first week of November work continued on the Forest Hall line, normally under cover of darkness to avoid more accurately targeted shelling. But while Blythe was toiling behind the scenes on this vital communications work, there were striking developments up at the Front. On 6 November the village of Passchendaele was over-run by the Canadians in a bloody battle. On 10 November, with the final securing of the ridge, the campaign was over.

On the evening of 8 November, a German shrapnel shell burst behind the allied line. Close by were a group of sappers, including two cricketers. Claud Woolley of Northamptonshire was wounded. Five men were killed, three instantly, and one of those was Colin Blythe of Kent. The shrapnel pierced his clothes, the wallets in his breast pocket, the photograph of his waiting wife, and then his body. One moment he was alive. The next he was dead.

The war diary of the battalion recorded simply

3 other ranks killed, 6 wounded, 1 missing. B Company.

Chapter 12

Legend

Thursday 10 June 1920. A passenger express plane is flying in the early evening from Paris to London with four passengers aboard. These are the first days of public air travel and the experience is novel and exciting – but also dangerous.

It is flying smoothly over the cricket fields of west Kent when, a few miles east of Tonbridge, it develops engine trouble. The pilot looks for a suitable place for an emergency landing, but finding no cricket field immediately to hand, comes down in an oatfield on Brandenbury Farm in Collier Street, near Marden. These are light planes and the landing procedure is safely executed. A young farmer and his wife, both in their late twenties, from Brook Farm next door, who have seen the plane flying low across their fields, rush out to the scene to check that all is well. No-one is hurt, but the passengers are shaken up and the plane needs some work on it. They arrange for the passengers to be taken to Marden station a mile away for the onward train journey to London.

Meanwhile the pilot and his mechanic, with the help of the farmer, spend the next three hours of a summer evening putting the engine to rights. About ten o'clock, as twilight begins to fall, all is ready for take-off. The plane now stands empty and the pilot, in the gathering dusk, makes an offer to his unscheduled hosts to thank them for their enthusiastic help: would they like to take the trip with him to Croydon airport? Being young and adventurous, and caught up in the excitement of this strange evening, they gladly accept. It was a fatal decision.

The plane takes off safely enough and heads north west for Croydon. Some time after ten o'clock it is seen flying low over Dartford, as if the pilot were searching for a place to land. The machine, hovering, passes away into the darkness. It has come too far north. The pilot realises that something has gone wrong with the compass and he has lost his bearings. A night flight is slowly turning into a nightmare.

The plane is seen again about 10.30 by two men at Swanley. It is clear that the pilot is in difficulties and coming down. They head in the direction in which it is falling. The pilot has seen in the darkness near Swanley Junction what he thinks is a meadow and drops down upon it. It turns out, however, a field of wheat. The wheat becomes twisted in the propeller and the machine, still travelling at speed, turns over. The three men are thrown clear, dazed but only slightly injured. The young woman is trapped in the wreckage. The farmer rushes to the plane and pulls his wife out, but finds her seriously injured. She has a broken collar bone, but her spine is badly fractured.

The two men from Swanley arrive at the scene and she is driven to Dartford Cottage Hospital. A specialist is summoned from London and she is treated so far as medical science will allow. Two days later she returns by motor ambulance to her home at the Brook in Marden where she lies for some while in a critical condition.

Her husband tends her there for almost a year, an invalid in that twilight world between life and death. In the spring of the following year, she develops a kidney infection as a direct result of her spinal injuries. It is nature's way of signalling the end. She dies of blood poisoning on the last day of May. She is 28 years old and leaves behind her two little girls of five and three.

———————

What am I doing here? On a blustery late June evening of leaden skies, a gale is blasting through the Menin Gate as we huddle together about a hundred of us, no more than a cricket crowd at Northampton, to watch the celebrated Last Post which has been played here every evening at eight since 1929. The music is played with panache and melancholy combined, and followed by a few minutes silence, occasionally broken by men passing and repassing across the road under the central arch in a home-made ceremony which, after seventy years, has found its own authenticity.

Despite the wind tunnel in which we stand, the silence is deep and strangely moving; everyone is thinking of someone else – you can read it on their faces. And me, of the man who has brought me here, whose grave I shall visit tomorrow. At the close of the ceremony and the formal recitation, with its own peculiar Flemish emphasis – "we *will* remember them" – we burst into a spontaneous round of applause, eager to be a part of it. Coming out of the Gate, the clouds have parted at last to reveal a blue promise of tomorrow.

I sit in the morning sun outside the Café Vivaldi (they're not playing the Four Seasons, thank God) in the Grote Markt at Ypres (or Ieper as we must call it now), wondering at the restored glories of the Cloth Hall across the square, which only seems a fake because we know it is one. What is fake, and what is true, in this world anyway? Before me, a glass of fresh orange, hot croissants with butter and a small espresso, as I ponder the strange story from the past of the night flight that went wrong. I think of the number of times I have eaten with my own lost angel this very same breakfast in the morning sun in countless small *places* in France, *plazas* in Spain and *piazze* in Italy. And always the same quiet joy in her eyes at the freshly exotic experience.

And I think of another woman too, with misty grey eyes, who came to this very square in the summer of 1919, and who had cause to ponder that night-flight story for the rest of her life. For in this first summer after the war, when English people could travel abroad for the first time in five years, this great old medieval cloth town, still in ruins, became the centre of a very strange tourist trade that was to flourish through the twenties and thirties, and is to some extent still flourishing today.

Colin Blythe

They flocked in their tens of thousands for a four-day package deal costing less than four pounds, packing the cross-channel steamers, pouring into trains at Ostend and pouring out again at the shabby little sheds that served as a temporary station. No Café Vivaldi on the Grande Place then; no Grande Place even, just the shattered remnant of the Cloth Hall pointing its skeletal finger angrily to the sky. They were put up in inns in the surrounding villages, or in hostels run by YMCA or Church Army, adapted from the old military canteens.

And most of them were women, come to see the last resting place of husband or lover, father or brother, or at least to touch the ground where it all happened – to put a closure on their loss. For Ypres was a symbol, not just of the generic horrors of the western front, but of the exclusively *British* war, the one place where the British had fought from the beginning right up to the end.

But Janet Blythe would have to wait almost two years before she could make her own personal pilgrimage. Her husband had died on a fine but dull and hazy Thursday, two days after the capture of Passchendaele. Ironically, the day he died was one of scarcely any activity on the salient; the official war correspondent reported: "There has been no further action, and the enemy still makes no serious attempt to recover Passchendaele".

It was not until the following Thursday that the news came through to Tonbridge, in the very unofficial shape of a letter from one of Blythe's fellow soldiers to the widow of another of the soldiers killed in the incident. Thus, when Blythe's death was reported in the newspapers the next day, his widow had still yet to receive official confirmation from the War Office. *The Times* carried a brief, rather spatchcocked, obituary notice, plundered from the much fuller notice in *Sporting Life*. It made the standard references to the Headingley Test of 1907 and the feat at Northampton four weeks before, but it did at least make one reference to his very personal skills.

In the last forty years we have had five left-hand slow bowlers of the highest class. Blythe was the youngest of the five, the other four being Peate, Peel, Briggs

190

and Rhodes. Blythe was not the least gifted of the five and had perhaps the most varied resources. Instead of pitching shorter when he was being knocked about, he would ask to be hit again, putting more and more spin on the ball.

Indeed *Sporting Life* gave him a mammoth spread which had been very carefully prepared. It spoke with more authority of his bowling prowess.

> Blythe cultivated spin and length, with "the ball that goes with the arm", and he became greatly dreaded. His best ball was, undoubtedly, of the latter class, but he could break both ways, and his variety was always puzzling and disconcerting. ... He was an adept at lulling a batsman into a sense of security – inducing the mood which drove them to take liberties. He did not mind being hit – he only put on more spin, and he generally had his way in the end.

It was this article which started the debate as to who was the greatest of the five recent left-armers, with the oft-repeated quote "If you asked Ranjitsinhji whether he would rather face Rhodes than Blythe, he would undoubtedly have said 'Yes'."

Writers in the latter part of the 20th century have not known enough about Blythe to contribute meaningfully to that debate. The judgment of his contemporaries, many of whom faced him at the crease, is all. Plum Warner clearly thought he was a greater bowler even than Peel – "the best of the lot". Gilbert Jessop saw him as "the best left hand bowler of my time". Home Gordon said he was "one of the greatest bowlers ever seen" and highlighted his most powerful claim on posterity – his incomparable skill on a good wicket: "he kept down runs on a batsman's wicket more skilfully than anyone else since Alfred Shaw". Philip Trevor, writing in 1908, encapsulated the contemporary view.

> In the dry English summer of 1906 and in the wet English summer of 1907, sober, serious expert opinion

Colin Blythe

would have ranked Blythe as the best of all our bowlers. He was, all things considered, better than any other bowler on a good wicket, and much better than any other bowler on a bad wicket.

Another contributor to *Sporting Life* in that dreadful week of his death summed up the spectator's view from the boundary.

> What a thrill would pass through one when Blythe made that half-shuffling, half-stumbling little run of his to the bowling crease when rain and sun had combined to prepare a surface on which the plainest bowler became difficult, and so skilful an one as Blythe was really terrible to the unfortunate batsman who had to face him. There was just that nonchalant delivery, the impish amount of finger spin imparted to the ball as it left his hand, the swerve in towards the wicket, and the break back when it came in contact with the ground. What numerous victims he has claimed with that ball which seemed certain to clear the leg stump and yet whipped back and took the off.

On the day the news came through, Lord Harris wrote a fulsome appraisal from his home in Faversham, full of boy scout rhetoric and bathetic cadence.

> Charlie Blythe has fallen. What that means to lovers of Kent cricket it is difficult to describe. His brilliant exploits with the ball will doubtless receive adequate description in due course. For all their lives his tripping up to the wicket will be a happy recollection. What can have been known only to his closer friends was his sterling character. He was an *influence amongst his class*, besides being a fine judge of the game. [*my italics*]

So despite all those lowly wrangles over money, his sportsmanship on the field and mild manners off set an example to other working class players, liable to misbehave in cheap hotels in Dudley. It is one way of looking at it.

But Harris's contribution is valuable above all for making perhaps the first public reference, albeit in very guarded terms, to his epilepsy. He felt moved to do so to counter possible future assertions that Blythe's departure from Test match cricket had been due to cowardice. But he felt *able* to do so because the subject of the illness was now dead.

> His retirement from the Inter-State matches was not due to any lack of courage, for he never failed in a crisis, but to a physical defect which followed on any severe mental strain.

It would not be long before other commentators would be able to voice the dreaded e-word itself.

Better writers than the affable Lord Harris were able to pay proper tribute to his personal qualities. He was ambitious and single-mindedly devoted to becoming the best bowler in the game, but he never let it show. He was keen on making and breaking records which would do the boasting for him. Amidst all the backbiting and jealousy of traditional pavilion life, he stood out as a simple nice man.

> His was a truly wonderful career, but it never spoiled the man. He remained, as always, simple and unassuming, loth to speak of himself and rather deprecatory of his own talents – if one could persuade him to talk of them… . His career in France was a short one, but one can imagine him contemplating the odds in that calm, reflective, and unflinching way of his which was so characteristic of the cricket field. Sgt. Blythe is dead, but his spirit lives, and his fame will endure for all time.

This flood of commendation, coming so soon after the news had broken, must have been a bitter-sweet pill to the new widow reading it at home in Tunbridge Wells – comforting to witness the world's respect and grief, but impossible to digest

Colin Blythe

on this day when there had yet been no time to take in the dreadful new reality.

There was nothing to help her on her journey – no funeral service, no grave to watch by. All that activity was taking place a hundred miles away on dangerous territory from which she was prohibited. For two years, her only contact with that past was an official War Office letter, and those small bits and pieces that had been salvaged from his body – the two precious wallets, moving in their intimacy but frightening in their redolence of death. And the chastened figure of Claud Woolley, who was transferred back to the KFRE in the course of 1918.

She kept in touch with contacts in France who told her of the grave and its emplacement. It was, therefore, a matter of both relief and apprehension when she heard in summer 1919 that she could go. In the post-war world of military and non-military zones, where national boundaries were not yet back to full normality, much time was needed to complete the bureaucratic formalities. Following a detailed application process, her passport was finally issued by the Foreign Office on 23 July, authorising her journey to Ypres by way of Boulogne. It took another fortnight to collect her visas from the French and Belgian embassies and on 9 August set off from Dover for Boulogne. Two days later she arrived at the goal of her pilgrimage, and made for the little cemetery on the north east outskirts of the town.

She looked at the letter sent the previous year by one of his comrades to guide her to the site.

> There is practically no one around the place. It is just between times when the troops have gone forward and the other units have not come up to clear the ground. [The second] grave in the second row from the s.e. corner of Plot No 1 Wieltje Cemetery, corner of Oxford Road and road leading n.e. from Ypres to Poelcappelle. The registration of the plot is C-28-BIH and I think this is the map reference but I am not sure until I have worked it out.

Painfully helpful and a little confused, but enough to get her there. She found the grave plot and the simple wooden cross, with its few terse lines of rudimentary identification, punched out on four fragments of aluminium tape from a slot machine like the one on Victoria Station in my childhood.

9 R U
49296 C Blythe
12/KOYLI
8 11 17

Just lines of numbers concealing a name that seems almost an afterthought. Nothing here of the human being behind it all, let alone the master-cricketer, praised and respected throughout the world. Yet perhaps more fulfilling in its simplicity than all the pomp and trumpets of praise. For this was still to come.

On the Saturday of the following week, a few days after her return, she arrived at the St Lawrence Ground for a one day match between the Band of Brothers and the Kent Club and Ground. It turned out a high scoring draw, with the Band of Brothers declaring on 320 for 6, thanks to a mighty 107 by Sammy Day which deprived Lord Harris of the chance to bat. The Club and Ground, with Wally Hardinge as its principal, replied with an uncompleted 289 for 6.

At the tea interval, that novel and controversial institution of Edwardian cricket, designed, some said, to ruin a batsman's concentration, a small party, with herself in place of honour, made its way from the pavilion to the north east corner of the ground to find awaiting them a small guard of honour of the Buffs, with arms reversed, surrounding an obelisk-shaped structure shrouded in the Union Jack and the Kent Flag.

The obelisk about to be unveiled was very different from the structure that we see today – not just a memorial, but a building with a very specific social purpose. This was, we must remember, some time before the days of Volvic and Evian, when water has become either a free good or a fashion accessory. It was then a precious commodity for which public provision had to be made, not just for vagrants or the poor, but for ordinary members of the public engaged in outdoor activities, like watching a cricket match. And such provision conveyed a sense of social responsibility and status, at a time when every horse-trough up and down the land carried the name of some high municipal dignitary of the recent past.

In short, the memorial to Colin Blythe doubled as a drinking fountain. What stood originally on the octagonal base was a marble basin with brass taps and cups on all four sides. It was an ingenious design with the overflow from the basin feeding down into four small troughs below for, as the local press delicately phrased it, "canine pets to quench their thirst". So ingenious, in fact, that it proved over time most impractical. Four years later a stoppage was reported in the overflow and a choking of the troughs through accumulation of leaves. Later, two layers of stone were added to the base to cover the taps and basin, and the dog troughs filled in. The functional purpose had had to give way to the purely presentational, but strangely the integrity of the whole was enhanced.

There had already been hiccups. As Lord Harris pointed out, in inviting the President of the Club to make the unveiling, it was a great disappointment that the ceremony could not take place as intended in Cricket Week that year, but some difficulty with the fittings had delayed the completion. The President, Lord George Hamilton, was quick to draw the analogy between the spirit of sport and the spirit of war.

> England is the home and nursery of sport, and no locality has more contributed to that proud distinction than the county of Kent. During the most critical phases of the war, the qualities engendered by sport were a great national asset. It matters not in what particular sphere of athletics a man has excelled, whether as horse-man, shot, boxer, cricketer or footballer, the ascendancy which he has attained over his competitors becomes more firmly established under the ordeal of war, and he becomes among his comrades the national guide and leader, and he is also the foremost "over the top" and the last to leave the trench.

At last Janet Blythe heard the name of her husband drawn from the list.

Legend

The first and foremost is the name of Sergeant Blythe. Kent has always been famous for its left-handed bowlers, and I can call to mind Willsher, Wootton and Woolley, but probably Sergeant Blythe is the best slow bowler Kent has ever produced. He was a remarkable personality, and although fragile in physique he had the heart and head of a lion. No man probably understood the game better, and no man had a greater control over the ball. When war broke out he was determined to go to the front and, having dodged the medical inspection, he rapidly established his position and became sergeant. He went to the front and was soon afterwards killed.

And finally, after further brief tributes to the others, the peroration.

To the memory of our lost comrades I now dedicate this fountain as a small permanent memorial of their gallantry, and in the belief that, erected here on the most historic ground in Kent, it will encourage future generations to practise on this cricket ground those great qualities of patience, self-denial and cooperation which are alike the essence of the true spirit of chivalry and the mainstay of public service.

Despite the traditional clichés and high-flown rhetoric, it had been a simple and moving ceremony. The flags were drawn down to reveal the Portland stone in the afternoon sun, and two trumpeters sounded the Last Post and the Reveille.

There was an even more moving sequel, moving because of its spontaneous and unrehearsed nature. In 1920 Middlesex beat Kent at Canterbury by just five runs on their way to taking the championship. On 5 August, it was reported to the Kent Committee, meeting as usual under Lord Harris in the middle of Canterbury Week, that the captain of the Middlesex team, Plum Warner, one of Blythe's warmest admirers, had laid a wreath on the memorial with a card "To the memory of Colin Blythe, a great cricketer and true sportsman, and to the members of the Kent Eleven who fell in the Great War".

It was agreed formally to thank the Middlesex captain and, informally, to take a leaf out of his book. Every year since, at Canterbury Cricket Week, a wreath of fresh flowers has been laid at the memorial, initially by the opposing captain, and in more recent years by the President of the Supporters Club. Though a ceremony for all the Kent players killed in the wars of the 20th century, for those taking part it is the memory of one player in particular that remains forever at the forefront of the mind.

———————

I rise from my seat in the Grote Markt and make my way slowly on foot out through the eastern suburbs of the town. I continue on along Brugseweg, with its beds of red and white roses along the verges, and through the tidy suburban village of Sint Jan (St Jean of Blythe's day), taking the right fork down the tree-lined lane, which the British named rather awkwardly Oxford Road, that leads to the little cemetery. Though more than eight hundred are buried here, it is smaller than I had imagined and a rather surprising shape, three arms branching out unevenly from the Great Cross at the centre. Plot I, containing little more than a hundred graves, was the original cemetery started in August 1917 – you can tell by the higgledy-piggledy alignments which point to a makeshift graveyard in a corner of a farmer's field; touching in their impromptu disorder, compared to the neatly symmetrical ranks of the plots added after the Armistice.

It is quiet here, and I am the only person so early in the day hunting for a grave. At last I find the stone I have come all this way to see, still standing like the cross in 1918, the second in the second row of the south east corner. But so different then from now. Now it has a formal identification marker, I. L2. The grass is mown like a bowling green and a jungle of large red begonias wave at the foot of each Portland white stone, like imitation Flanders poppies. The inscription today is more forthcoming than the citation on the old wooden cross.

Legend

49296 SERJEANT
C. BLYTHE
KING'S OWN YORKSHIRE L.I
8TH NOVEMBER 1917 AGE 39

And below the elegantly incised cross, a personal message.

IN LOVING MEMORY OF
MY DEAR HUSBAND
THE KENT & ENGLAND CRICKETER

She has given it the identity lacking before, but has failed once again to spot the deliberate mistake. Yes, the age is wrong here too, on the original gravestone itself. Is this just chance – or fate? A deliberate attempt by the gods to defeat that over-weening presumption of man, who brazenly aims to set the record in stone for all time, and achieve the perfection of accuracy too?

Next door lies the body of Private Salt of Tunbridge Wells, formerly Lance-Corporal Salt of the Royal Engineers, killed on the same day by the same shell, aged 19. I scout around to find his other working comrades of that day. There are two others here – Private Dye of Leeds, aged 27, joining his two brothers, Osborne and Fred, killed in 1915; and Private Bennett of Chatham, aged 21, whose headstone carries the inscription that applies to the lot of them – *all he had he gave*. Only the illustrious fame of their sergeant draws them to our attention now.

I sit down by the graveside to rest in the warmth of the morning sun. I see at once the link – not the clerical errors – between this memorial and its counterpart in Canterbury, whose image has remained with me for so much of my life. They both shine so vibrantly in the summer sun, they might well have been hewn from the same block of stone. I see clearly too how legends grow up from chance events – the death on the battle-field that freezes an image for all eternity, the spontaneous gesture of flowers on a memorial, creating a perpetual tradition that keeps the image alive, if not so fresh as the flowers that support it.

For with early death and no vested interest around to

promote the past as reality, the legend and image become so easily faded and stereotyped. Colin Blythe did not survive to write his own cricket memoirs, or make a celebrity appearance as an 80-year-old spectator on the boundary at Lord's. Thousands of words have been written about him in cricketing books, but mainly as passing references with the same narrow focus – his epilepsy, his violin-playing, his sportsmanship and "niceness" generally. And in cricket, it is the records – the game at Northampton, the Headingley Test, the consistent century of wickets each season. Little here to bring back the reality of the man and the style – the constant variation of delivery, the single-minded pursuit of the next wicket, the fearless response to being struck, the deliberate temptation of the overweening opponent, the nervous exhaustion of hours of concentration.

And when a real live recollection appears on the scene, threatening to shake up the time-worn image, it serves only to enhance the mythical ambience. Thus Cardus writing in the 1930s, in the context of class, of a character so distant and unapproachable he might have come straight from the Bible.

> One day I saw Blythe walking round a cricket field, and I followed him about. I never dreamed of asking for an autograph; I simply wanted to hear him speak. He was talking and laughing with a player from the Kent side, Seymour, who used to hold, and sometimes miss, his slip catches. And I heard Blythe say: 'I'll 'it yer on top o' the nose in a minute'. It was a shock, because a boy's romanticism is always snobbish.

And it was Cardus too, with his incomparable prose, who did most to sustain that romantic image, which has clung so powerfully to Blythe, of the dichotomy between the gentle summer game and the horrific violence of war.

> But he lost his life fighting for England, one of the first to join up. A shell made by somebody who had never known cricket and directed by eyes that had never seen a Kent field, fell on Blythe and killed him. On any of those quiet, distant, delicious afternoons

at Canterbury, when Blythe bowled his gentle spin and the summer blossomed all around, could even the ironic gods have discerned the course of events which was to take Blythe over the seas and leave him there part of the foreign dust?

Yet if the romantic prose and the stereotyped potted biographies, which the future will continue to churn out, leave us cold, we have still the solid reality of two lasting documents. As we leaf through the pages of the Kent record books, we meet at each turning the twenty odd bowling records that will not be extinguished and, perhaps even more potent because unexpected, that tenth wicket batting record along with Jack Mason at the Oval in 1909. Brief references, it is true, but ones that can lead us past the image to the reality of old matches actually played, the tough physical reality of ball upon ball, over after over, as we read it now through the hieroglyphs on the yellowing scoresheet.

And next the oil painting of 1906 with which we all started. Romantic in conception, it too was an attempt to burnish an historical image, but of a history too recent in time to suffer any distortion. It was, in fact, drawn from life, without any of the preconceptions with which it is now commonly saddled. And as we look into it too, we look directly into the life of the frail-looking bowler framed in the archway of the handsome new pavilion, a life as it was lived then without the clutter of future accretions – a real image founded in a real world.

I leave the graveside and wander slowly back into town. As a final act, I put my nose in St George's Memorial Church, built by Englishmen in the late 1920s to claim their citizenship of this place. I have come to see the small brass plaque – companion to the more elaborate memorial in Tonbridge church back home – which shares its space with many others on the long pew lectern at the back. It was dedicated at an evening service back in 1991, attended by a small band of the Kentish faithful. It contains two magic numbers – *8* November and *38* years. They have got it right at last!

Colin Blythe

With the memorial celebrations over, for Janet Blythe the vacuum left by his death remained the central feature of her life. In striving to fill it, she followed the traditional wisdom of mankind – sticking close to his friends and to the cricket club that had been his life, the one environment in which it was not a social crime to mention his name or stories from his past. Through the club and her husband's connections, she was well acquainted with Marden, the little village close to Tonbridge so cricket mad that it can still today boast three private cricket grounds on the local farms. Blythe's close colleague, Jim Seymour, was to move there after the war, and die there too in 1930.

One of these private grounds was on Blue House Farm, worked by Mercer Day of the well-known Day family who had farmed the village for centuries. No surprise then that Janet Blythe should eventually come in touch with Mercer's younger brother, Sibery Day, the young farmer whose wife had been crushed in a plane on that June night when a joy ride had turned to sorrow. They shared the common bond of premature loss in a world of sickening violence, and the knowledge, gently filtering through the tears, that when one door closes another creaks slowly open. They were married at Brighton in June 1923, and she went to stay on his farm where they lived as happily as life and the past would allow.

She did not get on so well with the two young daughters of her new husband, but her cricketing past brought her close to her new nephew, Frank Day, whose enthusiasm for the game was to lead in the end to his election as President of the county club in 1976, the year before she died. A little while after her marriage, she gave up to Frank those most painful remnants of the past, the two wallets taken on the field from her husband's still warm body. It was the final confirmation that she had come through. He presented them on her behalf to the county club, where tucked away behind glass in a corner of the pavilion they wait for us now – to confirm that the whole of this story is true.

Legend

This morning I walked out into the meadows at the back of the house to gather a handful of late August flowers – yarrow, camomile, ragwort, willow-herb, hogweed, jumping jack – the simplest and purest of birthday gifts. As I crossed the stone bridge at the bottom of the road, the bulrushes stood proud among the reeds in just a few inches of water. The grass in the churchyard crumbled like yellow parchment as I climbed the path through the tumbling old graves.

I filled the stone jug that had sat on her table with the now precious water and shook out the flowers into their natural shapes. Always a rushed action this, as if my only thought were to finish and get away. But today I sat down in the grass beside and read, for the first time it seemed, the two words on the simple headstone of blue Cornish slate which she had designed herself. The plan of it lay there at her bedside in those last days, her passport to another world and reassurance of remembrance in this. When things went wrong, she would take the piece of paper in her hand, study it silently… and breathe again.

As I read the words, the deep incisions of each letter shone silver in the sun. A small bird, one brown sparrow of nondescript lineage, alighted on the curved top of the slate and looked me straight in the eye, puzzling at the strange force of my attention. I looked down at the golden ring on my finger – and I smiled.

Career Record

Batting and Fielding

Season		M	I	N0	Runs	HS	Ave	100	50	Ct
1899		4	4	2	0	0*	0.00	-	-	2
1900		22	29	12	125	15*	7.35	-	-	11
1901		22	32	8	168	20	7.00	-	-	8
1901/02	Australia	8	14	6	62	20	7.75	-	-	3
1902		25	36	7	249	31	8.58	-	-	12
1903		22	30	10	254	28	12.70	-	-	14
1903	America	2	2	1	5	5*	5.00	-	-	1
1904		24	37	11	400	82*	15.38	-	2	9
1905		27	39	11	288	75	10.28	-	1	13
1905/06	S Africa	11	15	4	94	27	8.54	-	-	8
1906		18	25	3	246	53	11.18	-	1	9
1907		27	39	9	264	33	8.80	-	-	11
1907/08	Australia	11	14	1	145	27*	11.15	-	-	6
1908		28	32	6	241	27*	9.26	-	-	8
1909		32	38	6	263	38	8.21	-	-	12
1909/10	S Africa	10	12	8	60	14*	15.00	-	-	3
1910		28	38	7	400	37	12.90	-	-	15
1911		27	35	6	319	47	11.00	-	-	16
1912		28	32	7	196	26	7.84	-	-	16
1913		34	46	6	282	37	7.05	-	-	17
1914		29	38	6	382	61	11.93	-	1	11
Total		439	587	137	4443	82*	9.87	-	5	206

Bowling

Season		Overs	M	R	W	Ave	Best	5i	10m	SRate	Econ
1899		151.2	56	310	14	22.14	3/15	-	-	64.85	34.14
1900		842.1	232	2106	114	18.47	6/40	11	2	44.32	41.67
1901		878.5	261	2151	93	23.12	7/64	4	1	56.69	40.79
1901/02	Australia	316.5	103	711	34	20.91	5/45	1	-	55.91	37.40
1902		847	243	1965	127	15.47	8/42	12	3	40.01	38.66
1903		925.4	292	1953	142	13.75	9/67	13	7	39.11	35.16
1903	America	56	16	140	10	14.00	5/30	1	-	33.60	41.66
1904		1024.2	273	2705	138	19.60	9/30	9	2	44.53	44.01
1905		1195	327	3142	149	21.08	8/72	12	5	48.12	43.82
1905/06	S Africa	480.2	168	1046	57	18.35	6/68	4	1	50.56	36.29
1906		886.5	243	2209	111	19.90	7/63	10	4	47.93	41.51
1907		1136.1	291	2822	183	15.42	10/30	17	6	37.25	41.39
1907/08	Australia	393.2	97	935	41	22.80	6/48	3	1	57.56	39.61
1908		1366.4	386	3326	197	16.88	8/83	20	6	41.62	40.56
1909		1273.5	343	3128	215	14.54	9/42	23	7	35.54	40.92
1909/10	S Africa	382.3	120	783	50	15.66	7/20	3	1	45.90	34.11
1910		1043.3	274	2497	175	14.26	7/53	18	4	35.77	39.88
1911		1039.4	254	2675	138	19.38	8/45	10	5	45.20	42.88
1912		919.3	241	2183	178	12.26	8/36	16	8	30.99	39.56
1913		1120.2	290	2729	167	16.34	7/21	15	3	40.25	40.59
1914		1008.4	278	2583	170	15.19	9/97	16	5	35.60	42.68
Total		17288.3	4788	42099	2503	16.81	10/30	218	71	41.44	40.57

Sources

Minutes of the Managing Committee and General Committee of Kent
    County Cricket Club
KCCC scorebooks
KCCC Trials Book
KCCC Blue Books
Papers of Janet Blythe, in possession of Edward Gosnell
Papers of Phyllis Spellar
Scrapbook of Jim Seymour, in possession of Richard and Helen Seymour
Register of Alverton Street School
Pupil card index, Bloxham School
War Diary of 12/KOYLI, National Archives
Parliamentary report on Condition of the Working Classes in London, 1887

Daily Graphic, Daily Mail, Daily Telegraph, The Globe, Kent and Sussex Courier,
    Kentish Express and Ashford News, Kentish Gazette, Kentish Independent
    and Kentish Mail, Kentish Mercury, Kent Messenger, Manchester Guardian,
    Northampton Daily Chronicle, Northampton Daily Reporter and Echo,
    Northampton Herald, Northampton Independent, Northampton Mercury, The
    Times, Tuesday Express, Tunbridge Wells Advertiser

The Bloxhamist, Cricket, The Cricketer, Kent County Cricket Club Annual, Playfair
    Cricket Monthly, The Review - the organ (unofficial) of the Kent Engineers, The
    Sapper, Sporting Life

Bibliography

Altham, H.S., *A History of Cricket, vol. I*, Allen & Unwin, 1962
Ames, Leslie, *Close of Play*, Stanley Paul, 1953
Arrowsmith, R.L., *A History of County Cricket - Kent*, Arthur Barker, 1971
Barker, Ralph and Rosenwater, Irving, *England v Australia, a compendium of*
    Test Cricket between the countries 1877-1968, Batsford, 1969
Batchelor, Denzil, *The Book of Cricket*, Collins, 1952
Beldam, G.W. and Fry, C.B., *Great Bowlers and Fielders, their methods at a*
    glance, Macmillan, 1906
Birley, Derek, *A Social History of English Cricket*, Aurum Press, 1999
Bond, R.C., *History of the King's Own Yorkshire Light Infantry, vol. III*,
    Percy Lund, Humphries & Co., 1930
Bonjeu, *The 497th at Wipers, July 4th-7th 1935*, Finden Brown, 1935
Brown, Lionel H., *Victor Trumper and the 1902 Australians*, Secker & Warburg,
    1981
Cardus, Neville, *English Cricket*, Collins, 1947
Cardus, Neville, *Cardus on Cricket*, Souvenir Press, 1977
Cave, Nigel, *Passchendaele, the fight for the village*, Leo Cooper, 2000
Coldham, J.D., *Northamptonshire Cricket, a history*, Heinemann, 1959
Cottret, Bernard, Hearn, Michael, Mioche, Antoine, *Manuel de civilisation*
    britannique, 3e édition, Bréal, 2004
Coulter, John, *Lewisham and Deptford in Old Photographs*, Alan Sutton, 1990
Cowdrey, Colin, *MCC, the autobiography of a cricketer*, Hodder and Stoughton,
    1976
Cross, Tom, *The Shining Sands, artists in Newlyn and St Ives 1880-1930*,
    Halsgrove, 1994

Croudy, Brian, *Colin Blythe*, Association of Cricket Statisticians and
    Historians, 1995
Dews, Nathan, *The History of Deptford*, Simpkin, Marshall & Co.,
    1884
Edmonds, Phil, *100 Greatest Bowlers*, Queen Anne Press, 1989
England, R.E., *A Brief History of the 12th Battalion KOYLI (Pioneers)*,
    Wakefield, no date
Evans, Brian, *Woolwich in Old Photographs*, Sutton, 1994
Fox, Caroline, *Stanhope Forbes and the Newlyn School*, David &
    Charles, 1997
Frindall, Bill, *England Test Cricketers*, Collins, 1989
Frindall, Bill, *The Guinness Book of Cricket Facts and Feats*, 1991
Frith, David, *The Golden Age of Cricket 1890-1914*, Omega Books, 1986
Frith, David, *The Slow Men*, Corgi Books, 1985
Fry, C.B., *Life Worth Living*, Eyre & Spottiswoode, 1939
Gordon, Sir Home, *Background of Cricket*, Arthur Barker, 1939
Green, Benny, *The Wisden Book of Cricketers' Lives*, Queen Anne Press,
    1986
Green, Benny, *A History of Cricket*, Barrie & Jenkins, 1988
Harris, Lord, *A Few Short Runs*, John Murray, 1921
Hayes, Dean, *Kent Cricketing Greats*, Spellmount Books, 1990
*History of the Royal Corps of Engineers, Vol. 5, the Home Front, France,
    Flanders and Italy in the First World War*, Institution of Royal
    Engineers, 1952-58
Jefferson, E.F.E., *The Woolwich Story 1890-1965*, Woolwich and
    District Antiquarian Society, 1970
Jessop, G.L., *A Cricketer's Log*, Hodder & Stoughton, 1922
Kinross, Albert, *An Unconventional Cricketer*, Harold Shaylor, 1930
Lilley, A.A., *Twenty Four Years of Cricket*, Mills and Boon, 1912
Macdonald, Lyn, *They Called It Passchendaele*, Penguin, 1993
MacLaren, A.C., *Cricket Old and New*, Longmans, Green and Co.,
    1924
Martin-Jenkins, Christopher, *The Complete Who's Who of Test
    Cricketers*, Orbis, 1980
Martin-Jenkins, Christopher, *Cricket, A Way of Life*, Century, 1984
Meredith, Anthony, *The Demon and the Lobster*, Kingswood, 1987
Milton, Howard, *Cricket Grounds of Kent*, Association of Cricket
    Statisticians and Historians, 1992
Milton, Howard, *Kent Cricket Records, 1815-1993*, Limlow Books, 1994
Mitchinson, K.W., *Pioneer Battalions in the Great War*, Leo Cooper,
    1997
Moore, Dudley, *The History of Kent County Cricket Club*, Christopher
    Helm, 1988

206

Morrah, Patrick, *The Golden Age of Cricket*, Eyre & Spottiswoode, 1967

Paine, Philip, *Innings Complete, Vol. 7*, Mischief Makers, 2003

Peebles, Ian, *Woolley - The Pride of Kent*, Hutchinson, 1969

Porter, Clive, *Kent Cricket Champions 1906*, Limlow Books, 2000

Powell, William A., *Cricket Grounds, Then and Now*, Dial Press, 1994

Powell, William A., *Kent County Cricket Club*, Tempus Publishing, 2000

Sewell, E.H.D., *Cricket Up-To-Date*, John Murray, 1931

Sewell, E.H.D., *Who's Won the Toss?*, Stanley Paul, 1944

Sewell, E.H.D., *Overthrows*, Stanley Paul, 1946

Steel, Nigel and Hart, Peter, *Passchendaele, The Sacrificial Ground*, Cassell, 2001

Steele, Jess, *Turning the Tide, the history of everyday Deptford*, Deptford Forum Publishing, 1993

Stevens, Frank A., *Southborough Sappers of the Kent (Fortress) Royal Engineers*, Fast, 2000

Swanton, E.W., *Back Page Cricket*, Queen Anne Press, 1987

Swanton, E.W. and Taylor, C.H., *Kent Cricket, A Photographic History*, Birlings, 1985

Taylor, Christopher H., *The Story of Canterbury Cricket Week*, Geerings, 1992

Trevor, Philip, *With the MCC in Australia (1907-08)*, Alston Rivers, 1908

Trevor, Philip, *Cricket and Cricketers*, Chapman & Hall, 1921

Warner P.F., *Cricket*, Longmans, Green & Co., 1920

Warner P.F., *Cricket Reminiscences*, Grant Richards, 1920

Warner, P.F., *My Cricketing Life*, Hodder & Stoughton, 1921

Warner, Sir Pelham, *The Book of Cricket*, Sporting Handbooks, 1945

Warner, Philip, *Passchendaele*, Wordsworth Editions, 1990

Weigall, G.J.V., *Cricket, the art of "playing the game"*, Cricket Press, 1922

Wilton, Iain, *C.B.Fry, An English Hero*, Richard Cohen Books, 1999

Wisden Cricketers' Almanack

Woolgar, Jason, *England's Test Cricketers 1877-1996*, Robert Hale, 1997

Woolley, Frank, *The King of Games*, Stanley Paul, 1936

Woolley, Martha Wilson, *Early Memoirs of Frank Woolley*, The Cricketer, 1976

Wright, Gerry and Frith, David, *Cricket's Golden Summer*, Pavilion Books, 1985

Yapp, Nick, *Pictures from the Past, Cricket*, Select, 1991

Table of Matches

LANCASHIRE v
  Kent (1907) 79, (1909) 104-5, (1910) 133
  Somerset (1905) 85
LEICESTERSHIRE v
  Kent (1909) 117-18, (1911) 138, (1912) 152-3, (1914) 167
MCC v
  Australia (1909) 101
MIDDLESEX v
  Kent (1906) 66, (1909) 104, (1910) 132-3, (1914) 172
  Surrey (1897) 15
NEW ZEALAND v
  England (1988) 130-1
NORTHAMPTONSHIRE v
  Kent (1907) 79-88, 118, 129-30, 190, 200, (1909) 118-19, (1912) 153, (1914)
  168-9, (2004) 129-31
NOTTINGHAMSHIRE v
  Kent (1904) 57
OXFORD UNIVERSITY v
  Kent (1914) 166
QUEENSLAND v
  MCC (1907) 99
SOMERSET v
  Kent (1901) 38, (1904) 57, (1914) 166
SOUTH AFRICA v
  England (1906) 61, 93, (1910) 106,131
SOUTH AUSTRALIA v
  MacLaren's XI (1901) 39
  MCC (1908) 100
SURREY v
  Australia (1909) 101
  Kent (1901) 38, (1903) 49-50, (1905) 60-1, (1908) 109-10, (1909) 116-17,
  (1914) 168
  Northants (1905) 78
  Yorks (1906) 65
SUSSEX v
  Kent (1906) 63-4, (1914) 166-7
WORCESTERSHIRE v
  Gloucs (1913) 158
  Kent (1902) 41, (1907) 99, (1909) 116, (1912) 153, (1913) 158
YORKSHIRE v
  Kent (1900) 30, (1907) 88, (1908) 109, (1914) 167

Index

Main entries are highlighted in bold

211